The Sacred and the Impure in Judaism

The Sacred and the Impure in Judaism

Law, Food, and Identity

MARTA F. TOPEL

Translated by

MIRIAM ADELMAN

OXFORD
UNIVERSITY PRESS

OXFORD
UNIVERSITY PRESS

Oxford University Press is a department of the University of Oxford. It furthers the University's objective of excellence in research, scholarship, and education by publishing worldwide. Oxford is a registered trade mark of Oxford University Press in the UK and certain other countries.

Published in the United States of America by Oxford University Press
198 Madison Avenue, New York, NY 10016, United States of America.

Library of Congress Cataloging-in-Publication Data
Names: Topel, Marta F., author. | Adelman, Miriam, translator.
Title: The sacred and the impure in Judaism : law, food, and identity /
Marta F. Topel ; translated by Miriam Adelman.
Other titles: Sagrado e o impuro no judaísmo. English.
Description: [New York] : Oxford University Press, [2024] |
Includes bibliographical references and index.
Identifiers: LCCN 2023057254 (print) | LCCN 2023057255 (ebook) |
ISBN 9780197677674 (paperback) | ISBN 9780197677667 (hardback) |
ISBN 9780197677681 (epub)
Subjects: LCSH: Jews—Dietary laws. | Orthodox Judaism—Customs and practices.
Classification: LCC BM710 .T666 2024 (print) | LCC BM710 (ebook) |
DDC 296.7/3—dc23/eng/20240105
LC record available at https://lccn.loc.gov/2023057254
LC ebook record available at https://lccn.loc.gov/2023057255

DOI: 10.1093/oso/9780197677667.001.0001

Paperback printed by Marquis Book Printing, Canada
Hardback printed by Bridgeport National Bindery, Inc., United States of America

*For O.S., because without that hurried question, before my interview
with a ritual butcher in Jerusalem, this book would have been
totally different. Less relevant.*

*And for Dzioncio, because love of life is always among
the greatest of lessons.*

Contents

Acknowledgments

First, my thanks to Z'l Francisco (Chico) Moreno. Without him as an anchor, readily answering my questions about medieval Judaic sources and, more importantly, the "spirit" behind them, this book would not have been written. Without his scholarship, I would have been obliged to seek out other interlocutors to help me in deciphering the obscure passages of the codifications that I studied. Without the originality of his thought and his insights, this research would most probably have been much more limited. Nonetheless, I assume sole responsibility for the positions taken here—that is, after the enrichment obtained from my long conversations with Francisco Moreno and after his attentive, encouraging, and professional reading of parts of this book.

To Rabbi Oren Duvdevani and kashrut supervisor Hemda Shalom of the nongovernmental organization Hashgacha Pratit, who welcomed me with open arms in Jerusalem and were ever-patient with my questions.

My heartfelt thanks to the Orthodox men and women I spoke with in Israel and in Brazil: ritual slaughterers, kashrut supervisors, and housewives who went out of their way to clear up my doubts about kashrut and how it is put into practice today.

To David Lehmann, for the encouragement, and for his seemingly unconditional belief in the value of taking this journey all the way to its final port.

To Jan Szeminski, because his words, after reading certain chapters in the draft of this book—a sort of a ship that was refusing to set sail—were what sent the "vessel" out to sea and made sure it arrived at its destination.

To Daniel Bargman, for his interest in this research from day one, notwithstanding our distinct perspectives on anthropology and on Orthodox Judaism—and for the long conversations, which were always so very stimulating.

To Damián Dzienciarski, for his help with Mishnaic and Medieval Hebrew, the clarity of his explanations and interpretations, and his perennial willingness to step in.

And, as always, to my friends here and there and everywhere, without whom none of my intellectual adventures would be possible.

A special thanks to the FAPESP Foundation (Fundação de Amparo à Pesquisa do Estado de São Paulo) for funding my trip to Israel in 2014–2015, where I carried out a part of the field research for the present work, and to the PROAP program for financial support in translating this book from Portuguese to English.

Introduction

The idea of exploring kashrut, or Jewish dietary laws, was born of my earlier research on Jewish orthodoxy,[1] carried out over extensive periods in which I never ceased to ponder the hyperritualization that characterizes the daily life of Orthodox Jews. My fieldwork in Brazil and in Israel and my scouring of diverse materials—from medieval legal codes to manuals published today on different dimensions of Jewish Law—caused me certain discomforts: I found it difficult to understand how and why it was possible to sustain a lifestyle that was regulated even in its most minute details. This includes rules that govern the most insignificant facets of life—that is, facets that for a layperson would be insignificant—as well as those that are the most important. The Halakhah[2] or Jewish Law interferes in the seasonings to be used in the kitchen with the same verve as it guides the way that the rites of passage of Judaism should be performed. Nothing remains beyond its scope, nor is anything too petty a matter! I could add here that, at present, the widened scope of Halakhah has drawn in, under current and constant vigilance, dimensions that less than a century ago fell outside its realm of concern. Examples are politics (which candidates observant Jews should vote for), economics (which professions are permitted, which are prohibited, and which are seen as "problematic"), and the labor market (which people are exceptionally qualified to work, and who should be exclusively devoted to religious study), among others.

Long immersed, in one form or another, in the universe of Orthodox Judaism, both observing the behavior of Orthodox Jews and reading old and new interpretations on a wide range of topics—I could not refrain from pondering the existence of an obsessive component within Halakhah. Yet while this hypothesis is thought-provoking, it is also disturbing. Could one perhaps think of communities with hundreds of thousands of members spread all over the world for centuries upon centuries as communities of obsessive people or as obsessive communities?

If we were to start from the premise that obsession is an individual pathology, it would be daring, if not incorrect, to think of observant Jewish communities in such terms. On the other hand, I have a background in the social sciences, obliging me, for better or worse, to follow the approaches and

The Sacred and the Impure in Judaism. Marta F. Topel, Oxford University Press. © Oxford University Press 2024.
DOI: 10.1093/oso/9780197677667.001.0001

guiding premises of the field. At the same time, I have also explored works from ethnopsychiatry and psychology that study the incidence of obsessive-compulsive disorder (OCD) in Orthodox patients and expand my horizons for understanding the high ritual density that characterizes Orthodox Judaism in general and dietary law in particular.

The significant increase in the number of rules demanded by orthodoxy today, known as the "Around the Torah,"[3] has led different researchers to suggest some hypotheses on the origin of the phenomenon. From a sociohistorical point of view, Liebman (1983) analyzes the extremism of the Israeli Jewish orthodoxy of the last few decades, focusing on two major dimensions: Halakhah's expansion and orthodoxy's relationship to the outside world. On the first matter, the author emphasizes three components: the scope of Jewish law, as expressed in the political program of certain Orthodox currents; the elaboration of details that enable the consummation of commandments, limiting subjective, elective, and personal authority in their interpretation; and the rigor that is adopted in interpreting Jewish law vis-à-vis lenient positions. The second dimension of radical extremism is characterized by the growing isolation of the Orthodox groups that have become more radical in recent decades. According to Liebman (1983, 84), the extremism of orthodoxy results from the declining influence of external social factors that, in the past, led to the creation of liberal currents within Judaism, such as emancipation and the process of Jewish adaptation to greater European society and, later, to wherever Jewish communities had been established. Modernity and its growing secularism were fundamental in dismantling a large part of the orthodoxy of the nineteenth century, yet at the same time gave rise to sectarian groups, known as ultra-Orthodox. Ferziger (2004) scrutinizes the strategies through which the Great Rabbi Chatam Sofer, architect of Jewish ultraorthodoxy, modified the way in which the commandments were interpreted, promoting their radicalization. Their precedents within Jewish law were set aside, and a "meta-Halakhah," emerging from the desire to respect the commandments more strictly, became the interpretative basis not only for understanding existing commandments but for the creation of new and more detailed rules for adhering to them.

The extermination of entire communities of European Orthodox Jewry during the Nazi period is, without a doubt, a historical event that left its marks on the post-Holocaust reconfiguration of orthodoxy, both in Israel and throughout the diaspora. The mission to re-create orthodoxy as it existed prior to the genocide, and to strengthen it in the face of the threats of a largely secular world, were put into practice without making concessions. This led to the emergence and consolidation of fundamentalist Orthodox currents.

The zeal of the rabbis of recent generations in legislating more severely, known as chumratization[4] has led, paradoxically, to creating new subterfuges and transgressions that in turn become part of the system. At the same time, data indicate that one of their objectives is to effectively curtail the individuality and autonomy of observant Jews. Whether this is made explicit or not, it is surely something that Orthodox rabbinical authorities desire, which leads me to hypothesize that today's observant Jews are more subjected to constraints on individuality than were those of earlier centuries. At present, it is not enough to lead a life that unfolds according to the traditions and customs that have been handed down from one generation to the next, nor to resort to the Shulchan Aruch[5] for guidelines or occasionally consult a rabbi when doubts arise on how to proceed. Rather, one must regularly consult with experts on specific domains of the Halakhah and take part in courses on a wide and diverse range of topics pertaining to recent rabbinical decisions in different arenas of traditional Halakhic jurisdiction, or within domains in which the latter has only recently become involved. In the realms in which Halakhah has a long-standing seminal role, such as rules regarding Sabbath rest, kashrut, or familial purity, there are now a plethora of books, educational materials, videos, internet sites, courses, and talks designed to help Orthodox Jews follow precepts as strictly as possible.

My curiosity in understanding the chumratization of Orthodox rabbinical legislation, over the course of recent decades, could have remained circumscribed to research on laws regarding Shabbat[6] or family purity. I decided, however, to take Jewish dietary law as my object of study as it allowed me to analyze very specific topics that are a result of the incorporation of technology into the lives of observant Jews. Although Orthodox Jewry declared itself at war with modernity, closing itself off within ghettos and scorning values and symbols that were alien to Halakhah, there are arenas of life for those who live within these ghettos that cannot be cut off from larger society. This is all the truer in today's globalized world, in which technology occupies a relevant place within the diverse domains that are shared by all those who live in the same society. At the same time, talking to kashrut supervisors and kosher butchers allowed me to study the heightened interest in animal welfare that exists in Judaism, both past and present. In addition to rules regarding procedures to be adopted on industrial farms and in slaughterhouses where kosher meat is produced, the Hebrew Bible, the Talmud, and medieval codebooks all demonstrate explicit concern for protecting animals from the unnecessary cruelty that Halakhah prohibits. Rabbinical Judaism's sensitivity regarding the welfare of animals, domestic and wild, is, without a doubt, one of the findings of my research. So is the knowledge that—although it has been a concern corrupted over the course of the centuries—there are today Orthodox rabbis who condemn the consumption of meat and defend a vegan diet, to do justice to the principles found in Judaic sources in which sentience constitutes one of the parameters of the relationships established between human and nonhuman animals.

* * *

Unlike my previous work on orthodoxy, the primary source for this research came from books and websites on kashrut that Orthodox Jews from a wide range of currents practice. This approach might trigger some doubt regarding the scope of my conclusions, as I was unable to verify whether housewives really consult this material, or how closely they follow what is written there. The important and revealing distance between norm and conduct, so dear to anthropology, is thus clouded over. This was a dimension of reality that I was unable to explore further, or at least not much beyond the answers that my interlocutors gave me, when I asked whether they were familiar with or owned copies of the most popular books on kashrut—whether they understood the very detailed aspects of the rules explained therein and if they were able to put them in practice. Yet two particular situations became clear through my research. The first is that women and men know, have, and use up-to-date books on kashrut and, at the first doubt, ask for advice from kashrut supervisors and rabbis. The second is that to call the rabbi when a question regarding Halakhah (and in this case, kashrut) arises is part of the routine of observant Jews.[7] Rabbis and supervisors keep special cell phone numbers for these specific purposes. As an interlocutor from Jerusalem told me, "It's quite good for us since Rabbi X answers phone calls early in the morning and Rabbi Y answers in the afternoon and evenings, so we always have support." Furthermore, supervisors and ritual butchers are encouraged to consult with colleagues or professors who have more scholarly knowledge or experience than they do when issues arise.

For the purposes of this research, I interviewed seven kashrut supervisors in Israel, as well as a female kashrut supervisor for the nongovernmental organization (NGO) Hashgacha Pratit.[8] During the same period, I interviewed ten Orthodox women and seven men. My field research included a visit to

Rabbi Moshe Vaya's laboratory. He is considered the great legislator[9] of our generation on insects. I also paid a visit to the laboratory of Eda Charedit[10] and took part in the kosherizing of breads and cakes for Shabbat in an industrial bakery in the cities of Beitar Ilit and Jerusalem. During that same stay in Israel, I spent three days with Hemda Shalom, kashrut supervisor for *Hashgacha Pratit,* accompanying her as she provided guidance to restaurants and kosher grocery stores. Hemda Shalom's work is carried out in Jerusalem. I went with her to the *shuk* (city market) as she made her rounds of several restaurants and food shops, and to establishments in the center of Jerusalem and the Rehavia and Moshava Guermanit neighborhoods. I spent three weeks taking part in a course taught by Rabbi Moshe Vaya on kashrut rules for single women. In Brazil I interviewed three ritual butchers and a kashrut supervisor. Both in Israel and Brazil, I spoke with Orthodox women and men on a very wide range of topics related directly and indirectly to kashrut.

More than one reader may be surprised by the fact that the word *charedi* (or *charedim*)[11] does not appear later in the book. The absence of the term is intentional, for two reasons. The first has to do with the fact that this is not an ethnographic study of a specific current of Orthodox Judaism, a heterogeneous group within which several groups coexist (peacefully or not), from the most extreme, known as ultra-Orthodox Jews or charedim, to groups identified with modern orthodoxy. My research was encouraged as I discovered regular tendencies and patterns emerging from different contemporary Orthodox groups, which, despite their conflicts, have common denominators. They can all be considered as Jewish observers of Halakhah who follow Rabbinical Judaism. Furthermore, the term "charedi" may breed misunderstandings or make reading harder for an English-language audience.

This is a book about Jewish dietary laws or kashrut. But it is also about religion and religious fundamentalism. It is a book about food and the respect for nonhuman animals that some Jews are striving to put into practice, following the intimations of medieval philosophers and legislators who interpreted the Hebrew Bible. Hence, this book also serves as testimony of Judaism's own inexhaustible power of renewal.

1

Orthodox Judaism

The two reasons why Jews for thousands of years have kept kosher is because Jews believe: 1) There is a God who created the world, sustains and supervises it. 2) God entered into a covenant with the Jewish people, and gave the Torah, obligating Jews to uphold and fulfill its commandments. The kosher laws are a part of that covenant.

Rabbi Kalman Packouz

Historical context

Modernity created several challenges for traditional Judaism. The emancipation of the Jews in western Europe as of the eighteenth century brought major changes to Judaism that, little by little, spread throughout central Europe, and later, by the mid-nineteenth century, to eastern Europe as well. Some researchers argue that the revolution that Rabbinical Judaism underwent during those centuries was no less relevant than the one that Biblical Judaism suffered with the destruction of the Second Temple in Jerusalem, in the year 70 CE. If in antiquity the religion of Israel was a sacrificial one, in the first century Judaism became a ritualistic religion in which time and body took the place of the Temple. The emancipation of European Jews undid the millenary symbiosis between ethnicity and religion that was a characteristic of Judaism, enabling the creation of new Jewish identities, many of which were detached from religion or even opposed it. To be a Jew within modernity no longer had self-evident meaning, and groups that were led by people guided by diverse ideals, sometimes in contradiction with one another, gave rise to different ways of being Jewish. As of this time and place it becomes possible to speak of Judaisms, made up of different identity references or endowing different (or even antagonistic) meanings and functions to the same ones (Sacks 1993). Reform Jews, liberal Jews, Zionist Jews, and Jews who sympathized with the Bund[1] as well as secular Jews began to interact with society in general and among themselves. The aforementioned forms of

The Sacred and the Impure in Judaism. Marta F. Topel, Oxford University Press. © Oxford University Press 2024.
DOI: 10.1093/oso/9780197677667.003.0001

Judaism—which in no way exhausted the new expressions of Jewish identity of the times—shared a common denominator: an openness to larger society and the incorporation of its values and symbols.

In this context, the Jewish ghetto—the structure that over the course of many centuries was taken as "the face of Judaism," if I may use such an expression—was emptied, as the vast majority of Jews in western and central European countries left it, settling in neighborhoods in which, before their political emancipation, they were forbidden to reside. Now considered equal citizens before the law, European Jews began to develop closer and more intense exchanges with the wider society. Their new activities—as they attended public schools and universities, worked in the civil service, exercised new professions, and defended national states in times of war— left their mark on Judaism and on the sociodemographic structure of Jewish communities. The Haskalah,[2] the Jewish enlightenment movement, assumed singular importance within the new configurations of modern Judaism and Jewish identity (Jewishness). Inspired by the Europe enlightenment movement, the *maskilim*[3] set themselves the goal of reforming Judaism and the structure of Jewish communities, modernizing both. However, the Haskalah should not be understood as a movement of total assimilation, that is, the disappearance of Judaism itself. On the contrary, the aim of the maskilim was to make the old and the new, particularism and universalism, compatible— that is, to integrate Judaism within the new winds of modernity that were blowing over the European continent. The incorporation of vernacular languages, and more importantly, as Eisenstadt (1997) points out, Jewish participation as coauthors of the Western narrative, were two important changes resulting from the emancipation of European Jewry and the Haskalah.

At the same time, a group of Jews opted to remain outside the realm of transformation and changes of the epoch, choosing the Jewish modus vivendi that had reigned over the centuries. Tied to religion as it had been conceived since the creation of Rabbinical Judaism, its members became known as Orthodox Jews. In general terms, Orthodox Jews can be characterized as a group that submits to fundamental practices of the Jewish faith and to Jewish ritual practice, although orthodoxy is not monolithic and groups that are different and even antagonistic coexist within it. Yet despite the disagreement and discord that inheres among the multiple Orthodox currents, Heilman (1977, 230) highlights their shared trait of support for a totalizing ideology, based on the Torah[4] on the one hand, and on the teachings of the Great Rabbis, on the other. From the Orthodox perspective, any deviation from this belief suggesting that the Torah can be reformed or revised in accordance with the demands of our times is the same as a partial or complete questioning of its divine origin, and is therefore considered heresy.

Rabbinic Judaism's identity was shaped from a conception that the Jews were a chosen people and from a series of myths and beliefs, rites, and practices (such as dietary laws and endogamy) that upheld the separation between the pure and the impure, the sacred and the profane (Sorj n/d). Biblical practices regarding purity were to a large extent radicalized by the diaspora rabbis, in order to award continuity to a religious and ethnic group that, with the destruction of the Temple in Jerusalem, lost its religious and political epicenter. As Sorj argues,

> The lack of a common geographic space that could serve as a natural boundary between Jews and non-Jews led to the extension of rules of purity/impurity to almost every act, ritualizing daily practices and thus working against the natural mingling that life in the diaspora encouraged. (Sorj n/d)[5]

The orthopraxis that characterizes Judaism, one of the pillars of the religion of Ancient Israel, was intensified over the course of the centuries. The rabbis had a fundamental role in this process, both in the passage from Israelite religion to Rabbinical Judaism as well as the postemancipation, and later post-Holocaust, radicalization of orthodoxy (Liebman 1987; Heilman 2000; Slifkin 2011).

With the modernization of European society, religion became a voluntary choice (Berger 1985), and as in the case of other religions, orthodoxy was obliged to compete with other forms of Judaism so as not to lose members. This situation weakened rabbinical authority, which was based on the study of canonical texts—that is, on tradition. Modernity, future-oriented and taking progress as its ultimate goal, thus became an assault on traditional Judaism, which defended the principle that was known as *ieridat ha´dorot* (generational decline). According to this principle, past generations are inherently wiser than their successors, each of which is born further from the moment of epiphany when God bestowed the Torah on the people of Israel, sealing a pact that made the latter into a people of priests, a holy people.

Faced with a scenario that celebrated the future and progress, the rabbis' strategy was to distance themselves completely from everything that was alien to the Torah, as well as from all forms of Judaism originating in the nineteenth and twentieth centuries. Hence, they separated themselves not only from the Gentile[6] other but also from Jews who were on different paths. The famous phrase pronounced by Rabbi Chatam Sofer,[7] known as the architect of postemancipation orthodoxy, expresses the whole of the Weltanschauung that shaped post-Haskalah Orthodox Judaism and dominates important segments of contemporary orthodoxy: *chadash assur min ha'Torah* (Innovation is biblically forbidden).

Yet not all rabbis took a position that negated modernity as a whole, and in the twentieth century there were Orthodox rabbis who defended leniency in the interpretation of the Halakhah, seen as the best way to avoid greater loss of followers in times of lassitude. The debate that took shape through figures such as the radical rabbi Chatam Sofer and Rabbi Hayyim Hirschensohn, the latter willing to make concessions, can be summed up in the following questions: Should rabbinical authorities legislate with leniency in the hope that Jews with waning religious observance thus refresh their commitment to Judaism? Or, on the contrary, assuming the premise that leniency brings more leniency, is it necessary and imperative to legislate with severity (Ackerman 2002, 261)?

In addition to imminently Halakhic issues, at stake in the approach of Hirschensohn and his followers was the notion of Halakhah as a cohesive factor for the Jewish people, rather than the other way around (Ackerman 2002). This issue is vitally important because it refers to a phenomenon that I analyze throughout this book: the division of orthodoxy into increasingly fragmented groups as a result of chumratization, that is, the choice to legislate in the most severe way.

In his article "Extremism as a Religious Norm," Liebmann does an in-depth analysis of the extremism that took over traditionalist Judaism, which had previously understood moderation and leniency as a fundamental instrument for the conservation of communal unity within a hierarchical context that was hostile to Jews. The author does not rule out the existence of extremist figures and tendencies during the European pre-emancipation period. Nonetheless, Liebman draws attention to community leadership, conscious of the danger that such positions represented for the group, and thereby attempted to coopt or excommunicate those who defended extreme positions (Liebman 1987, 80).

Yet, as mentioned, in the nineteenth century Rabbi Chatam Sofer's strategy took precedence, and the groups known as Orthodox instituted a symbolic separation from every new form of Judaism, also departing from any interpretation of the world and of Judaism inspired by sources outside Jewish tradition. At the same time, the most severe form of commandment compliance was instituted as rule, dictating that when several ways of following a precept are possible, the strictest one must prevail. The strategy of protecting Halakhah from the creation of new customs and legislating in the most stringent ways became known by the social actors themselves as the "Fence around the Torah." Alongside it, actions were implemented for the concrete separation from the Jews now considered as apostates, expressed in the prohibition of marriages and commercial relations with Reformist Jews, the interdiction of their burial in Jewish cemeteries, and the fortification of the Orthodox ghetto, that is, creation of their own neighborhoods and their isolation within them.

Contemporary or post-Haskalah orthodoxy is different from its premodern precursors, despite the fact that Orthodox rabbis present themselves as bastions of a past that they claim to re-create exactly as previous generations experienced it. An important innovation of modern orthodoxy was the creation of the full-time *yeshivot*[8] for young men, a fundamental strategy meant to give concrete shape to the desire to distance the latter from the values of modernity. This was a system of education guided by the goal of keeping youth free of the tentacles of the times, among which the role of the university stood out. The *kolelim*,[9] set up in eastern Europe at the end of the nineteenth century and in Israel during the early decades of the twentieth century, were extremely important in the process of the radicalization of orthodoxy. Defined by Tikochinsky (2007, 77) as an "a-geographical" Orthodox institution bringing together students from different regions of eastern Europe, the *kolelim* functioned as boarding schools. From the end of the nineteenth century, the kolelim became the heart of Orthodox life. This strengthened the position of their directors, who became the major leaders of Orthodox communities as a whole; their authority allowed them to establish community guidelines, not only on religious matters, but also on social, political, and everyday issues (Topel 2011, 113–114). It is important to point out that the directors of the *kolelim* had a stricter view of orthodoxy than did the families of the young men who studied there, exercising the role of spiritual guides over these youth first and over their communities as a whole second. The creation, crystallization, and spread of the kolelim led Heilman (2000) to refer to contemporary Orthodox society as a "society of scholars." This invokes the ideal of the Orthodox man that took hold from that moment onward: a man who dedicated his whole life to the full-time study of religious texts.

In relation to the kolelim and to segregation in neighborhoods of their own, Heilman and Friedman (1991, 214–216) assert that this strategy—which they define as "passive traditionalist," characterized by the rejection of the modern secular tradition of the outside world—did not prove to be enough to combat the unwanted intrusion of the latter, thus leading to the emergence of an "active and aggressive" traditionalism. Furthermore, in the words of Heilman and Friedman,

> The activists moved beyond traditionalism and towards what may be called active contra-acculturation, or something akin to what today is called "fundamentalism." As those Jews demonstrate, fundamentalism as such is not identical to traditionalism, in that it is not content with mere emphasis of the positive elements of tradition but focuses equally, or even more intensively, on the negative aspects of modern secular culture. Fundamentalism is thus essentially a movement of active and aggressive opposition. (Heilman and Friedman, 215)

Orthodoxy, possessing the characteristics of a fundamentalist movement, was fueled by the establishment of the State of Israel and by the catastrophe that devastated European Jews during World War II. The end of the war and the dissemination of knowledge regarding what the Nazi genocide had done[10] awakened a sense of mission among Orthodox survivors—both those who emigrated to the United States and those who made it to what was first Palestine and, later, the State of Israel. Orthodoxy's self-imposed mission was to re-create the past of European Orthodox communities in their new places of residence, a mission seeking to honor the memory of those who had perished, on the one hand, and to revitalize traditional Rabbinic Judaism in the new countries, on the other. Yet the survivors' past was cast in an image that had little to do with actual historical past, a point on which Heilman and Friedman (1991, 257) insist. It was portrayed as a glorious past that, according to rabbinical leaders, would be the basis for the establishment of a post-Holocaust orthodoxy.

Menachem Friedman (1990) argues that the major difference historically between premodern and contemporary orthodoxy is their approach to Halakhah. Along these lines, Friedman refutes authors who assert that the Orthodox emphasis on the rigid application of the law (*chumrah*) is a characteristic of traditional Judaism. In opposition to such a view, and as mentioned earlier, Friedman, a historian at the Bar-Ilan University, maintains that in premodern Judaism the efforts that rabbis made to adopt rigid interpretations of the Halakhah were contested by community authorities based on social considerations, among which the most significant was the wish to avoid intracommunity rift.[11] Nonetheless, the erosion of traditional Judaism wrought by Haskalah made way for the blossoming of strict interpretations of Jewish law within Orthodox communities.

Another innovation of the ultra-Orthodox in twentieth-century Israel, was the imposition of the *Daat Torah*[12] doctrine, currently in force. According to this new approach to Judaism, the authority of the Great Rabbis awards them decision-making power in matters pertaining to the public and personal lives of their followers that have nothing to do with Halakhah, that is, with religion. One example of how this doctrine functions is the lack of autonomy that Orthodox Jews are given regarding their choice of political parties and candidates to support in Israeli elections.

Brown (2014) describes three stages that Daat Torah went through, showing how the original nature of the doctrine underwent gradual transformation. From a concept that emphasized the magnitude of the Torah, it became a model that gave salience to the greatness of the authorities who interpret it, culminating in the obligation of the faithful to unconditional obedience. The figure who solidified and monopolized the doctrine of Daat Torah in Israel was the rabbi Elazar Menahem Mann Schach, whose influence was instrumental in the configuration of contemporary Israeli ultra-Orthodoxy. Slifkin (2012, 9) argues that the Daat Torah is presented not as advice but as mandatory prescriptions and proscriptions. Finally, in contrast to the approach consecrated over the centuries through rabbinical response, the Daat Torah provides no explanation for the tools it uses, whether Halakhic or based on other sources.

Contemporary orthodoxy, child of the ultra-orthodoxy born in Hungary at the end of the nineteenth century, is, as diverse authors argue, a new form of Judaism, despite its claims to be the only authentic and true one—that is, Judaism as it was practiced before the political emancipation of European Jewry. In Slifkin's words (2012, 14),

[The charedi orthodoxy] had its nascent roots in the early twentieth century, but emerged more clearly as something distinct from its predecessors after the Holocaust. In its most distinctive characteristics—the prominence of the yeshivah and Rosh Yeshivah, the notion of Daat Torah, the role of the *kollel*, and its extreme traditionalism—it is markedly a new approach to Judaism.

Halakhah: A manual for life

Religious fundamentalism is defined as a movement that defends literal interpretations of the sacred texts in the desire to resume a type of religiosity and community that, from a historical point of view, never existed. This characteristic of religious fundamentalisms, which seek to impose a single interpretation of canonical texts, places them in confrontation with exegetic traditions that developed over the course of the centuries. This explains why renowned authors emphasize that fundamentalisms should be seen as modern, traditionalist movements rather than traditional ones (Appleby and Marty 2002; Ruthven 2007). Caplan (1987) adds that we distinguish a fundamentalist movement through its relationship to a "significant other" to which it is antithesis and with which it engages in constant counterargument. In his view, insofar as fundamentalism is a product of modernity, it cannot be seen as its binary opposite.

Rabbinical Judaism, which we know today as Orthodox Judaism, is an eminently orthopraxical religion, based on strict conformance to the commandments and rules of Halakhah or Jewish law. These commandments, to which over the course of the centuries new rules and customs were added, appear in the Hebrew Bible, particularly within the books of laws such as Exodus, Leviticus, Numbers, and Deuteronomy.

Halakhah in Hebrew means "road": those who follow the steps that God has indicated will be forever blessed, while those who violate the Halakhah will be the target of terrible punishment. The Halakhah is part of the Talmud or Oral Torah, an enormous corpus of literature written and organized over the course of centuries by different generations of the Great Rabbis and codifiers.

The Halakhah is composed of mitzvot or precepts, taken from different sources. Hence, Halakhah includes most of the mitzvot of the Torah (*d'oraita*), that is, commandments that are found in biblical texts, the mitzvot instituted by the rabbis (*derabanan*) and the customs (*minhagim*) established by different diasporic communities throughout history.

From the perspective of the rabbinical tradition, the commandments found in the Hebrew Bible and those instituted by the rabbis both have their origin in the revealed word; consequently, they must be fulfilled by all Jews indistinctly.[13] In addition to this first classification, there are several ways of organizing the commandments. The most common is to distinguish between positive commandments, such the obligation of men to put on phylacteries every day except Saturday, and negative ones, such as the prohibition of certain foods. Another classification is the one that separates ritual and ethical commandments. In the former category are those that relate man to God, such as lighting candles at the beginning of Shabbat and eating matzah[14] during the eight days of Passover. The latter govern the relations between human beings, such as the prohibition of demanding debt payment from a poor person who is unable to comply or the prohibition of lusting after the wife of one's neighbor.

In his clear and interesting article "Commandments" (1987), Yeshayahu Leibowitz explains that commandments should not be understood in terms of underlying philosophy, but as a matrix that guides the daily actions of Jews who bind their lives to the law of the God of Israel. He puts it this way:

> As a religion of mitzvot Judaism is an institutional religion: its institutions, viz., the mitzvot—not its dogmas and values—define its spiritual content. Accordingly, Judaism is not an abstract or confessional faith, but is rather an emphatically concrete faith grounded in a complex of well-defined religious deeds and ritual practices. (Leibowitz 1987, 67)

Halakhah governs the most insignificant facets of life—or those that a layperson would regard as insignificant—as well as the most important. Halakhah sets out when and how Jewish marriage and burial should be performed, what professions men and women should and should not practice, how to treat domestic animals, and how and why certain fruits and vegetables should be washed in a specific manner. Nothing escapes the gaze of Halakhah.

We could add here that, at present, the widening reach of Halakhah has brought under constant surveillance dimensions that less than a century ago were not in its scope. What the Orthodox eat, and where and with whom they eat, are Halakhic questions of core importance, as is the information on whom they marry and at what age they do so. Certain books are permitted while others are prohibited, as is the case for professions and hobbies. There are specific times for the three prayers of the day. Holidays demand specific behaviors. How to dress, with whom to fraternize, and with whom not are matters regulated by Halakhah with the same precision as ways of organizing kitchen cabinets. The same strictness applies to rules for mourning the death of a loved one and the different Jewish rites of passage.

In the earlier-mentioned article, Leibowitz defines Judaism in strictly rationalistic terms as a mundane religion that busies itself with the concrete goals, obligations, and responsibilities of the common man, a man devoid of any special spiritual disposition that would distance him from daily duties through the illusion of reaching higher realities. The mitzvot are followed for the sole purpose of worshipping God, rather than for the satisfaction of human needs. Furthermore, "Based on mitzvot, Judaism makes religion the prose of life: a religion of worldliness. This is the very strength of Judaism" (1987, 68). Yet, Leibowitz adds, Judaism's attachment to the everyday, to the simple acts of life, does not make it a religion that minimizes the poetic and the extraordinary. Moments of spiritual elevation have their value, yet life is built around the prosaic acts of daily life.

In his work *Halakhic Man*, Soloveitchik (1983, 19) emphasizes the fact that the observant Jew approaches the universe through the Halakhah, as if it were a lens through which life and the world could be deciphered. The essence of Halakhah, seen as divine, consists of the creation of an ideal world and of rules that relate such a world to our concrete one. Thus,

> When halakhic man approaches reality, he comes with his Torah, given to him from Sinai, in hand. He orients himself to the worldly by means of fixed statutes and firm principles. An entire corpus or precepts and laws guides him along the path leading to existence. Halakhic man, well furnished with rules, judgments, and fundamental principles, draws near the world with an a priori relation." (Soloveitchik 1983, 19)

There are no phenomena of life that observant Jews do not see through the aprioristic lenses of Halakhah: human organic functions (eating, sex, all bodily needs), the rights of landlord and tenant, which days are holidays and how to respect them, ritual practices, interactions with geographic space and the measurements of grapes and dates—all these subjects are covered by Halakhah.

As already mentioned, in current times, the growth of the mitzvot or commandments that must be strictly followed by Orthodox Jews has reached an unprecedented level, the result of a historical process begun in Europe—more precisely, in nineteenth-century Hungary—and crystallized in twentieth-century Israel. Paradoxically, from the perspective of its architects, this change was intended to continue traditional Judaism at a time when the emancipation of Jews in Europe provoked a "alluvium of heretics" within

Jewish communities. Convinced that there was no way to keep the thousands of Jews who opted for Reformism or neo-orthodoxy within Rabbinical Judaism, figures such as Rabbis Chatam Sofer and Akiva Yosef Schlesinger made historic decisions that led to the creation of what is known today as ultra-orthodoxy. One of their concerns was to face the challenge of individual autonomy in a world permeated by uncertainty and constant change, to which they responded by reaffirming rabbinical authority.

Two major steps in this direction were taken. The first, to which I have already pointed, was to isolate Orthodox communities from individuals and groups who opted for a more liberal Judaism. The second step was the transformation of the Jewish way of legislating that had been in force for centuries. Legal codes with clear rules like the *Shulchan Aruch* were chosen over polysemic Talmudic deliberations in which opinions are always in dispute. The uncertainties that modernity produced in Judaism led the Hungarian rabbis to eliminate any manifestation of pluralism in fulfilling the commandments. Based on the premise that all elements of tradition are equally sacred, there would be no reason to distinguish between different strata, relativizing the value of each one (Ackerman 2002). Schlesinger, in turn, made a statement that would become one of the keys in the creation of post-Holocaust orthodoxy: "Every rule contained in the *Shulchan Aruch* is equal to the Ten Commandments, and every Jewish custom is equal to the Ten Commandments" (Silber 1992, 49).

In their desire to avoid any type of interference coming from outside Judaism, or any deviation from it, the ultra-Orthodox rabbis ignored the Jewish tradition that had been built over the centuries: to ponder, discard, or reconcile with assertions that disagreed with canonical texts. At present, a clear example of this trend comes from the compendiums of laws put out by transnational publishers that circulate among different currents of orthodoxy and around the globe. These manuals and codifications, among which those by the publisher ArtScroll[15] occupy a prominent place, have created a clear tendency toward standardization, relegating the *Sifrei Minhagim* (Books of Customs) to the background. These books had been part of Jewish communities for centuries, revealing their singularities and specificities. On the other hand, and as Waxman points out,

Whereas historically, the traditions of both the family and the local community played a central role in setting the standards of proper behavior within the religious realm—minhag, custom, often took on the authority of

Halakhah—with the growth of the yeshiva *gedola* a new pattern emerged. The rosh yeshiva now determines proper behavioral norms, and the folkways and mores of the family and local community are often not taken very seriously. (Waxman 1991, 17)

Waxman (1991, 15–16) is vehement in his assertions that within today's Orthodox communities there is a consciousness, and almost an ideology, that aspires to fulfillment of commandments as strictly as possible. Kashrut is one of the realms in which severity in following the precepts is consensual, as is the case in two other pillars of Orthodox Judaism: the Sabbath rest and laws of family purity.

As stated above, kashrut concerns Halakhic laws on food and food preparation, in addition to many rules regarding foods that can be eaten together or the mixing of utensils used to cook and prepare them. Kashrut's scope, and the way it is interpreted by social actors—that is, rabbis and others responsible for its codification—as well as scholarly interpretations, are essential to our understanding of the intricacies of contemporary dietary laws. And although definitions of and critical reflections on kashrut are many—not only diverse but sometimes contradictory—without understanding them it is impossible to even begin to think about the different issues that it raises.

2

From Jewish tradition to anthropological tradition: Kashrut today

> It is easy to understand why kashrut is often considered the most far-reaching of mitzvah. History has shown that when kashrut observance is strong, Jewish identity remains strong.
>
> Chabad rabbi

The laws of kashrut: Emic viewpoint 1

The kashrut[1] is a dimension of life in which the transformations in orthodoxy and, consequently, of Halakhah—can be observed. It is common for Orthodox Jews to define themselves as *shomer mitzvot*[2] (those who respect commandments) or as Jews who respect kashrut laws, Shabbat laws, and laws of family purity: the three pillars of rabbinical Judaism. This definition is fundamental, insofar as it expresses the Jewish Weltanschauung regarding who is a good Jew. Consequently, kashrut should not be understood as a facet of Orthodox Judaism or as an addendum to Jewish religion. Kashrut is one of the foundations of Judaism, one of the prisms through which Orthodox Jews codify their daily lives; it governs their everyday existence. As is written in the Hebrew Bible, the people of Israel become holy through fulfilling commandments.

There are some seminal works on the dietary laws of the book of Leviticus. Among them, research by Mary Douglas (1966; 1993/4), Jacob Milgrom (1991; 1993), and Howard Eilberg-Schwartz (1990) stand out. The empirical universe that these scholars worked with was the Hebrew Bible and, in some cases, medieval codifications. Their work is based exclusively on written sources. Although much has changed since the dietary laws were compiled by biblical scribes, these works cast light on aspects of kashrut that my own research intends to discuss.

The Sacred and the Impure in Judaism. Marta F. Topel, Oxford University Press. © Oxford University Press 2024.
DOI: 10.1093/oso/9780197677667.003.0002

The first and simplest definition of kashrut refers to a set of rules that Jews use to identify foods that are ideal for consumption, according to a corpus of religious laws that have been developed over the course of Jewish history. In Leviticus 11 and 14:2–21, there is a long list of clean and unclean animals from the three cosmic domains (land, water, and air) and the requirements that each one demands in order to be approved for consumption. In the following chapters of this book, interdictions regarding the eating or touching of dead animals are also enunciated, as well as the prohibition against ingesting blood and particular types of fat.

Jewish dietary laws seem to be characterized by a certain arbitrariness. At different times, and despite the fact that the laws of kashrut were considered chukim,[3] some key figures, among whom Maimonides stood out, attempted to decipher their underlying logic. Yet it was not until 1966, with the publication of the chapter "The Abominations of Leviticus" by Mary Douglas in her *Purity and Danger* that we were provided for the first time with a model that attempts to account for the logic governing Jewish food laws. Douglas argued that these laws must be understood within the broader context of the idea of holiness and separation espoused by the rabbis who wrote the book. I return to Douglas's approach, and that of the other authors I have cited, after a brief presentation of how contemporary rabbis and Jewish thinkers understand and explain kashrut.

The first chapter of third edition of the book *Cashrut e Shabat na cozinha judaica: leis e costumes* (Kashrut and Shabbat in Jewish cooking: Laws and customs)—written by Rabbi Shamai Ende, affiliated with the Chabad-Lubavitch[4] movement of Brazil—is titled "Cashrut: qual é a razão?" (Kashrut: What's the reason for it?). We find there the following ideas: over the course of centuries, different functions and meanings were attributed to the laws of kashrut, such as caring for the physical health of Jewish people and fomenting their hygienic practices. Before the author goes on to discuss the meanings of kashrut, he makes a point of stating that the only reason to follow dietary laws is to maintain unrestricted obedience to the covenant made between God and the people of Israel when they were bequeathed with the Torah.[5] This leads him to conclude that kashrut was instituted by God for reasons that only he knows (Ende 2006, 9). *Naasa ve'nishma* (First we do and then we listen)[6] is the saying that best expresses the need for the chosen people's total obedience to the God of Israel.

A compilation by Rabbi Eliahu Birnbau and the philosopher Shalom Rosenberg (2020), published by Sêfer[7] under the title *O que é cashrut?* (What is kashrut?) presents a variety of interpretations of Jewish dietary laws, ranging from the most rationalistic to the kabbalistic, including contemporary interpretations that demonstrate a sensitivity toward animals such as found in vegetarianism. The book is brief and includes names as varied as Shalom Rosenberg himself, Aaron Barth, Martin Buber, and Rabbi Chayim HaLevy Donin. Rather than a manual for those who want to follow kashrut strictly, the volume provides a view of the multiple horizons from which these laws can be pondered and understood.

On the Beit Chabad do Brasil website, in the section titled "*Cashrut: a 'dieta' judaica na teoria e na prática*" (Kashrut: Jewish "diet" in theory and practice), we read the following definition on the meaning of kasher:[8]

A product that is apt, appropriate for consumption, that is, that fills all the requirements of the Jewish diet. Kashrut is the set of these laws that God bequeathed to the Jewish people through the granting of the Torah, on Mount Sinai. Kashrut belongs to the category of the chukim, for which the Torah gives no rational explanation. It describes the type of foods that the law of the Torah considers adequate for ingestion, as well as how they should be prepared.[9]

The authors then go on to assert that, according to tradition, the home of each Jew is like a "small sanctuary," the abode of the Divine Presence, and that a Jew's table can be compared to the altar of the Holy Temple. The authors point out that just as the greatest care was taken to ensure that only that which was in accordance with Jewish law be given as an offering at the altar of the Temple, so with its destruction it becomes the duty of all Jews to ensure that only suitable foods are placed on the table, defined as "a miniature altar."

In turn, in the general introduction to the hefty volume *The Kosher Kitchen: A Practical Guide,* published by Mesorah (Halachah Series), author Rabbi Binyomin Forst introduces the reader to theoretical issues surrounding kashrut, sharing diverse interpretations on its meanings and functions. "Medicine for the Body or Salve for the Soul?" and "People of Holiness" are the titles of a few of the sections into which it is divided. Forst's arguments are consistent and anchored in diverse Jewish sources, including the written Torah, the Talmud, medieval codifications, midrashim,[10] and kabbalah wisdom. In his introduction, the author establishes connections between the history of creation, the laws of kashrut, and his readers:

> As we face the test of our fealty to the laws of kashrus, we reenact Adam's challenge in the Garden of Eden. We are once again charged with the mission of partaking from the plenty offered to us by the Creator, and to eschew that which He has forbidden. Man's malchus and subsequently God's Malchus waits for the outcome of that decision: *u'bacharta ba'chaim.* (Forst 2013, xxviii)

The book *Kashrut: Guidelines and Orientations on Kashrut: Cuisine and Food*[11] by Rabbi Yitzchak Yacov Fuks (2002), like many manuals on Halakhot, adorns its first pages with blessings from Great Rabbis who testify to the author's erudition on the subject and extol the book's relevance. The introduction, titled "The Theory of Kashrut," covers different topics, as the section headers indicate: "Food—Nourishment for the Soul," "Distinguishing between the Sacred and the Profane," and "The Key to Respecting the Precepts." The second section, titled "Sanctions and Supervision," contains topics such as "The Kashrut System," "Sovereign Rabbinical Authority," "Institutional Management," and "Information and Media."[12] In the early pages of the book, Fuks claims that he wrote the manual not only for the *chozrot bi'teshuvah,*[13] but also for observant women, because even those who are born into Orthodox Judaism are continually faced with challenges. To illustrate this phenomenon, Fuks (2002) raises the following issues that often plague those who are born into observant Judaism: finding oneself unable to pray with the necessary *kavana*[14] or losing the desire to study the Torah. The solution to these problems is simple and definitive, and is sustained by the Holy Torah and the Great Sages. Literally,

> Open, please, your kitchen cabinets, check your refrigerator and your freezer, and ask yourself: Am I in fact careful with kosher food? Or, God forbid, do you err with foods that contain prohibited ingredients—especially in our generation, in which problems related to kashrut are more complex and difficult, and this may, possibly, be the cause of your spiritual descent and your weakness in serving God? (Fuks 2002, 4)[15]

The introduction ends with a systematic and thorough glossary of the basic concepts of kashrut.

Having come this far, what I would like to emphasize here is that both manuals—similarly to the way manuals regarding other areas of halakhah are written—devote their first pages to reflections that are spiritual in nature and to biblical interpretations, then move to technical questions meant to help readers comply adequately with the commandments of daily life. The two kashrut manuals that were the major sources for this research expound in their respective introductions on the spiritual relations between the food ingested by Jews and their state of spirit, the importance of food to the relationship with God, and the consecration of the Jewish people through food, among other topics. Thus, we read in *The Kosher Kitchen*, "We will see in the overview that our spiritual purity and ability to properly serve Hashem are directly influenced by the food we eat" (Forst 2013, 16). The author addresses this issue in different ways and asserts that the objective of the human experience is to subdue the animal that exists in man and live life according to a special standard for human beings. Yet, he claims, the objective of a Jew is larger: to bring the sanctity of the soul to the body, elevating the mundane to the level of the spiritual and transforming the temporal into the sublime (Forst 2013, xxvii). A few pages later, Forst asserts that forbidden foods induce the negative to take over, subverting man's nature. Yet the laws of kashrut govern the intake of food in such a way as to allow the spiritual life that was nourished by the positive to connect with everything that is divine in man. (Forst 2013, xxxii).

The laws of kashrut: Emic vision 2

Readers of the prefaces or introductions to the manuals analyzed here (and many others) note the difference that separates their style from that of the chapters that follow in those manuals, as if they were works with different objectives written by different authors. Interest in relating kashrut to the spiritual dimensions of Judaism have a fundamental role in the first pages, a focus that then shifts drastically. Complex and detailed explanations of each one of the mitzvot that are eminently practical and technical move center stage, alongside the respective customs, discussions on the Great Rabbis and their views regarding the mitzvah, as well as innovations in the way some of these mitzvot are consummated, given the influence of processes of industrialization in food production. All these pages include various and extensive footnotes. The Fence around the Torah comes to life in these books, in all its vigor and dynamism.

In order to facilitate the reading of his manual, after explaining the concepts, strategies, and care necessary to respect a particular commandment, Forst

(2013) regularly adds graphics highlighted in gray under the title "Practical Applications." Yet it may be possible to argue that such explanations provide little help to a layperson—or to a Jewish researcher who is fluent in Hebrew and has been doing research on orthodoxy for more than a decade!—in understanding the laws, rules, customs, and advice found in the work. The first thing that struck me as I pored over Orthodox Halakhot manuals was the range and diversity of topics, subtopics, and their respective ramifications. It seems that the capacity of lawmakers to imagine unreal or even outlandish situations is infinite. Or almost infinite.

In the section devoted to the use of vegetables at the Passover table, Fuks (2002, 360–367) lists the types that are available on the market and the forms they come in. Celery can be found frozen, dried, or "worm free"; lettuce can come from a regular or "worm-free" planting. The term "worm-free vegetables" refers to the Israeli company Gush Katif,[16] which produces vegetables and fruits for the Orthodox public. However, the author uses quotation marks around "worm free" for Gush Katif products because the assertion that they are supposedly not infested with insects should not exempt housewives from taking proper care. To reinforce his advice, Fuks (2002, 364) explains that although the vegetables are grown in greenhouses, the environment is not airtight; black flies often enter greenhouses and cling to plant leaves. Thus, Fuks writes, in the specific case of vegetables from Gush Katif, a deep washing is enough to cleanse them, unlike the thorough verification needed in the case of vegetables from common farms. The rabbi goes on to recommend placing leaves of lettuce under a strong jet of water, then leaving them in a basin full of water for another three to five minutes and finally washing each leaf again on both sides under a heavy spurt.

On another aspect of kashrut—the utensils used directly or indirectly in preparing food, and how they should be kosherized[17] or handled—Forst, in the section "Adjacent Sinks" (2013, 241), explains that housewives must be careful. When washing the dishes and utensils used with meat, the dairy dishes and utensils stacked in the other sink should be protected from the splash, and vice versa. His advice for avoiding this problem, which would transgress the mitzvah that forbids mixing dairy and meat products, is to cover the sink that is not being used or build a stone separation between the two sinks. I remember that when I interviewed an Orthodox woman in Jerusalem and was invited to visit the kitchen of her apartment, my hostess proudly showed me two adjacent sinks separated by a marble plank about a foot high, telling me that this was a gift from her mother-in-law that greatly eased her daily labors in the kitchen.

I later compared these randomly chosen examples with hundreds of others found in the two works that I analyzed. Clearly the conduct regarding food that was considered kosher enough several decades ago—such as the care that needs to be taken in washing vegetables and produce and keeping two adjacent sinks—is no longer seen as sufficient, creating the need to implement new behaviors and strategies in verifying foods and utensils being kosher. Throughout his vast manual, Forst (2013) advises his readers that they must follow a path of greater stringency in fulfilling precepts and customs. He provides arguments and justifications in this regard throughout the text. Interestingly, in an illustration highlighted in gray and appearing under the title "Non-Kosher Medications," readers encounter four pieces of advice to avoid transgression when confronted by the need to take medications that for one reason or another are not ideal for consumption by observant Jews. There are rules and lists of medications that circulate within Orthodox communities clarifying which should be avoided or prohibited. The fact that Forst includes this advice in a book on kosher cooking is one more indicator of the severity of his views on kashrut and how kashrut has expanded the scope of its mandate, if I may say so. Forst's last two pieces of advice (2013, 62) in relation to nonkosher medications are the following: (1) pills that must be ingested that are pleasant-tasting but coated with a film made of nonkosher components should be wrapped in a very thin layer of tissue paper and swallowed with a glass of water, and (2) the content of medicines coated in nonkosher film should, after purchase, be transferred from the nonkosher capsules[18] to vegetable ones. It goes beyond the objectives of this work to discuss the seriousness and dangers implicit in conducts such as this one, endorsed by Forst and a significant number of Orthodox rabbis; I mention them here to illustrate the spirit of contemporary orthodoxy in its zeal for chumratization.

Forst's *The Kosher Kitchen* (2013) is 576 pages long, divided into nineteen chapters and concluded with two appendices. In an attempt to provide more examples that illustrate the spirit of the work, not very different from other Halakhot manuals, I offer here the heads of the subsections of Chapter 8 (again, randomly chosen) appearing under the title "The Kashrut of the Knife" and divided into three sections, as follows:

    I. General Principles
        A. The Unique Ability of a Knife to Transmit or Absorb Taste
        B. The Retention of Residue on a Knife Surface
        C. The Method by Which a Knife Is Koshered
    II. Practical Kashrus Situations
        A. A Knife Used to Cut Cold, Non-Sharp Foods
        Summary of Section A
        A. A Knife Used to Cut Cold Foods
        B. A Knife Used to Cut Hot or Warm Foods, or a Hot Knife Used to
           Cut Cold Meat
        Summary of Section B
        A. A Knife Used to Cut Warm Foods
        B. A Knife Used to Cut Sharp Foods—*Davar Charif*
    III. Koshering a Knife: A Unique Method (Forst 2013, overview)

The thirty pages of Chapter 8 are sprinkled with a variety of expressions and concepts. If I were obliged to follow all the rules in Chapter 8 to kosherize a knife, I confess that the suggested call to a rabbi—a recommendation that the author constantly repeats—would not be enough to solve my doubts; rather, I would be lost in an entire labyrinth of them. I do not hide my own ignorance of Halakhic language in general and of kashrut in particular: during the years in which I carried out my research on orthodoxy, I sought assistance whenever I ran into difficulties in understanding a text in Mishnaic[19] or Medieval Hebrew. Nonetheless, at the same time, interaction with the Orthodox led me to expect that understanding a kashrut manual written in the twenty-first century—after all, it was just a manual, not a treatise!—could not be so terribly difficult (which is to say impossible) for a person interested in and exposed to the numerous materials distributed by orthodox institutions. Yet what seems most relevant to the goals of the current research is the fact that this experience led me to corroborate that the two sources that I was working with were not addressed to the chozrim bi´teshuvah—or at least not to novices, who would have experienced the same difficulties that I did in understanding the content of these kashrut manuals. Furthermore, Forst and Fuks both point out that although their books can be useful to Jews who turned to orthodoxy as adults, Jews who have been observant from birth are obliged to read them for purposes of *leitchazek*[20] (spiritual strengthening), thereby avoiding any failures in mitzvot compliance.

In turn, a kashrut supervisor at the nongovernmental organization (NGO) Hashgacha Pratit mentioned studying these books to obtain her kosher supervisor's certificate and begin to work. Another interlocutor, who worked for several years as a kashrut supervisor in a small city in the north of Israel, told me that he received the ArtScroll kashrut book as a wedding present, and that he resorted to it constantly while working in the field.

The production of this type of reference work has grown considerably over the last two decades, and its circulation within Orthodox communities is well attested. The manuals can be found on bookshelves at the homes of Orthodox families, organized according to theme. They can also be found at the yeshivot, and those who visit the bookstores in Orthodox neighborhoods in Israel may have the impression that each week another new book appears on the different areas of Halakhah jurisdiction. In turn, Jewish bookstores of the diaspora have sections specifically devoted to Halakhot manuals, the number of which have grown over the last two decades. The fact that use of the internet is in principle off limits to most members of Orthodox communities—except for those who need it for specific work purposes—confers a prime position to printed texts and newspapers.

Three decades ago, Waxman (1991, 20) had already awarded a significant role to technology—in this case, books and the telephone—regarding the speed with which Halakhic decisions were being disseminated, in comparison to the way new works circulated within observant Jewish communities of the nineteenth century. Within his analysis, Waxman draws attention to the fact that, although publishing books on Halakhah bequeaths prestige to legislators, having published a Halakhot manual is neither a prerequisite for nor proof of the scholarship and recognition of the authors involved. Obviously, legislators who bring together both scholarship and analytical depth in specific fields of knowledge and transform their knowledge into books have a greater probability of being recognized as Halakhic authorities.

In that same text, Waxman mentions the publisher ArtScroll and argues that, although the quality of its books is questionable, the major impact of what he refers to as the "ArtScroll phenomena" is not (1991, 21). At the same time, as he goes on to argue, the manuals from this publisher rouse the consciousness of more than a few Jews who are ignorant in Halakhic matters, and who, after reading them, seek out rabbis and kashrut supervisors, eager to become observant Jews or more stringent in their observance than they had been prior to their contact with ArtScroll books.

In an interesting article, "Holy Pleather: Materializing Authority in Contemporary Orthodox Jewish Publishing," Stolow (2007) analyzes the central role of ArtScroll publishers in the standardization of contemporary orthodoxy, as its books are read and purchased by members of different Orthodox currents—and can also be found in diverse synagogues affiliated with the Conservative movement. During my fieldwork in Israel, I was able to verify that the publisher' books could be found in Orthodox neighborhoods, as well as in some of the homes that I visited. Kashrut supervisors, rabbis, and ritual butchers with whom I spoke in Brazil and in Israel know these books and manuals and use them in study. This gives eloquence to Stolow's observation:

> The spread of ArtScroll books thus evinces what critics see as a haredi assault on Jewish traditions that stress autonomous powers of reason, pluralism, and enlightened acculturation. From this perspective, ArtScroll books epitomize a dangerous drift toward punctiliousness, interpretive rigidity, and unreflective obedience to the literal wording of the text itself. (Stolow 2007, 318)

Furthermore, standardization according to the model of a publisher that is considered radical in its interpretation of Jewish law, expressed in its choice of greater zeal in complying with mitzvot, leads the author to conceive of it as an important element in a marked fundamentalist tendency within contemporary Jewish orthodoxy and neo-orthodoxy.

The laws of kashrut: An enigma for scholars

In her first foray into Jewish dietary laws, in her well-known essay "Abominations of Leviticus," Mary Douglas attempted to uncover the logic behind the dietary laws of Ancient Israel. This objective was part of a broader inquiry into the rules concerning cleanliness/dirtiness and purity/impurity that dominate both Western societies and so-called primitive societies. According to Douglas (1966), the deeper we delve into these rules, the more evident it becomes that we are dealing with symbolic systems.

Regarding the laws of Leviticus, the British anthropologist makes a historical analysis of the interpretations that have accumulated over the centuries and comes to the conclusion that most suffer great disadvantage by not attributing meaning to the rules. On the other hand, such interpretations appear more as commentaries, as they are neither consistent nor comprehensive: an ad hoc interpretation is provided for each animal, and there is no end to the number of interpretations that are made in relation to each animal, as there is no limit to the number of interpretations that can be given for each one of them. Discarding existing interpretations, Douglas points to the fact that if each prohibition includes the imperative to be holy, interdictions must be explained by taking the category of the holy or the sacred as their point of departure. Leviticus 11:43–47 enables us to understand Douglas's insight:

> You shall not eat, among all things that swarm upon the earth, anything that crawls on its belly, or anything that walks on fours, or anything that has many legs; for they are an abomination. For I יהוה am your God: you shall sanctify yourselves and be holy, for I am holy. You shall not make yourselves impure through any swarming thing that moves upon the earth. For I יהוה am the One who brought you up from the land of Egypt to be your God: you shall be holy, for I am holy. These are the instructions concerning animals, birds, all living creatures that move in water, and all creatures that swarm on earth, for distinguishing between the impure and the pure, between the living things that may be eaten and the living things that may not be eaten.[21]

Inquiring into the sacredness of kashrut allows us to account for each and every one of its rules, detecting a consistent system in which the sacred is the attribute of God that necessarily opposes that which is considered abominable. Sacred—in Hebrew: *kadosh*—means to separate, to set apart, and this is what is required of a holy people: the people of Israel, the people chosen by God, must separate from all others to fulfill the divine desire to be a people of priests (Douglas 1966, 49). Another issue analyzed by the British anthropologist is the physical completeness that is required of permissible animals, directly linked to the sanctity required of the Israelites. Thus, men who go to war must be noble in the same way as animals who are sent to sacrifice. Consequently, the idea of the sacred and the pure is revealed in the physical dimension that permeates animal and social realms. Douglas points to yet another issue: hybrid animals are considered incomplete, abominable, because they lack one of the attributes required by the Levitical laws. These observations lead her to conclude that the sacred requires that individuals belong wholly to a single class; the sacred requires that different classes of objects or individuals not be confounded (Douglas 1966, 51–52).

On the other hand, there is a relationship between the cosmic categories of creation and the social categories. If we understand the idea of the sacred as the idea of order, of nonconfusion, we can understand the logic underlying dietary laws: they show the path of righteousness, and contradicting them is a way of tainting the sacred. The sacred is the unity, integrity, and perfection of the individual and the species, and dietary laws constitute a metaphor for the sacred in this same sense. "Holiness means keeping distinct the categories of creation. It therefore involves correct definition, discrimination, and order" (Douglas 1966, 53).

As I have already mentioned, to be fit for consumption an animal must belong to its class in full, and the pig—an animal that has become the symbol of Jewish food prohibitions—is exactly the opposite: it represents ambiguity. Pigs have cloven hooves but are not ruminant. Impure species are seen as imperfect members of their class and pose a threat because of their power to wreak havoc to the established order. If this interpretation of the forbidden animal is correct, Douglas continues, Jewish dietary laws should be understood as "signs that inspire meditation on the uniqueness, purity and completeness of God" (57). Through laws prohibiting certain species or incomplete members of a species, the sacred takes physical expression in every encounter with the animal kingdom, and at every meal. Douglas's text ends with an observation that waxes poetic:

been a meaningful part or the great liturgical act of recognition and worship which culminated in the sacrifice in the Temple. (Douglas 1966, 57)
The terror that is generated by ambiguity is a central component of Jewish culture. It is present in the Halakhah in different ways. The Fence around the Torah expresses this fear and constitutes a mechanism to keep Jews as far as possible from ambiguous situations, conditions, and foods.

At the same time, separation from the non-Jewish other was a constant in diasporic Jewish history and, beyond doubt, the food laws fulfilled this function. However, as Alter (1979, 47) points out, although the rabbis took advantage of the isolation effect produced by kashrut, there is no evidence that this was the main objective of the food laws. With some caveats, particularly in relation to certain excesses he attributes to Mary Douglas's symbolic approach, Robert Alter agrees with the main ideas of her analysis. However, the interpretations of Jewish food laws listed by Jean Soler[22] seem to him most instigating and closer to the way of thinking of those who wrote Leviticus. The French scholar Soler insists on Israelite rejection of everything that is hybrid, further pointing to an interesting phenomenon: the decisive break between Judaism and Christianity came from the latter's conception of Jesus as God/man, a hybrid that violates thousands of years of the Israelite imagination that encompasses narratives, institutions, and food laws.

At the end of the text, Alter (1979, 51) signals to a question of extreme importance:

> Dietary prohibitions, then, may well express a sense of taxonomic necessity in the world, built on a solid principle of differentiation. Yet far from differentiating man from God, they [dietary prohibitions] are intended to bring man into a greater likeness to Him. This is a point upon which the biblical legislator insists, through the emphatic repetition of a key term of connection at the beginning of the formal conclusion of the food code in Leviticus 11: "For I am the Lord your God; you must become holy and be holy, for I am holy."

In the article "Atonement in Leviticus," written in 1993, Mary Douglas resumes her analysis of the pure and the impure as they were conceived of and legislated by the authors of Leviticus, signaling a singularity of the laws of pollution of Ancient Israel: these are universal laws that do not intend to separate different groups into hierarchical categories and do not establish, as other cultures do, internal social boundaries. All are compelled to follow the laws of purity: "There are classes of defilement, but no classes of persons are more defiling than others" (Douglas 1993, 114). The analysis is dense and detailed, but for the purposes of this research, what is important is the anthropologist's conclusion that the authors of Leviticus built, through the rules of purity, the body as sanctuary and the sanctuary as body. The consequences of this phenomenon allow us to understand the importance of dietary laws and their central position within the Judaic worldview:

> [Thus] taking into the worshipper's body the meat of an animal which has taken blood into its body is equivalent to the worshipper eating blood directly, and taking unclean food into the human body is made equivalent to taking uncleanness into the sanctuary. (Douglas 1993, 121)

God is holy, God is pure, and to the extent that the people of Israel are consecrated through laws of purity—among which dietary laws play a fundamental role—they become a holy people in a process that brings them closer to God and makes them similar to him. In turn, starting from the premise that *tuma* (ritual impurity) and *kedusha* (holiness) are semantic opposites and that the source and quintessence of holiness is God, Milgrom (1993, 110) concludes that the people of Israel have the obligation to control the incidence of impurities. This approach contains a new element: the conception of impurity as a threat contained within death. Milgrom justifies his conclusion in the following manner:

> The explicit sources of impurity detailed in Leviticus 11–15: carcasses, scale-disease, genital discharges, together with corpses (Numbers 19), are all founded in this postulate, i.e., they symbolize the forces of death. (Milgrom 1993, 110)

On the other hand, the Israelite conception of an ethical God that reveals himself in history put an end to the cosmic struggle between good and evil deities, a notion that is typical of the peoples of the Fertile Crescent. This in turn engages the forces of life and death, in a dilemma that sows in human beings the need to employ their free will to either obey or break from the divine commandments. Those who follow the commandments of the God of Israel are bequeathed with blessings and long life; those who abandon them are punished by death. Furthermore,

> Of all the diachronic changes that occur in the development of Israel´s impurity laws, this clearly is the most significant: the total severance of impurity from the demonic and its reinterpretation as a symbolic system reminding Israel of its imperative to cleave to life and reject death. (Milgron 1993, 110)

The life force, which might seem to be part of the logic that underlies the biblical laws of purity, comes close to the vital God that Alter observes (1979, 51) in his reading of kashrut: a dynamic quality that the North American critic adds on to the static qualities (unity, integrity, and the perfection of the species and the individual) that Douglas envisions (1966, 51–52).

More recently, in the analysis of the theories that Mary Douglas and Jacob Milgrom point to, Kramer (2009, 14–15) argues that Milgrom's great contribution was the observation that, within Judaism, the sacred is opposed not to the profane but to impurity (1991). Based on this premise, Kramer states that if the impure represents death, the sacred represents life. In his words, "The eating laws, which demand that Israel be holy by separating herself from that which is impure, must be an affirmation of life and a repudiation of death" (Kramer 2009, 14). Both Milgrom and Kramer remind us that the interdictions in Leviticus 14 did not begin with an enumeration of prohibited animals, but with banning the consumption of animal blood. To eat bloody meat is equivalent to spilling blood, to taking a life. Thus, in Leviticus (17:14) we read that

> For the life of all flesh—its blood is its life. Therefore I say to the Israelite people: You shall not partake of the blood of any flesh, for the life of all flesh is its blood. Anyone who partakes of it shall be cut off.[23]

The prohibition against the ingestion of blood is an open expression of concern over life and death. To abstain from its ingestion is a movement toward the sanctification of life, of taking distance from death, of rejecting it (Kramer 2009, 15).

The theories that are briefly discussed in the pages just cited here break down dietary laws, particularly as they appear in the Hebrew Bible, and focus attention on the logic or system that underlies them. The arbitrariness that characterizes them has not been fully resolved by the analyses of the authors we discuss; thus, why these animals were chosen rather than others—and why these rules and not others were instituted to mark the identity of a group as a sacred people with an ethical mission—has not been resolved. And most likely it is not even very important. Yet for our understanding of the zeal with which Orthodox Jews follow the laws of kashrut today—their belief that the blessings bestowed on those who follow the dietary laws and purity interdictions symbolize life, while the maledictions that come with breaking such rules amount to death—is fundamental. Orthodox Jews' almost blind obedience to rabbinical guidelines may be interpreted as the action of those who try to hold on to life in a firm, unambiguous, and protected way: following the kashrut to the letter amounts to choosing life, and to a consequent distancing from death.

The analyses that have been expounded in this chapter constitute one of the perspectives from which it is possible to understand the logic behind Jewish dietary laws and their functions, both for the people of Israel in antiquity and for Orthodox Jews today. However, other perspectives elucidate different facets of kashrut, especially when our analytical focus becomes the institutions that are currently responsible, among other things, for attesting that a certain food is kosher, such as the certifying agencies that grant kashrut seals and the experts who work for them. Chapter 3 is devoted to the analysis of these phenomena.

3

Tradition, experts, and certifying agencies: Advances and setbacks in kashrut practice today

In principle—it should be clear—Judaism offers no middle ground: either something is kosher or it isn´t. There is no "part kosher" because "part" is the same as "not kosher." The yellow list is kosher. The green list has some peculiarities that we will explain below.

BDK Brasil website

I'll tell you more than that: there is no halachic ban on a woman being a kashrut supervisor. In all of our history as a Jewish people, who did this work? Women!

Chemda Shalom, supervisor of Hashgacha Pratit

Kashrut in practice and the practice of kashrut

To follow a kosher life in our times means having the needed information on foods that are considered fit for consumption by observant Jews—a task that is not always easy, considering the large number of foods that are part of our daily diet. Industrialized foods are a complicating factor, given the amount of ingredients and nutrients that they are composed of, making it hard for a layperson to determine if they are kosher, problematic,[1] or not kosher. The long list includes preservatives, flavorizers, and stabilizing agents, among others. A Jerusalem kashrut supervisor explained the issue to me this way:

In the past, when you baked bread, there were only three basic ingredients: flour, water, and salt. And how long did your bread last? Three days maximum. Today you buy a loaf of bread in the supermarket and it

The Sacred and the Impure in Judaism. Marta F. Topel, Oxford University Press. © Oxford University Press 2024.
DOI: 10.1093/oso/9780197677667.003.0003

lasts more than two weeks. But just look at the list of ingredients: you will find more than eighteen of them! And not all kosher.

The constant change in the composition of certain industrialized or semi-industrialized foods has become another problem, dealt with through the creation of a list of industrialized kosher food products (from juices to different brands of mineral water and even canned fish, pickled vegetables, jams and jellies, bread, cereals of different types, and a wide variety of other edible goods). These lists—generally posted on websites and made available as print flyers for those who don't have internet, or as *pashkevilim*[2] on the streets of Orthodox neighborhoods in Israel—undergo frequent change because of the varying composition of products used in particular brands of industrialized foods. It is therefore common to find "alerts" on food products that are no longer kosher, as well as new products that have been added to the list of the permitted.

In medium-sized and large diasporic communities, as well as in Israel, there is no single regulating body on kosher foods; rather, a number of certifying agencies compete among each other. They are usually overseen by a rabbi who is a kashrut expert, or by a particular Orthodox current that has its own customs for fulfilling precepts. Many and costly are the human resources deployed to enable the Orthodox to diversify its diet and consume processed food. Kashrut certifiers and supervisors, ritual butchers, kosher meal makers, and farmers devoted to growing fruits, vegetables, and produce that are insect-free[3]—it all makes kashrut into a big business.[4] Kosher hotels and restaurants, kosher cruise ships, bars, and bakeries are just a few examples of the variety of places that Orthodox Jews have created to enjoy the pleasures and demands of modern life despite the strict diet they must follow. Kashrut is not only a business; above all, it is a system that in recent decades, in addition to its exponential growth,[5] has diversified and given rise to new institutions. Because without these certifying agencies, Orthodox Jews would be obliged to spend most of their time in their own strongholds—unable to travel or use halls and facilities to celebrate rites of passage—they would be prevented from enjoying outings to gourmet restaurants, and—worse yet—their diet would be extremely simple and based only on products in their natural and unprocessed state.

The current reality, however, is relatively novel, if we look at the scenario from a historical point of view. For many centuries, kashrut responsibilities in Jewish communities belonged to the community rabbi, ritual butcher, and the housewives whose mission it was to keep a kosher home, in practical and spiritual senses—that is, a Halakhah-respecting household. In the absence of a ritual butcher and the presence of impediments to the purchase of meat in neighboring communities, not few were the times throughout history when religious Jews were obliged over relatively long periods to abstain from consuming beef.

Fishkoff (2010, 47) informs us that until the decade of the 1930s, the North American housewife made practically all that her family consumed, yet as of the 1960s, over 90 percent of what North Americans consumed involved some degree of industrial processing. As of this decade Orthodox Jews began to concern themselves with food preservation, assembly lines, and other technologies used in food processing. Fishkoff states that

> They [observant Jews] had to wonder whether the beef soup mix they bought in the supermarket had been freeze-dried in machines previously used for cream soups, a violation of the prohibition on mixing meat and milk. They had to determine the kosher status of chemicals used to make artificial flavorings and preservatives. The congregational rabbi was no longer enough of a guide; hence, the emergence of the kosher expert. (Fishkoff 2010, 47)

Nonetheless, by the end of the 1980s, there was a boom in kosher food certification in the United States, a tendency that did not stop growing (Selby 1997; Kramer 2009; Fishkoff 2010). In smaller Jewish communities, such as the Brazilian one, the widening of networks for processed kosher foods took two more decades to emerge and was the direct consequence of the teshuvah[6] movement (Topel 2005; Geraldo 2010). In Israel the situation is different because since the State was created, the Central Rabbinate[7] has kept the process of supervising and certifying kosher foods consumed in public institutions under its own wings.[8] Later, due to the questions raised by Orthodox and ultra-Orthodox communities on the stringency of the rabbinate's kashrut, alternative certifying agencies began to emerge, stricter in the criteria they used to inspect foods. Among them, two agencies— that of the Eda Charedit and of Rabbi Landau—stand out. The certifying agencies, whether multinational companies or local rabbis, award seals that are placed on food packaging (whether foods are processed or not) informing consumers that production has been supervised according to the Halakhah interpretations of the respective rabbis. There is another special seal, glatt kosher—extra kosher. Glatt in Yiddish means smooth, and in the context of kashrut, it refers to the animal's lungs—usually in reference to cattle—as free of lumps or sores that could potentially turn the animal into nonkosher. Originally, glatt was only applied to beef, never to poultry or nonmeat products. Consequently, defining chicken, fish, or dairy products as glatt, as is done today, is a misuse of the term and yet another indicator of the chumratization process that Orthodox communities are going through. Furthermore, as far as meat is concerned, the glatt seal refers only to the animal's lungs and provides no references to other details, such as strict procedures of slaughter. At present, misconceptions regarding the meaning are widespread, and for many, glatt has come to signify a higher standard of kashrut, like the term *mehadrin*.[9] Yet in this latter case, higher standards of kashrut supervision are in fact ensured.

The economic consequences of these classifications are many. Besides, the kashrut industry has significant economic dimensions that extend over the different stages of certification for each product. An illustrative example of the dimensions and scope of the kashrut industry is the relocation of US and Israeli supervisors to China and other countries in the Far East with the aim of inspecting all food production and processing procedures from these countries aimed at kosher certification for different Jewish communities (Fishkoff 2010). Ritual supervisors and butchers from Israel and the United States also often travel in groups to South America to verify all stages in the production of kosher meat on farms and slaughterhouses in Brazil, Argentina, Paraguay, and Uruguay.[10] There are cases in which local certification is not accepted; the Israeli rabbinate then sends ritual butchers and supervisors to kosherize meat that will be sent to Israel, from the moment of slaughter to the freezing of different cuts.

Fishkoff (2010) and Kramer (2009) highlight the momentum that kashrut picked up in the decade of the 1980s, with the creation of certifying agencies and the subsequent confrontations in which competitors attempted to delegitimate one another. Furthermore, it was during this period that new criteria for kosher certification were established. This criteria is that kosher certification seals—and, above all, the *kasher le´mehadrin* seal—must be emitted exclusively by those who follow kashrut procedures most stringently. In other words, the discussion is not forged around technical questions that refer to diverse aspects of kashrut but centers around levels of religious observance on the part of kosher supervisors and those who sell kosher products (Fishkoff 2010; Kramer 2009).

Based on articles published in the Orthodox Jewish press of North America over the course of these years, Kramer (2009, 147, 155) provides detailed descriptions of accusations regarding kosher seals in the United States whose kashrut procedures were questioned by major North American certifying agencies. Veritable scenes of battle are evoked. In a general sense, accusations focus on the degree of religiosity attributed to ritual butchers and owners of stores devoted to kosher products, rather than on the technical processes of product certification. Kramer (2009, 155) sees this novelty as expressing one of the particularities of contemporary orthodoxy, its chumratization. For Kramer, emphasis on extreme rigor generates even further subdivision within the ongoing fragmentation of Orthodox groups. He puts it this way:

> This author recognizes that the divisions are rarely about kashrut as such. What divides the groups of supervisors, and necessitates the proliferation of supervising organizations, packaging, etc., is the politics of religion—often motivated by fine differences in religious outlook, but also—no less significantly—by economic and other more worldly factors. Whatever the precipitating forces, the outcome is the same: as one author quoted earlier commented: "kosher is no longer kosher" (and, we might add, observant is no longer observant, Orthodox is no longer Orthodox, and so forth). The Jewish world is divided against itself, and these divisions show up, first and foremost, in their grocery stores and on their tables. (Kramer 2009, 154)

Some consequences of Kramer's insights are analyzed in Chapter 5, taking other contemporary ramifications of kashrut into account, indicating a clear fragmentation process that takes hold of orthodoxy.

In her monumental work, Fishkoff (2010) analyzes the delegitimizing of kashrut supervisors and certifying agencies on the part of the four major North American certifying agencies: four powerful groups that have succeeded in imposing their severe vision on the levels demanded of kosher foods in that country. In the chapter "Kosher Law and Its Discontents," Fishkoff gathers several accounts on this topic, in which the most recurrent situations refer to kosher stores that were obliged to close for lack of clientele after the chumratization process became the norm. The author reports that as of the year 2000, signs began appearing in the windows of kosher businesses warning consumers that their Jewish owners were not sufficiently observant (Fishkoff 2010, 269). Hence, although the products themselves continued to be kosher, the fact that the owners did not follow certain precepts to the letter—such as respecting the Sabbath—dealt a death blow to many businesses.[11] Protests coming from several segments of the Jewish community managed to get the signs removed, but considerable damage had already been done.

Kashrut experts: Some data

When I asked several of my interlocutors why they chose a particular kashrut seal (through my experience, from fieldwork and prior to it, I understood that each family chooses a seal, or at most two kashrut seals), the responses were quick and simple: "My rabbi urges me to buy only from Rav Landau"; "Because we, from Chabad, prefer to consume products supervised by Chabad staff"; "In my family we consume only Eda Charedit products and fruits and vegetables from Gush Katif because they are the most rigorous in their inspection. Everyone knows that, and we want to be able to rest assured." As I went deeper into my fieldwork, I realized that there was a certain complicity or closeness among persons who chose products with the same seal— or perhaps more than complicity, a common identity that enables people to gather without any worries regarding the kashrut level that is offered by their host (whether in private residences or in public spaces or salons), a behavior that enables them to avoid involuntary transgression. Most importantly, it enables them to avoid ambiguity.

If we extrapolate from analyses of biblical food–law scholars to the scenario of kashrut laws among Orthodox Jews today, following especially the conclusions of Jacob Milgrom and Robert Alter, could one conclude that this conduct—consciously or unconsciously—distances Orthodox Jews from death and brings them closer to life?

To eat together, and more precisely, to be authorized to eat together, has significant meaning when the people it brings together are friends, relatives, and neighbors: it is sharing a table, and with it, a singular culture. I remember one night I was invited to take part in a study group made up of women identified with Chabad. It was winter, and we were in Jerusalem. Together with Myriam, an interlocutor with whom I spoke several times before and after this encounter, I went to the apartment of the person who had offered her home that evening—a very generous woman who became a key informant of the highest caliber. After I had been introduced to the other women, we sat down at the table to commence with the study session that was to be led by one of the participants. There were five of us, and before the session began, our hostess made a point of showing us the seal of the cake that was on the table, certifying the supervision of a particular rabbi. She then picked up the cake, still wrapped in cellophane, to show us how it was hermetically sealed; it was not until she had finished this explanation that she opened the package and invited us to help ourselves. I was surprised by the fact that, although all those who were present belonged to the same Orthodox stream, none of them even tasted the cake. They did no more than occasionally sample the grapes that had been placed on a tray with other fruit. The same type of scene repeated itself in different ways throughout my field research with observant Jews.

On another occasion, while I was interviewing a *mashguiach*[12] in Betar Illit, the telephone rang. The mashguiach answered immediately, and little by little I was able to glean that on the other end of the line was a person with lesser kashrut knowledge who kept asking him questions. The supervisor gave explanations and attempted to assure his interlocutor but did not seem to be having much success: the questions kept coming, and with them, doubts and fears. When the mashguiach got off the call, he shared with me details he felt would be of interest to an anthropologist who was researching kashrut. They had been discussing a religious ceremony that was to take place in an Orthodox setting, and the other person, also a kashrut supervisor, was upset. He had been made responsible for the food and drink at the festivities yet was not certain if the meat supplier really worked for the certification agencies that the family hosting the bar mitzvah identified with.[13] This was undoubtedly a very serious question, more so considering existing frauds in the kosher meat industry (Fishkoff 2010; Lytton 2013ab; Hornstein 2013). I sensed anxiety coming from the other side of the line, given the fact that the mashguiach repeated each answer several times. A follow-up call for purposes of information checking made it clear to me that kashrut has many embroilments, going beyond the political confrontation between different certifying agencies and the economic dimensions of a growing, expanding industry. Kashrut stirs anxieties and fears, which, if not constant, are certainly persistent on the part of those who wish to follow its laws and rules as stringently as possible, yet feel threatened by the numerous possibilities of transgression.

The existence of certifying agencies with different types of staff reflects the level of complexity of the process that certifies a certain food as kosher.

The larger and more diverse their areas of expertise, the more powerful and rich agencies are. Data from Fishkoff (2010) reveal that in the United States, although numerous small agencies are run by local rabbis or specialized in certain segments, there are currently four North American agencies that dominate the kashrut industry.[14] According to Fischer (2015, 1), the certification, regulation, and inspection of kosher food have been a response to the increasing level of awareness on the part of Jewish consumers.

Examination of the political and economic dimensions of kashrut go beyond the scope of the present research. Such aspects demand a broad analysis from different perspectives in order to understand, for example, the diverse dynamics of certification processes in the diaspora. In Israel, the role played by the Central Rabbinate in kosher practices becomes a fundamental element in explaining any kashrut-related phenomena. Although some topics discussed in the present work touch upon the political dimensions of kashrut, they are not our focus.

The entanglement of people, institutions, and strategies implicit in the kosherization of natural and processed foods, public and private spaces, utensils, and meals constitute a complex universe that has consequences in several areas of life, often making it difficult to distinguish between what is political within the economic realm and what is economic within the religious one. Kashrut is a universe in which commandments of purity and petty economic interests converge, as do struggles for the establishment of monopolies and battles between important rabbinical authorities who seek greater power and prestige.

At this juncture, a series of questions come to the fore: What institutions train kashrut experts—that is, supervisors, inspectors, and ritual butchers? How many specializations are there today? Finally, must kashrut experts be male?

It could be said that until the 1980s, communities had only a ritual butcher, and in some cases, a kashrut supervisor whose task was to inspect problematic foods. The development of food processing brought with it the type of person whom Giddens (1991) refers to as an expert. Today there are numerous specializations in kashrut supervision, such as those who oversee poultry farms, cattle ranches, restaurants, bakeries, dairy processing plants, and factories that make parve[15] goods or different types of animal protein. Some supervisors specialize in kosherizing homes, a process that is put into practice when an Orthodox family moves or when people who have become

Orthodox as adults decide to set up a kosher home. There are also specialists for detecting insects on vegetables, fruits, seasonings, and other produce, as well as experts in the koshering of Passover utensils for Jewish families that do not have a special set of dishes for the occasion.[16]

There is a hierarchy among kashrut supervisors that depends on their level of scholarship in a particular field, and there are also kashrut inspectors who have the last word when problems or doubts emerge over the aptness of a particular food or utensil. In addition to these experts, a kosher diet is contingent upon a community that is concerned with the continuous training of ritual butchers.

The road to becoming an expert in kashrut varies from country to country and according to the stream of orthodoxy for whom the personnel are working. The level of institutionalization of studies needed to officiate as ritual butcher or as kashrut supervisor depends on the size of a community. Thus, in the diaspora, except for the United States (a country that, after Israel, has the second-largest Jewish community in the world), to be a ritual butcher or kashrut supervisor demands technical knowledge, obtained by working as an assistant to learned staff already established in the market. It is a tradition that is transmitted from one generation to the next, free of bureaucratic requirements. When a student reaches a level that is qualified enough to become a ritual butcher, the mentoring rabbi vouches for the person's ability to act as a ritual butcher of cattle or poultry. The theoretical study of the laws of slaughter, as well as other laws and rules relating to kashrut, are carried out informally. In the case of the mashguichim or inspectors, the title of rabbi may also be demanded, although it is not a sine qua non in all Orthodox communities.

In Israel, the Central Rabbinate offers frequent courses for mashguichim and ritual butchers. These courses are similar to vocational or technical training programs that award titles endorsing those who have completed them to supervise the kashrut field in which they have specialized. The vast majority of those who finish the program work for the rabbinate, since many of the streams known as ultra-Orthodox have their own staff who enter the kashrut market, much like those who carry out these functions within small diasporic communities. In 2006 the Orthodox Union,[17] a North American giant in kashrut supervision, began to offer summer courses for the future mashguichim of different countries. According to their site, more than seventy students have registered for these courses, which were theoretical and practical in nature:

> There are lectures on the cheese industry; chemical and pickle companies;
> Passover issues (when the laws of kosher become even more complex); the
> baking industry; the oleo chemical industry; oils and shortening; enzymes
> and emulsifiers; the egg industry and the blood spot; machinery; the flavor
> industry; ingredient research, and similar topics, all of which are discussed
> at length.

This passage provides an example of the level of sophistication that kashrut has achieved. Yet this complexity is not only the result of the industrial processing of foods, but also, as stated, of chumratization, the dominant tendency in Orthodox communities today, both within and outside the diaspora.

There is a vast technical bibliography on the problems raised by kashrut today, particularly regarding processed foods.[18] Some examples of the minutiae of the kosher gaze are the supervision of the use of renin, gelatin, lactose, sodium caseinate, and vitamins. In turn, naturally occurring microorganisms or microflora are considered kosher if they emerge from a kosher environment (Fischer 2015).

At this point I believe it is important to give salience to two specific phenomena. First, as I pointed out in the Introduction, orthodoxy is not homogeneous. Second, over the last decade, the hegemony that stringent interpretations of Halakhah have gained has been questioned by spokespersons of the younger generations who have, in different ways, confronted the leadership of the Great Rabbis. This phenomenon is manifested in the claims of young Israeli Orthodox regarding their right to enter the labor market. The younger generations no longer accept the interpretations of religious leaders about the causes of the Holocaust, in the absence of hostility on the part of members of the first generation born in Israel toward the country's army and its soldiers, and, finally, in the revolt of more than a few sectors over how kashrut is being practiced. In this terrain, the infeasibility of certain mechanisms that characterize the process of certifying food and public spaces such as restaurants and hotels is questioned. Criticism of the Central Rabbinate takes place mainly in Israel, as a direct consequence of the various scandals that have occurred over the last decade, in which Central Rabbinate kashrut supervisors and inspectors were accused of blackmail, negligence, and corruption (TOI Staff 2019; Sharon 2020). Another recurring topic that expresses the discontent of important segments of the country's population with the rabbinate's modus operandi in relation to kashrut—in secular and traditionalist sectors—is the increasing price of hotels, restaurants, cafés, and so on, resulting from the kosher seal that they exhibit. Rising prices (linked to the imposition of a seal), in turn, are seen as an expression of what in Israel is known as religious coercion; large segments of non-Orthodox Jews in Israel, known as "traditionalists," respect the rules of kashrut but do not follow them strictly and feel constrained by the severity of the Central Rabbinate.[19]

I believe it is important to point out that in Israel, unlike what has happened in the diaspora, eating kosher is the rule, since most businesses that make or sell food work exclusively with kosher products. The reason for this phenomenon is the basic law known as the Status Quo, signed in 1947 between David Ben-Gurion and the Orthodox party Agudat Israel. The document made four concessions to the Orthodox sector of the future State of Israel, among which was the stipulation that in all state institutions, including the country's army, only kosher foods would be served. This concession ended up going beyond the main objective its principal target and, for political and cultural reasons that escape the scope of this book, the private food sector also fell rapidly, first, under the monopoly of the Central Rabbinate and later under that of ultra-Orthodox certifying agencies. It would be no exaggeration to say that purchasing nonkosher foods or meals in Israel demands access to information on the few businesses that sell nonkosher products, whether supermarkets, convenience stores, stalls, restaurants, or hotels.

Technology and kashrut: The Sabbatical Year of the Land

Over the course of the fieldwork I carried out in Israel in January 2015, I was frequently informed that we were currently in the Sabbatical Year,[20] which, according to my interlocutors, multiplied the problems related to kashrut along all the links of the production chain: from farmers to food processing plants and, finally, housewives.

It is written in the Pentateuch (Leviticus 25:1–7) that every seven years the land must lie fallow for a whole year. During this year nothing should be planted. After seven cycles of seven years, the fiftieth year is called the Year of Jubilee. On that date, all slaves must be freed and all debts cancelled.

The complexity of rules related to the Sabbath Year and their number are so great that the ultra-Orthodox group Eda Charedit publishes, every seven years, a *Kashrut Guide for the Sabbath Year.* I was given one as a gift by a rabbi whom I interviewed in a kashrut laboratory, an experience that I discuss later in this book.

The guidebook is written in a didactic style, and its target audience—members of Eda Charedit or ultra-Orthodox Jews—are given detailed instructions as to which fruits and vegetables they are permitted to consume throughout the Sabbath Year and which establishments they should go to for duly certified foods. Nonetheless, the goals of the manual are broader since, as early as page 4, readers are alerted that there are not only interdictions regarding fruits and vegetables but also in relation to grains, condiments, vitamin complexes, dried fruits, jams and marmalades, shampoos, and body lotions and perfumes. This becomes an issue because all these products often contain fruit essences, whose origin is not always known. In the introduction to the guidebook, we learn that in the Old Yshuv (the Jewish settlement in Palestine before the State of Israel was established), the Sabbatical Year was not a problem; the Jewish community was small and had easy access to fruits and vegetables acquired from Arabs. The situation took a drastic turn when the first agricultural colonies were created in Palestine. Interestingly, at the end of the nineteenth century there were already a number of controversies around the Sabbatical Year. Secular Jews knew that following the Orthodox and religious nationalist models would deal a hard blow to the newborn agricultural activity of the first Zionist colonists or perhaps even lead to their bankruptcy, as well as representing a concession to religious groups (Cohen and Susser 2010).

It is not my purpose to go deeper here into the many and intertwined laws in reference to the Sabbatical Year, but to point to yet another paradox enshrouding kashrut today: the dependence of Orthodox sectors on Palestinian farmers in ensuring that the different types of agricultural products that reach their tables are kosher. According to the Jewish tradition, through its own sources, fruits harvested from outside the Land of Israel are fit for Jewish consumption, as are agricultural products planted and harvested in Israel by foreigners on their own properties. Based on such sources and in order to reassure Eda Charedit consumers, on page 5 of the guidebook we read the following:

> We have worked tirelessly over many years to research into crops planted on farms that belong exclusively to foreigners and on which only foreigners work, rather than any indication of joint property-holding by Jews and foreigners. The *Commission of the Sabbatical Year* has held numerous

meetings with farmers, with factory owners, with retail sales and all relevant parties in order to identify exactly who property owners are and what their boundaries are. We did vast research sweeping across the entire country on two, three occasions to study the situation properly.[21]

Visits to registry offices (to certify that Palestinian property is registered in the Palestinian farmers' names) and negotiations with Israeli security forces[22] to coordinate visits by kashrut supervisors to Palestinian farmers were part of the Eda Charedit rabbis' strategy to ensure the kashrut status of agricultural products during the Sabbath Year.

Yet Eda Charedit's work goes even further. When I visited the laboratory of the group to interview the rabbi responsible for kashrut, the latter showed me the room he worked in alongside several kashrut supervisors and their assistants, having to redouble their efforts because in June 2015, when this interview was carried out, according to the Jewish calendar we were right in the middle of the Sabbatical Year. I admit that I was stunned by what I saw, a feeling similar to what my secular Israeli friends expressed when I recounted my experiences. In a relatively spacious room, sitting in front of tables with state-of-the-art computers, I saw three ultra-Orthodox youth who were rapt with attention, eyes fixated on six huge TV screens placed on the wall in front of them. The images moving across the screen showed farmers collecting fruits and vegetables. The rabbi explained to me that these youth were following the footsteps of Arab farmers of different regions of autonomous Palestine, to make sure that the produce being harvested was not to be found on lands that the ultra-Orthodox considered to be the biblical Land of Israel. Alongside each screen was a GPS whose purpose was to provide the precise location where the farmers who supplied fruits and vegetables to Israeli Orthodox communities were working. The rabbi also showed me the complete kit of the Sabbatical Year, in which I was able to see the vest used by Arab farmers, connected to the GPS meant to transmit the location of their wearers to computers in the Jerusalem building that I was in with the rabbi. In the face of my wonder and perplexity, I was informed that this surveillance goes on twenty-four hours a day during the entire Sabbatical year, allowing the Orthodox to ingest fruits and vegetables without infringing the kashrut precepts that apply to Jews living in Israel. Before leaving, the rabbi gave me a copy of the Kashrut guide for the Sabbatical Year.

These data, together with the fact that some Orthodox rabbis do not eat meat when in Israel but may consume it when in the diaspora, led me to the following question: In the twenty-first century, is it easier to follow a kosher diet in the diaspora than in Israel? If the answer to this question is affirmative, does this then mean that the diaspora is holier than the Land of Israel itself? It should be noted that, unlike the *shabbos goy*,[23] instituted to alleviate the burden of observant Jews in the fulfillment of certain commandments, during the Sabbatical Year of the Land in Israel, dependence on foreigners is total and offers no choice, neither regarding countries from which agricultural products are imported nor the Palestinians living in territories that are considered to be beyond the boundaries of the biblical Land of Israel. In short, in the twenty-first century, without significant cooperation from Gentiles, Israeli Orthodox Jews would be unable to follow the rules of the Sabbath Year.[24]

Common sense versus chumrah: Hashgacha Pratit and renewal in kashrut

In opposition to the Central Rabbinate, in 2012 the NGO Hashgacha Pratit was created in Jerusalem by the Orthodox rabbi Aaron Leibowitz. According to the organization's website, Rabbi Leibowitz led the opening of the kosher food market to competition in a clear and open challenge to the Central Rabbinate.[25] One of the first steps taken by the organization was training kashrut supervisors to begin overseeing food establishments and restaurants from an approach based on the co-participation of interested parties.[26] Women make up the vast majority of the NGO's supervisors. Another important Hashgacha Pratit innovation was to include the owners of restaurants and food stores in the kosherization process by teaching them the corresponding procedures. Thus, instead of feeling victimized by supervisors, and obliged to pay for services that are not always performed, businesspeople are involved in a partnership with their supervisors. Notably, the NGO develops its work based on the Orthodox interpretation of Halakhah yet lacks the rigor or chumratization that characterizes most Orthodox currents today.

Another factor of fundamental importance in the modus operandi of Hashgacha Pratit is that while the rabbinate staff is paid by business owners—a situation that raises questions regarding the transparency of their work—Hashgacha Pratit supervisors are paid by the NGO itself, helping to avoid misunderstandings and fraud.

During my stay in Israel for the purposes of field research, it was easy to establish contact with Hashgacha Pratit, to get to know their supervisors and conduct a long interview with Rabbi Oren Duvdevani, renowned kashrut expert who oversees the NGO's work in that terrain.[27] From my first contact with the NGO it became clear to me that the staff carry out a job that they consider doubly important: on the one hand, they verify the kashrut practices of particular establishments, and on the other they attempt to establish a link between the interested parties: salespersons, kashrut supervisors, and consumers. This stands in open contrast to the low credibility of the rabbinate regarding its kashrut supervision activities, for which there are diverse reasons: the precarious state of poultry farms and slaughterhouses in which animals are consistently mistreated and issues of corruption regarding supervision in the latter stage of certification of businesses such as restaurants, bakeries, hotels, and street stalls that sell juices and falafel.

During my fieldwork in Israel, I had the fascinating opportunity on two occasions to accompany one of the Hashgacha Pratit supervisors on the job. This was in Jerusalem. Both workdays began very early in trendy city neighborhoods with visits to numerous bars and restaurants, including the Shuk Machane Yehuda,[28] and ending up downtown in an area also marked by a significant number of bars, food stalls, and restaurants of varying sizes and price ranges. The first establishment we visited in the Shuk Machane Yehuda was an Italian restaurant. The owner was waiting for the supervisor and had already prepared some plastic bowls of sauce, cilantro, and a series of vegetables. The supervisor sat down on a chair and, looking at the diverse greens that were piled in the bowls by holding them against the light, she began to examine them leaf by leaf to make sure they had no insects on them. While she was at it, I took advantage to pose a few questions, learning that the owners of this restaurant purchased their vegetables from Gush Katif, but nonetheless followed NGO guidelines to leave produce in vinegar and water for around three hours.

In all the places that we visited (restaurants, bars, and food stalls), the Hashgacha Pratit supervisor was welcomed. After her tasks were completed, her hosts signed an NGO handout containing the statement that the staff member had done her kashrut supervision work in the establishment on the agreed-upon date.

Hashgacha Pratit has a social and religious agenda that is reflected not only in its majority hiring of women to work as kashrut supervisors, but also in its objective to create a bridge between the Orthodox and secular worlds.

This last objective is expressed in their a priori rejection of imposing laws and religious customs on owners of food businesses who are not Orthodox, who understand little or nothing about kashrut, and who are fed up with paying fees and fines to rabbinate kashrut supervisors, for demands that are often beyond their understanding.

As stated earlier, trust is the basis of Hashgacha Pratit work, which, in its early days, underwent confrontation with the rabbinate, the latter attempting to discredit Hashgacha Pratit even through the use of legal mechanisms. According to the explanation I received from the NGO supervisor whose rounds I accompanied, the term "kashrut" has been monopolized by the Central Rabbinate, an institution that, on the one hand, reserves the right to impose fines on those who employ the term without its consent, and on the other, turns a blind eye to ultra-Orthodox certifying agencies that stick the word on their seals without authorization. Yet Hashgacha Pratit was subjected to fines and to disagreements that took it all the way to the Supreme Court. Finally, on September 12, 2017, Hashgacha Pratit returned to the Supreme Court with the support of over fifty restaurants. The court ruled that the authority to concede certification using the term "kosher" continues to pertain exclusively to the rabbinate, but that food industry establishments have the right to choose their own kashrut standards. The Supreme Court decided that the "Law against Kashrut Fraud" is to ensure that kosher foods receive careful supervision. This sentence may not seem particularly favorable, but in the Israeli context, it signifies a victory over religious coercion and the Central Rabbinate monopoly over kashrut.

As a result of the situation that I have described briefly here, Hashgacha Pratit drafted the Reliability Pact, which expresses mutual trust between the parties regarding the kashrut of the establishments supervised by the NGO. The pact functions as a kashrut certificate, and like the certificates granted by the rabbinate or by ultra-Orthodox currents, it is hung on the walls of the restaurant or the like. It seems that more and more food businesses—not only in Jerusalem but in other cities across the country—are using the NGO's services, and, little by little, customers are starting to consider these spaces just as kosher as those the Central Rabbinate has certified.

The name chosen by the NGO, Reliability Pact, expresses the strong commitment on the part of the founders and employees of Hashgacha Pratit to their work, in taking responsibility for the kashrut of food and meals in a context dominated by the presence of the rabbinate. The trust of the business owners who choose Hashgacha Pratit services is probably somewhere between the type of trust typical in traditional societies—in which individuals presume others are trustworthy, and the type that prevails in modern society—in which the trustworthiness of individuals flows from "symbolic tokens" and expert systems, and does not necessarily imply a meeting between responsible individuals or groups (Giddens 1991, 82–89).

The difference that Bildtgård (2008, 117) establishes between the credibility of the certificates issued by food certifying agencies in modernity and late modernity is an interesting one. If the seal in most modern societies becomes the only real contact between the consumer and food processing, in late modernity or postmodernity the position of science and experts begins to be questioned. Furthermore, consumers come on the scene and show that the decisions made by experts, or based on specialized knowledge, do not always have beneficial consequences. In some cases, their consequences may even be disastrous. In analyzing the intricate paths to the certification of kosher meat and the role of specialized kashrut supervisors in certifying meat, it will become clear just how disastrous expert actions may become.

One way or another, the recurrent scandals and frauds in kashrut,[29] both in Israel and in diverse diasporic locales, suggests that there "is something rotten in Denmark." It may be for this reason that the Hashgacha Pratit supervisor whom I accompanied as she went about her tasks in Jerusalem made a point of emphasizing the specificities of the NGO's modus operandi, giving salience to their work in education and their collaboration with the owners of the businesses they supervise. She contrasts this with the imposition, sometimes arbitrary, of the supervisors who work for the Rabbinate. In her words,

> Luckily for me, the NGO that I work for isn't out there to scare people. I don't go somewhere to make people throw out all the food just so that they tremble whenever I come near. We don't work like that. Our view is that we are part of the business, and that when we get to a restaurant or a bar, we not only help to discern what is or is not kosher, but we set ourselves to the task. I clean vegetables, answer questions, I look at what is going in the kitchen, I supervise the labeling of products that the business owner has purchased, I open refrigerators and look for things that are not kosher. We obviously encounter flaws because we are all human, and the important thing is that all mistakes are corrected. Our view is that a flaw is not the end of the world, and we try to solve the problem because in Halakhah there is a solution for almost everything.[30]

In fact, the supervisor who so kindly received me to make the rounds of the workday with her and talk about kashrut in Israel does her job with method, precision, and rigor, but without any behavior resembling obsessive involvement in the arduous task of identifying tiny insects in heaps of vegetables.

The NGO Hashgacha Pratit's arrival on the scene as a new social actor can be considered a milestone in the history of kashrut in Israel. Yet the situation is different in diaspora communities, where certifying agencies follow the guidelines of Orthodox rabbis identified with the most stringent approaches to Halakhah.

There are times and situations in which chumrah gains prominence. Regarding kashrut, the Jewish Passover may be cited as one of those times, eight days in which leniency is frowned upon or seen as a major threat. As a result, before and during Passover, Orthodox communities put a series of customs and rules into practice so that no commandments and customs are transgressed. Concern for festivities and preparations for them are so great that many observant women feel overwhelmed in the face of these exorbitant demands. The pointillism that characterizes contemporary orthodoxy in general and the Passover festival in particular has led some researchers to consider the existence of an obsessive component in Halakhah , which, in turn, would lead to a higher incidence of obsessive-compulsive disorder among Orthodox Jews.

4

Ritual density or obsession? Pointillism in kashrut

Take the same care in performing a "small" mitzvah that you would a "big" one, since we cannot know the reward that each of them deserves. Calculate the cost of a mitzvah versus the reward, and the gains of sin versus the loss it brings. Reflect on three things and you will not fall prey to sin: knowing that above you there is an Eye that sees, an Ear that hears, and that all your actions are recorded in the Book.

Pirkei Avot, Mishnah 1

Remember to be positive and focus on the holiness of your efforts. Never let your husband, or especially children, hear you kvetch (complain) about how hard you're working, how dried out your hands have become, how tired you are, etc. If you must vent, talk to your sister, Rebbetzin, mother or friends. Your family will appreciate the holiday much more if they have the sense that you enjoyed preparing for it.

Stephanie Savir (Aish Ha´Torah)

Remember, clean, and eat: Jewish Passover

Pesach or Jewish Passover is a celebration that many Jews know as one of the major festivities of the Jewish calendar. For many, these major holidays are their only link to the Jewish religion, or to Judaism itself, in a broader sense; there are as many ways of celebrating Passover as there are ways of expressing Jewish identity. There are those who choose to celebrate Pesach through a feminist and vegan take on Judaism, those who follow Halakhah to the letter, and others who venture beyond the Jewish law, putting the Fence around the Torah into practice . . . from a height that would cause dizziness to many others. There are Orthodox Jews who add to the Shulchan Aruch the age-old

The Sacred and the Impure in Judaism. Marta F. Topel, Oxford University Press. © Oxford University Press 2024.
DOI: 10.1093/oso/9780197677667.003.0004

customs of the rabbis who gave birth to the Hasidic[1] dynasty to which they now belong. There are liberal religious Jews who follow the Passover commandments less stringently. Many secular and ethnic Jews get together with the family to enjoy the typical delicacies of the Passover supper without worrying about how kosher the food or the wine used for the various blessings is, yet insist on intoning some prayers, the melodies reminding them of their childhood. In such homes, there is a link to tradition, yet religious ritual has undergone wide transformation.[2] There are also Jewish families who gather on Passover for a special dinner but sing no prayers. And then there are Jews who do not even celebrate the date. But among those who do celebrate Passover there is a tacit agreement: the typical foods of Passover—whether Ashkenazic in its many variations, Sephardic in its wide range of possibilities, or oriental in its rich assortment—are exquisite in taste.

As so magisterially explained by Yerushalmi (1992), Jews transmit their history through two primary channels, the ritual and the narrative. Passover dinner is an emblematic example of how this transmission took place, and how it continues to do so. The eight-day Passover cycle is marked by commandment and ritual, and the Seder[3] follows an order that take the Haggadah[4] as its compass. Yerushalmi points out that the command to remember is an imperative in the Hebrew Bible, even though it does not concern all the events narrated by the Book of Books. To put it another way, the Israelites were compelled to remember only the events in which God acted on behalf of the people of Israel and honored them with his blessings, or the events in which God unleashed his wrath on his people.

On the fifteenth of Nisan, the first day of the Jewish Passover, according to the Hebrew calendar, Jews celebrate their departure from Egypt, a moment that announces the end of their enslavement in the hands of the Gentiles and their search for freedom in the promised land. Passover also recalls the unification of the Jews into a nation that, in its entirety, had witnessed the greatest of all epiphanies. This refers to the covenant that the God of Israel established with his people, which from that moment on became a people of priests, a holy people, a chosen people with a unique and singular relationship with their God.

It is common for rabbis of all currents, from the most Orthodox to the most liberal, to emphasize that Jews during Pesach not only commemorate a miraculous event from the past that they feel proud of; the celebration of Passover is also a way of retracing the spiritual path of their ancestors.

Thus, on Passover, Jews celebrate being freed and again liberate themselves. Another metaphor often used by rabbis refers to people's spiritual freeing from their inner bondage—from their own ghosts.

The Passover Seder is made to revive a singular and fundamental process in Judaism: the exit from slavery toward freedom. Like many Jewish rituals, the Seder is held in the heart of the home and revolves around two main actions: the story of the exodus from Egypt, with its implications and importance, narrated by the eldest for the sake of the youngest; and the ingestion of certain foods that have symbolic meanings, such as matzah (unleavened bread), maror (bitter herbs), charoset (date and walnut or apple and walnut paste), and wine. Each of these elements represents specific levels of freedom and slavery.

Different streams of Judaism have their own ways of carrying out Pesach rituals and each family uses its own ritual and gastronomic traditions, as well as certain Haggadah to carry out their ritual. In turn, the duration of the Seder is directly proportional to the level of family observance. Thus, while for a secular family the Seder may be no more than a festive supper, for Orthodox Jews it is the consummation of a religious ritual, the consummation of Jewish Law, and can easily last for four hours.

According to the canonical sources of Judaism, the Torah stipulates five mitzvot in the celebration of Pesach:

1. the complete absence of chametz (leavening ferment) on the premises (Exodus, 12:15)
2. to partake of the Passover lamb (Exodus 12:43–49)
3. to partake of matzah (Exodus 12:16)
4. to partake of maror (bitter herbs) (Numbers 9:11)
5. to tell the children the story of the Jews' exodus from Egypt using appropriate symbols (Exodus 13:8)

The Torah not only prohibits the "consumption" of chametz (leavening) during the eight days that Passover lasts but also introduces two other commands: no bit of chametz may even "be seen" (Exodus 13:7) or "had" (Exodus 12:19) during the entire Pesach period. Thus, every fragment of chametz must be removed or eliminated before Pesach begins. Based on these commandments, the wise men of Israel formalized the process of removing and eliminating leavening through a systematic and ritualized search for chametz on all Jewish properties, objects, and items of clothing.

Similar to what happens in relation to other commandments, Jewish sources explain what should be done and how it should be done, but giving no reason as to why.

In an extremely summarized version of the Shulchan Aruch, from the 1960s,[5] the mitzvot concerning Passover are divided into five parts that take up more than ten pages. The second item[6] of our interest here is called "the search for leaven"; as mentioned above, it is one of the commandments that must be completed before beginning the celebrations. It has nine sub-items explaining the correct rules that allow for its performance. The reader is informed that the search for leaven must begin on the eve of Passover, and must be done with a candle made of wax, not of tallow; that all rooms where there may be leaven should undergo supervised inspection; that before the search a certain prayer must be recited; and that it is customary to leave pieces of bread in visible places so that, in case no particle of leaven is found, the prayer has not been recited in vain. Other rules are to put all the yeast found in one room, that is, what is to be burned and what is to be sold,[7] and "to nullify" the leaven, which in this context means "to proclaim that any fragment of leaven left on the property no longer exists," and that "if it exists, is no more than mere dust, it has a value comparable to dust." The leaven must be nullified again the following morning and followed by a formula that is pronounced aloud, the "Kal Chamira." Finally, the day before Passover Eve, all dishes used throughout the year must be thoroughly washed and kept in a room during the eight days of Passover, preferably one that is kept locked.[8]

The title "Shulchan Aruch," which in Hebrew means "the set table," alludes to Halakhic law, made easy so that any Jew of the time would be able to understand it. It was written in Safed in 1563 by Yosef Karo and published two years later in Venice. Its significance comes from the fact that its Halakhic resolutions are accepted by rabbinical authorities of all Orthodox streams. The book is a compilation of laws taken from the Torah and the Talmud, as well as from other books of codification. The goal of the Shulchan Aruch, as well as earlier and later codifications, was to facilitate future generations' understanding of the Laws. In 1864, on an identical mission, the rabbi Shlomo Ganzfried[9] published the *Kitzur Shulchan Aruch* (Synthesis of *Shulchan Aruch*), targeting those whose knowledge was insufficient to enable them to study the original and its respective commentaries. This manual, easy to understand, became immensely popular due to its simplicity, making Jewish laws regarding daily life more accessible.[10]

The long journey from Purim to Pesach

The high-density ritual that characterizes Rabbinical Judaism manifests itself in a concentrated manner in Passover preparations. Pesach constitutes a milestone on the Jewish holiday calendar, not only because of the importance and joy of the festival, but also due to the energy and time it consumes on the part of observant Jews. It is not by chance that the trend nowadays toward chumrah, followed by the vast majority of segments of orthodoxy and neo-orthodoxy, has made Pesach not only a joy for Orthodox women but also, at times, a burden that is hard to bear, given the number of steps, rules, and customs that must be followed to avoid transgressions.

The tasks are so many, the risks of violating commandments so great—beyond the requirement to follow the customs of the group or families involved—that the "eve" of Pesach begins, in many observant Jewish homes, when the Purim[11] celebration ends, and not—as the Shulchan Aruch stipulates—on the day that precedes it. In other words, housewives begin to concern themselves with Passover preparations a whole month in advance. Thus, if, as the Torah claims, to follow the mitzvot is to bear a burden or wear a yoke, the correct organization of the Pesach celebration as attempted by Orthodox Jews today becomes a significant part of that burden. And in the Orthodox world, everyone knows and is aware of this.

Awareness of the considerable time and energy that turn Passover Seder preparations into an especially difficult period– whether due to the chumratization of Halakhah, on the one hand, or the incorporation of technology into everyday life, on the other, led different figures from the Orthodox universe to write about the topic, drawing up guides to facilitate housewives' tasks. Not only rabbis, but also observant women have taken part in this endeavor.

In an article titled "Ten Tips for Reducing Pesach Pressure," with some of those tips originally published on the site of the Aish Ha'Torah[12] congregation, author Stephanie Savir shares practical advice and tips—as its title suggests—to lighten the burden of the Orthodox housewife. Her tenth piece of advice appears as the third epigraph of this chapter. The task here is not to go into each of them; suffice it to say that they are varied in theme, from the purchase of clothing for the Seder celebration to the choice of recipes to be made and deep cleaning of home and care in search of leavening. At the end of the article the writer vehemently urges housewives to put together a calendar of personal activities to be carried out starting the seventh week before

Pesach, that is, two months before it, giving the example of that which can be done seven weeks prior to the fourteenth of Nisan.

In the article's header is a photo of a woman with her hands on her head and her eyes bulging—a woman on the verge of a nervous breakdown. And although the idea is to add a humorous tone to the text and lighten up a situation that is considered stressful, the fact is that the Jewish Passover celebration can trigger anxiety-producing situations, especially among Orthodox women.

Similarly, several websites and internet forums cite the ideas of Rabbi Chaim Pinchas Scheinberg (2009), who explains that today's observant Jews are caught in a trap. He argues that while "in times of yore," pre-Passover cleaning in wealthy households was done by servants and in small, poor homes, by household members themselves, today's homes—comparable to those of the wealthy Jews "in days of yore"—have no maids and all tasks must be done by the housewives themselves. Rabbi Scheinberg goes further to say that today's housewives feel obliged to clean and scrub as was done in the past "on stone or rough wood floors," although today there are "laminate and ceramic floors," making this type of cleaning unnecessary. Finally, Rabbi Scheinberg warns that this phenomenon creates a paradoxical effect that can be summarized in the observation that excessive zeal (chumrah) in the fulfillment of certain commandments can preclude the fulfillment of others. In his words,

> One might be tempted to insist on doing the extra work anyway—to be "*machmir*" (stringent). However, in these stringencies lies the grave danger of causing many laxities and brushing aside many *mitzvohs* completely, Torah and Rabbinic obligations which women are required to do on Pesach and particularly during the Seder.[13]

Two centuries earlier, demonstrating greater empathy toward the anxiety some people experienced regarding stringent Seder preparations, Rabbi Nachman of Bratslav[14] used the words "confusion," "melancholy," and "madness" to describe those who demanded too much of themselves in complying with the commandments. He argued that when meticulous observation is so much that it begins to cause suffering to people and families, leniency should be allowed. His own suffering over the fear that the water consumed during Passover might contain some remnants of flour, and strategies needed to avoid it, convinced Rabbi Nachman that restrictions, excessive meticulousness, and melancholy were not the right way to perform the mitzvot.[15]

As I write these lines, I recall an interview I did with an Orthodox couple in Jerusalem. While we spoke about a variety of themes, the husband recounted experiences working as a volunteer on a telephone hotline set up for Orthodox persons with suicidal thoughts. The largest number of calls, he told me, came on the eve of Passover from women whose physical and emotional exhaustion were at their limits.

In an article published in *Ha'aretz* in 2012 and titled "How Passover Rules Strike Fear in the Heart of the Hasidic Community," Tamar Rotem, a journalist who covers themes related to Israeli Orthodox communities and was herself once Orthodox, recalled that "the very idea of physical contact with or even verbal mention of leavened foods during the holiday wreaks hysteria on Haredi streets." Rotem explores the specific customs of different Hasidic groups whose observation of Pesach rituals are extremely stringent, principally those that involve food interdictions meant to avoid the consumption of leaven. Her choice of the word "hysteria" does not seem unwarranted.

Yosef Lindell, one of the editors of The Lehrhaus,[16] an online forum that promotes discussion of Orthodox themes from diverse perspectives, wrote an article providing a detailed analysis of the evolution of Orthodox Passover guidebooks, beginning with the first of them, composed by Rabbi Blumenkrantz, disciple of the renowned North American rabbi Moshe Feinstein, and published in 1981. Lindell states that the first manual, running fifty-two pages, was in only a few decades turned into a guidebook of over two hundred pages, going on to say,

> While the Blumenkrantz guide was growing in readership and size, other Passover materials were following a similar trend. The Star-K's 50-page handbook and medicine list debuted in 2002, and by 2018 had swelled to over 200 pages. The Orthodox Union's (OU) glossy magazine now runs over 100 pages. Since the year 2000, there has been a virtual explosion of frequently updated books and online resources about how to keep Passover from halakhic figures across the Orthodox spectrum and beyond. (Lindell 2020)

Yet, curiously, Lindell observes the following: although, as of the 1980s, guidebooks reveal a tendency toward chumrah, widespread within the Orthodox universe, as of the year 2000, there is a demonstrable inclination toward leniency.[17] The author cites Passover guidebooks by North American ultra-Orthodox rabbis—such as Yaakov Forchheimer, Dovid Ribiat, Elozor Barclay, Yitzchok Jaeger, and Pinchos Yehoshua Ellis—and asserts that the books written by these rabbis, although longer, demand less stringency in fulfilling the Passover precepts, as compared to forerunner Rabbi Blumenkrantz. Lindell attributes this leniency to two internet-related factors. First, since anyone can publish material online at low cost, the production and distribution of Passover guides is no longer the monopoly of kashrut agencies and major figures in the Orthodox world such as Rabbi Blumenkrantz. Rabbis at lesser synagogues may post their own practical guides on the web that, for some reason that Lindell does not explain, are less stringent than those that came out two decades earlier. The second reason is the opportunity that the internet offers to observant Jews, not necessarily affiliated with a specific current, to question the chumrah that has been generally established in Orthodox communities.[18]

Thus, in Lindell's (2020) view, the increased length of Pesach guides should not be taken as an indication of chumrah, at least not as of the year 2020. The example that Lindell brings out to prove his thesis on flexibility is the precise definition of the *ke'zait* measure in the newest Pesach guidebooks.[19] After pointing out that each year, complying with minimum amounts of matzah and maror to be consumed at the beginning of the Seder causes much distress among observant Jews, Lindell signals two facts. The first is that the latest English-language guides have not gotten any stricter. He notes that they have been relatively consistent about measurements for half a century. Second, he argues, in recent years more lenient alternatives have started to appear online, options that reduce the ke'zait measure. Thus, in his view, it would be a mistake to presume that the longer a guide, the more stringent its requirements. Yet one issue that should not escape our attention here is that Lindell writes from the perspective of an Orthodox Jew. In other words, that which for him suggests leniency may represent, for people coming from other cultural and religious perspectives, nuances that are nothing more than an example of the constitutive filigree of Jewish Law, characterized by legal and ritual density.

Whether in recently published voluminous guidebooks or in brief guidelines with no more than several dozens of pages—as in the case of the Passover section of Forst's book (2013) *The Kosher Kitchen*—the rigor in Halakhot consummation during festivities remains visible. It is no coincidence that the latter begins with a short prologue titled "Preparing for

Pesach—Finding the Balance" (Forst 2013, 374). Once again, we encounter references to the intrinsic difficulties in preparing a Seder that follows the Halakhah, to the anxiety that this tends to provoke in housewives and the danger that the exhaustion it breeds leads to neglecting other commandments: a housewife may doze off during the Seder or get irritated with the family and not be the cheerful person she is expected to be.

The text, like others of a similar kind, is ambivalent because at the same time that it exalts the balance that is needed for an observant woman not to drown emotionally in a sea of demands, it also reminds us that "While one is obligated to follow Halakhah in all its details, one may not accept chumros that are beyond one's limits" (Forst 2013, 374). At the same time, the author does not miss the opportunity to warn that families who choose to spend their Pesach in a hotel (a choice that is ever more frequent among wealthy families who want to avoid the headaches of preparing for celebration) deprive their children of learning about the Passover mitzvot through the tasks carried out by their mothers and even by helping her at them—perhaps a steep price to pay for comfort and convenience. Also in the prologue, Rabbi Forst explains that "for our grandparents, preparation for Passover were easier, as life was more frugal and simpler." In this regard, the author is explicit in that the complexity of social life and an easier economic situation today come together to complicate the stringent cleaning that the celebration demands. And although he makes no direct reference to technology, over the following pages, in the list of objects that have to be supervised and how this should be done, the rabbi makes clear that new technologies, rather than easing the burdens of observant Jews, become a compounding difficulty, at least with regard to kashrut.[20]

Fridge, freezer, electric oven, gas oven, microwave, stove cover, dishwasher, mixer, blender, coffee maker, dishwashing soap, thermoses, and coffee pots: these are just some of the objects of the modern kitchen that must be strictly kosherized. Several of them, such as the microwave and the freezer, require special cleaning methods, and there are controversies among different rabbis about how to carry them out correctly. Appliances are contemporary additions to kitchen furniture such as the sink, pantry, table and chairs, dishes and silverware, strainers, and oven mitts. In turn, the *haggalah* (a way of kosherizing some utensils by means of boiling water) consists of twenty-three steps.

The book written by Rabbi Fuks (2002) is more complex, perhaps because it was thought up for an Israeli readership—implying a singularity related to the peculiarities of kashrut in that country—or because ArtScroll publishers, which printed Rabbi Forst's book, also has a book of 172 pages devoted specifically to Pesach.

As I have mentioned in my analysis of Rabbi Fuks's book, in chapter 3, also in the pages devoted to Passover preparations, the way each page is divided in two parts stands out: a smaller part consists of texts, and a longer one is made up of footnotes. The latter, extremely complex, demand scholarly knowledge in the reading of Halakhot books. The author begins the introduction to chapter 6, titled "A Kosher Kitchen for *Pesach*,"[21] with the following reflections:

> Commitment to kashrut in a Jewish home is the key to its sanctity, as well as that of those who live in it; thus, the acquisition of food and the correct use of appliances and utensils to serve it is a mission of extreme importance that requires investment, efforts, perseverance, and attention throughout the year. This becomes even more so as Pesach approaches, the celebration of freedom that all preparations seek to exalt, like a diamond in a crown. The central target of activities is the kosherization of the kitchen and utensils as well—of course—as the purchase of kosher Passover food that bears reliable seals.[22] (Fuks 2002, 162)

The big leap that the author takes between the spiritual realm (holiness) and the sphere of daily life (devices and utensils for food preparation) is interesting, as the latter are neither symbol nor part of extraordinary ritual paraphernalia, but simple, everyday objects. Yet it is through the objects of everyday life that Jews are sanctified on a day-to-day basis. Also in the introduction, Rabbi Fuks reminds us that the yoke of Pesach preparations falls on all members of the family, although in this particular chapter and throughout the book as a whole, the targeted reader is presumed to be female.

Similarly to the ArtScroll book, written by Rabbi Forst (2013), Rabbi Fuks's (2002) manual begins with instructions on how to clean kitchen furniture. Several sub-items devoted to discussion of the sink consider how new it is and what material it is made of (marble, ceramic, stainless steel). After furniture come appliances such as stove, refrigerator, freezer, and so on, and utensils. The passage "Kosher Utensils for Passover" refers to utensils that have not had any contact with yeast and can thus be used without concern. Examples are new cutlery, pans, and cleaning basins. Yet even when these objects are new and have never had any contact with yeast, some rules for their correct use apply. Finally, the author makes a curious observation: new utensils purchased for Passover, even if purchased from a Gentile, may be considered kosher.

From the chapter's start—and throughout the book as a whole—each problem dealt with multiplies, making it impossible to write a rule without use of footnotes. Thus, the section headed "Types of Kosherization" mentions three types: haggalah (putting in boiling water utensils used for liquids that had contact with yeast), *libun* (putting in boiling water utensils that touched nonliquid yeast), and *ashrayah* (putting in boiling water utensils that had contact with cold yeast for twenty-four consecutive hours). Another danger comes from kosher Passover utensils that have unintentionally been mixed with nonkosher ones. In this situation, and where there is uncertainty regarding which kosher utensil was contaminated by a nonkosher one, none of those potentially affected can be used during festivities.

In the section "Pesach Purchases," the author advises shopping for the holiday in leaven-free stores[23] and explains that the shopping bags used throughout the year should be methodically cleaned and aired out. In "Last Preparations in the Kitchen, Reminder for Passover Eve," Fuks (2002, 189) calls for a thorough cleansing of the telephone (if there is one in the kitchen), calendars, and cookbooks. Finally, he warns that both the housewife and her daughters should kosherize the rings they wear on their fingers, explaining that in the preparation of bread, which takes place before Passover, there is a high probability that particles of leaven have remained in them. In fact, the author advises keeping rings in a place in the house chosen for keeping all the chametz during the eight days of Pesach and keeping this space under lock and key, if possible.[24] An entire page is devoted to a possibility that may become a real nightmare for Orthodox housewives but happens every few years: Shabbat's overlapping with other festivities, and in this case with Passover. This convergence of the calendar is extremely demanding, as the commandments for one festival may conflict with those of the Sabbath. One example is the obligation to fast and engage in a process of self-reflection on Yom Kippur and the obligation to eat three meals on Shabbat, which also requires feeling and showing joyousness. In the case of Pesach, complication comes from two conflicting mitzvot: eating baked bread on Shabbat and the Pesach prohibition of ingesting anything that contains yeast.[25]

Technology, strict religious observance, and the body: Indications of OCD in contemporary orthodoxy?

Passover is the celebration that most demands that observant Jews remain attentive to any possible transgression of precepts and is, at the same time, the most densely ritualized of holidays. Even Orthodox rabbis remind us that on Pesach the mitzvot must be very thoroughly performed. On ordinary days, of course, there are many commandments to be followed, and Shabbat prohibitions and obligations have multiplied significantly, as modern life further penetrates the daily life of Orthodox Jews. Thus, manuals such as *Do You Know Hilchos Shabbos? Practical Questions for the Whole Family* (Fletcher 2013), as well as many others that deal with issues of Halakhah, are emblematic of the new winds that began to blow over the Orthodox universe some three decades ago. Fletcher's book contains five hundred rules (commandments, Halachot, and customs) that must followed to the letter in order to respect the Sabbath as the day of rest. In his introduction, the author asserts, "The *sefer* [from the Hebrew: book] does not claim to be exhaustive but hopefully it could encourage people to study the halachos in more detail if they have the opportunity" (Fletcher 2013, 24). Like many others, the book is written in the form of the questions or doubts of an Orthodox man or woman, followed by the clarifications of the author, Rabbi Michoel Fletcher. I cite two examples from this kashrut manual, noting that given the meticulousness of the answers and the halachic categories which are referred to but not always explained, I was often at a loss in my comprehension of the problem at hand (without consulting some Orthodox person), albeit managing to imagine the spirit of the question.

I've always wondered about this: Can I eat the hot meat with the cold carrot salad together?

A number of factors in this situation could result in a lenient conclusion. It is doubtful that hot meat, if it is no longer in a kli rishon, can cook anything else. You don't intend to cook the carrot salad and even if it happened, it would spoil rather than improve the taste of the carrot. For these reasons, we cannot say that somebody who is lenient has done wrong. Even so, some say that lechatchilah we should try to avoid allowing hot meat to touch raw vegetables (Fletcher 2013, 157)

I was warming up Avi's milk bottle in some hot water when Chani told me she heard that it's not allowed. Is she right?

You could both be right. Indeed, to submerge Avi's bottle totally in hot water, even in a kli sheini, is not allowed because of hatmanah. If it is only partially submerged, that is not hatmanah and it is permitted. (Fletcher 2013, 164)

The rules that the parturient and the sick must respect regarding diet, prohibited drugs, and what is allowed or not allowed to be done in a hospital on the Sabbath, have also filled hundreds and hundreds of pages of guidebooks and manuals. Equally prolific are guidebooks, tutorials, classes, and courses on family purity and on different aspects of kashrut, such as the special commandments for the Sabbatical Year and the extra care that must be taken to eliminate insects and any "traces" of insects from vegetables for consumption. In other words, as I have reiterated, the ritual density that characterizes Halakhah permeates not only extraordinary moments such as Passover and rites of passage but daily life as well.

On this basis, I believe that it is already feasible to outline some of the hypotheses that undergird this research. First, is it possible to say that in Judaism there are not always clear boundaries between the sacred and the profane (as the anthropology of religion usually argues)? An alternative to this hypothesis would be that, as a religion whose objective is to create a holy, priestly people, no dimension of life remains entirely profane. Second, would it be possible to understand the dense ritualization of everyday life as a process of sanctification, whose opposite is the impure, rather than the profane? If these questions challenge some of the assumptions of anthropology and studies of religion and thereby become particularly provocative, to answer them demands analysis of other dimensions of kashrut and of how kashrut reflects concerns of and innovations in contemporary orthodoxy.

Yet before sketching some responses to these questions, I feel it is relevant and enlightening to take a brief look at the consequences of excessive demands made by other religious groups, particularly within the sphere of ritual, but also regarding faith. This means entering a terrain that lies somewhat outside the social sciences in order to gain broader understanding of the phenomenon of ritual density within Orthodox Judaism and ponder whether we can identify an obsessive structural component in Halakhah that has intensified, along with recent decades of the radicalization of orthodoxy.

A number of studies that originated in psychiatry, ethnopsychiatry, and psychology have addressed the relationship between religious rituals and certain types of neuroses. These studies try to identify similarities and differences between obsessive-compulsive disorder (OCD) and religious rituals. And although Orthodox Judaism is cited in many articles whose objective is to identify cause/effect correlations between a particular religion and OCD, Islam and Christianity have also been the subject of research. In a certain sense, what draws my attention in the vast bibliography on the subject is authors' conclusions that there is no causal relationship between degrees of religiosity (within any of the religions considered) and the incidence of OCD. Thus, in a much-cited article, Greenberg and Huppert (2010, 282) point out that "despite the similarities between religious ritual and compulsions, the evidence to date that religion increases the risk of the development of OCD is scarce." Further on, the authors make the vehement statement, "No study to date has found that a religious upbringing induces OCD" (Greenberg and Huppert (2010, 283).

Case studies, most frequently focusing on Orthodox Jews, Muslims, and Christian fundamentalists, come to similar conclusions. In their analysis of Muslim Turkish patients, Tek and Ulug (2001) were unable to identify a significant relationship between religiosity and the presence of religious obsessions. This led them to believe that instead of functioning as a determinant of OCD, religion is merely one of the dimensions in which OCD manifests itself. Regarding Orthodox Jews, conclusions are the same: there is no cause/effect relationship linking Judaism and OCD in Orthodox patients (Greenberg and Witztum 2001; Huppert, Siev, and Kushner 2007; Pirutinsky, Rosmarin, and Pargament 2007; Zohar et al. 2005).

Given these data, a question arises: why have so many studies been carried out on the incidence of OCD among members of different religions, if all of them conclude that religion cannot be considered a cause of OCD? A plausible answer is the fact that scrupulosity, a subcategory of OCD, was identified in the history of psychiatry prior to OCD itself. Furthermore, according to the specialized literature, when a very religious individual develops OCD, there is a high probability that this religiosity will express itself in the form of scrupulosity. In other words, in very religious individuals, scrupulosity is more likely to become their prime OCD symptom. Among the most common manifestations of scrupulosity in religions with a strong orthopractic base such as Orthodox Judaism and Islam are excessive care with the cleanliness of different parts of the body, strictness in compliance of the respective dietary laws (halal and kashrut stand out), and the fear of individuals' insufficient concentration when reciting daily prayers. Besiroglu, Karaca, and Keskin (2014, 4) point out that other common religious obsessions include fear of having committed sins (or of committing them in the future), intrusive mental images of a sacrilegious or blasphemous nature, and fears that one might be punished by God or go to hell because of undesirable thoughts. In turn, the most recurrent religious compulsions include constant repetition of prayers, repetitive cleansing rituals, and excessive attention to small details of religious tradition (Besiroglu, Karaca, and Keskin 2014, 4).

Studies suggest that individuals who suffer from OCD in its religious variant—that is, who are scrupulous in their compliance with of certain commandments and ritual rules—demonstrate a tendency to treat their own thought as if it were action. This trait, known as TAF (thought-action fusion), is more common in the Christian religion, which awards a seminal place to the strict relationship between thought and action, particularly regarding thoughts that are considered sinful and actions that are subject to condemnation. An emblematic example is the following passage from the Gospels: "You have heard that it was said, 'You shall not commit adultery'; but I say to you, that everyone who looks on a woman to lust for her has committed adultery with her already in his heart" (Matthew 5:27–28).

The articles cited here, and many others as well, tend to end with suggestions for the best ways of treating religious OCD patients. In the case of Islam, similarly to what can be observed in Orthodox Judaism, we find interesting recommendations on the best therapies to be used in treating patients. They suggest a type of cognitive therapy in which, in addition to the therapist, a religious authority is also brought in. The latter is deemed necessary because, in orthopractic religions characterized by ritual density—and hence, highly detailed ritual consummation—it may be hard for a therapist to tell whether apparently compulsive behavior is part of the religion or the expression of pathological behavior (Nabil et al. 2019, 19).

In addition to research that merely mentions Orthodox Judaism as an example, there are publications devoted to the analysis of OCD prevalence among Orthodox Jews. They attempt to identify cause-effect correlations between OCD and Orthodox Judaism itself (Greenberg and Shefler 2008; Huppert, Siev, and Kushner 2007; Pirutinsky, Rosmarin, and Pargament 2007; Zohar et al. 2005). Whether explicitly or implicitly, these works dialogue with the Freudian theory according to which there is more than a superficial similarity between the obsessional acts of neurotics and religious practices (Himle et al. 2011; Tek and Ulog 2001; Freud 1959). However, interest in establishing analogies and comparisons between religious rituals and mental illness is broader, encompassing a wide range of options. There are, for example, works that seek to reveal the therapeutic value of ritual, as in the case that interests us: the therapeutic value of Jewish rituals. Along these lines, Dein and Loewenthal (2013) highlight the benefits of Orthodox Jewish Shabbat celebrations, despite the word "costs" that is included in the article title ("The Mental Health Benefits and Costs of Sabbath Observance among Orthodox Jews"). Spero (1977) distinguishes between existential and neurotic types of anxiety; based on an analysis of canonical Jewish texts, he comes to the conclusion that Rabbinic Judaism stimulates existential anxiety, as cause of individual growth and a generator of creativity. The author clearly differentiates both types of anxiety in order to argue that from the perspective of Rabbinic Judaism, existential anxiety has a positive dimension. He sees it as a trigger for reflections on guilt and regret, which in turn clear a path in the direction of the Creator.

In this chapter I have chosen to analyze Pesach manuals because they constitute a sort of vox populi, including both Orthodox and liberal secular Jews, on how laborious it is to organize a Seder properly. Furthermore, as I have already explained, among Orthodox Jews in particular, the anxiety that Passover preparations arouse becomes an object of reflection and discussion, given the vast number of prescriptions and proscriptions, customs and idiosyncrasies that must be accounted for. In Chapter 5, I analyze commandments regarding the fruit and vegetable cleaning, in an effort to scrutinize and better understand the pointillism of the Jewish kashrut rituals.

There are few groups whose daily lives are as ruled by a ritual density as intense as the one that characterizes Orthodox Judaism. We could consider Islam, Jainism, and ancient Hinduism as religions in which orthopraxis plays an important role, yet the number of rituals they include is not as vast and decisive as in Rabbinic Judaism. In turn, Judaism is unique not only because of the quantity of rituals it comprises but because the latter apply to the entire group, rather than just a specific caste of individuals or priests. This feature of Rabbinic Judaism is its pillar, and mitzvot, rather than doctrine, are its matrix. Faced with this reality, which has increased due to the current tendency in Orthodox communities to execute mitzvot in the most stringent ways, two questions arise: What is the point of ritualizing the daily life of an entire group so meticulously? Could the pointillism that characterizes Halakhah be interpreted as an obsessive component of Orthodox Judaism and, consequently, of Halakhah?

Regarding the meaning of a ritualization so heavily connected to daily life and so loaded with detail, I believe that a plausible response is to understand ritual, less in its symbolic function—as anthropology has traditionally done[26]—and more as a performative act whose goal is to impose a singular type of discipline. In his work on medieval Christian monasticism, Asad (1987; 1988) suggests that the rituals developed by Catholic monastic orders, such as the liturgy, are necessary for the acquisition of Christian virtues. Thus, the liturgy cannot be separated from a broader program. It does not constitute a symbolic action that can be separated into technical actions, such as rules that establish correct ways of eating, sleeping, working, and praying. All such actions are part of a program, a pedagogy, and a disciplinary order that crystallize around the imitation of an exemplar model (Asad 1988, 80). Furthermore,

> The virtues were thus formed by developing the ability to behave in accordance with saintly exemplars. Acquiring this ability was a teleological process. Each thing to be done was not only to be done aptly in itself, but done in order to make the self approximate more and more to a pre-defined model of excellence. . . . In this conception, there could be no radical break between "outer behavior" and "inner motive," between "social rituals" and "individual sentiments," between activities that are "expressive" and those that are "technical." (Asad 1988, 80)

Asad (1987) uses the term *gestus* to refer to a correct attitude that is simultaneously physical and psychological. Regarding the institution itself—that is, the medieval Benedictine monastic orders—the central idea was to establish a disciplinary program, one of whose goals was to organize certain emotions, such as desire, humility and repentance, that the Christian virtue of obedience depends upon (Asad 1987, 166–167).

Despite the significant differences between the Catholic monastic orders of the Middle Ages and Rabbinical Judaism, Talal Asad's theoretical approach is more than relevant for beginning to understand the pointillism that characterizes Jewish Law in general and contemporary manuals in particular. Asad uses the term "reorganization of the spirit" to refer to the result of the ritual, gestural, and discursive practices that sustain the disciplined body, giving order to the spirit that must face the constant temptation of original and current sin (Asad 1987, 171). The monastic program, in turn, is anchored in texts whose authority varies according to temporal context. Therefore, in the case that Asad (1987) studies, the manual *The Rule of St. Benedict* substitutes the Bible, earlier manuals, texts written by the Church Fathers and breviaries, analogous to the replacement of Torah and medieval Jewish codifications by contemporary Halakhoth manuals. Furthermore, it is the program that tells disciplines what must be done, how, in what order, and by whom (Asad 1987, 171).

Finally, the program should not be interpreted simply and automatically as a way to repress socially perilous psychic forces or to inculcate new values: people here should not be seen as "active" versus "passive" social actors. Also governing a number of technical activities such as work, the program is meant to foster certain Christian abilities, among which the most important is the capacity to aspire to obedience (Asad 1987, 183).

It is not uncommon for Orthodox rabbis to approach the Halakhah as a program. Rabbi Noach Weinberg's well-known manual titled *Instructions for Living* is an emblematic example of such understandings of Jewish Law.[27] He offers videos and talks in synagogues, at yeshivot and on the internet, using the above-mentioned title repeatedly. No less important is the *naase ve´nishmh* (we do first and listen later), conceived by observant Jews as the only reason for following commandments: absolute obedience to the path that God has drawn for his people.

Research carried out with Orthodox people who suffer from OCD reveal four areas of religious observance in which the symptoms of obsessive-compulsive disorder are manifested: devotion to prayer (repetition of particular prayers of the liturgy in the belief that they were not said with sufficient devotion), meticulous observance of dietary laws (fear of mixing dairy with meat and derivatives, as well as obsessive behavior in pre-Passover yeast removal), stringent observance of the laws of family purity (women who have unfounded doubts regarding the state of menstrual purity), and laws regarding the hygiene of the male body before prayers (men's feelings that they are not clean enough to pray[28]). Such researchers work with small samples of patients who show up at the offices of their respective therapists and all come to the conclusion that it is not possible to establish cause-effect relationships between orthodoxy and OCD. Among these works, the most wide-reaching and instigating is the book *Sanity and Sanctity: Mental Health Work among the Ultra-Orthodox in Jerusalem*, written by Greenberg and Witztum (2001). I draw attention to the chapter "Ritual as Psychopathology, or Is the Code of Jewish Law a Compulsive's Natural Habitat?" in which the authors delve more deeply into Orthodox Judaism in their quest to understand the extent to which a religion that encourages verification and repetition in multiple areas of life has the potential to cause pathological behaviors such as OCD.

Regarding the laws of kashrut, the examples given by the authors refer to what they call "the battle between milk and meat" and the stress that precedes Pesach. Interestingly, the authors point out that the Mishnah injunction to follow reasonable standards of cleanliness seems to contrast with chumrah, that is, the general rigor of contemporary manuals (Greenberg and Witztum 2001, 117). In their conclusions, Witztum and Greenberg state,

> In the cases of OCD with religious content, the fear was religiously consistent—for example, the fear of being in contact with feces before prayer. The underlying logic was also religiously consistent: the understanding that if there is a speck of feces in the anal region, prayer is forbidden. (Greenberg and Witztum 2001, 124)

Yet immediately afterward, the authors assert the existence of important differences between Orthodox patients with OCD and extremely devoted religious individuals. Among the patients with OCD, the religious ritual that they fixate on is one of trivial religious importance, as in the example cited in the article in which a patient obsessively cleans his anal region before engaging in specific prayers. In the second type of situation, people with OCD are generally concerned with a determined type of observance; whereas groups or people who are more extremist in fulfilling the mitzvot follow all precepts strictly.[29] Third, patients with OCD, attempting to follow a particular mitzvah, often neglect others or lose track of their objectives, the result of compulsive fixation on the consummation of but one mitzvah among many (Greenberg and Witztum 2001, 124). Finally, Orthodox patients with OCD also tend to show compulsive behavior in other arenas of life that have nothing to do with religion (Greenberg and Witztum 2001, 130). Nonetheless, Greenberg and Witztum do not discount the chance that, in spite of the nonexistence of quantitative data on the prevalence of OCD among Orthodox and non-Orthodox Jews within the Israeli population, future research that is quantitative in focus may reveal that an education carried out under the influence of stringent compliance with Jewish law creates a predisposition to OCD on the part of members of Orthodox communities.

In order to find another way to argue the nonexistence of a correlation between Jewish orthodoxy and OCD, Witztum and Greenberg bring in the example of two of the Ten Commandments: respecting the Shabbat and honoring one's parents, asserting that neither of them triggers OCD-type conduct. (Greenberg and Witztum 2001, 128). I would, however, take issue with their choice of examples. If one of the ways of classifying mitzvot distinguishes those that deal with the relationship between human beings and God (cultural precepts) and those that regulate types of relationships among human beings (ethical precepts), throughout history it was those of the first type that were the target of legislators of different generations (in particular, those of more recent generations) in their attempts to intensify chumrot. Thus, it is difficult to imagine obsessive behaviors in relation to precepts such as honoring one's parents, helping the poor, refraining from false witness and many other commandments that govern the conduct among human beings. As for Shabbat, although the authors' conclusions probably come from the clinical samples they worked with, or from research found within specialized literature, it is important to keep two issues in mind: (1) samples of clinical cases of Orthodox Jews with OCD are small, and (2) there are numerous Shabbat Halakhot manuals, such as the one mentioned earlier, that demonstrate extreme concern for detail and encourage readers to take a hard line in fulfilling mitzvot.

Huppert and others (Huppert, Siev, and Kushner 2007, 930–937) did research on the same phenomenon and warned that therapists who treat Orthodox patients with OCD should be in touch with the patients' rabbis, since those whose are unaware of the detailed rules that govern Orthodox Judaism can easily confound religious commandments with OCD symptoms. The meticulous rules for washing hands when one gets up in the morning is an example given by the authors regarding the hygiene-related repetitions that characterize Orthodox Judaism and that an unknowing therapist might take as signs of compulsive behavior.[30]

Another function of rabbis who are involved in therapy, in their attempt to collaborate in the cure, is to offer patients with OCD more lenient interpretations of the mitzvot that the patients pursue compulsively. As mentioned on numerous occasions throughout these pages, rabbinical authority is of seminal importance within Orthodox communities. Manuals on kashrut and other types of Halakhot constantly remind their readers to consult rabbis who are known for their scholarship and authority in the area in which questions have arisen.

Returning to the issue of whether Orthodox Jewry has an obsessive component, despite all the reservations enunciated by the above-mentioned authors, the function that rabbis play in therapy, as expressed in the following account, seems particularly revealing:

> Ultimately, religious and halakhic standards are best defined by the patient's rabbi. This is important because built into the halachic system are leniencies that can be applied in difficult circumstances, and rabbis, when provided with appropriate information, may feel that they can provide lenient rulings that still do not violate the letter of the law. . . . Some rabbis will want time to examine the issues prior to answering. *This is not deferring the therapist, but standard for difficult questions. They may even recommend consultation with a rabbi of greater authority.* (Huppert, Siev, and Kushner 2007, 937–938, emphasis added)

I believe that if the therapist and the OCD patient are not sure about the definition of what a symptom is, and more importantly, if the patient's rabbi is not sure whether a particular behavior is a neurotic symptom or a mitzvah—or even a radical way of consummating a mitzvah, to the point where it becomes necessary to consult a learned rabbinical authority on the matter—this in itself is strong enough evidence of an obsessive component in Orthodox Judaism. If not the case for Rabbinic Judaism as a whole, it is certainly so for Rabbinic Judaism in its contemporary expressions.

Initial conclusions

As demonstrated in this chapter, Pesach manuals are becoming ever more voluminous and detailed. One of the reasons lies in the fact that each generation of observant Jews faces new challenges for stringent compliance with the Halakhah. Consulting the Shulchan Aruch[31] in the twenty-first century in order to solve a problem related to the Passover Seder or how to proceed in order not to infringe a Passover mitzvah is not the easiest or most efficient way to rigorously respect Jewish law in this day and age. There are, for example, no answers to be found in Josef of Karo's work regarding which food groups seeds such as chia or quinoa should be included in,[32] or whether one can open a PET bottle during Shabbat, questions that concern today's observant Jews. The same can be said regarding the Passover Haggadah, which, although not appearing in the self-same format throughout history, did not usually exceed thirty pages. Nowadays, as stated earlier, it is possible to find a Haggadah of more than two hundred pages. In other words, the Haggadah, a small manual that organizes the ritual of the Jewish Passover meal, can contain so many commandments, customs, rules, and logistical matters that it becomes an enormous book, similar to a treatise.

Considering the above-described scenarios, I see Asad's (1987; 1988) analysis of the disciplinary system of the medieval Benedictine order as a first step toward understanding Halakhah functions and characteristics. The "reorganization of the spirit" mentioned by Asad is related to Christian doctrine and practice that consider sin to be a constant threat to the soul.[33] In the case of Orthodox Judaism, the *yetzer ha'ra* (in Hebrew, "evil inclinations") refer to those whom deviations in the fulfillment of the Law are attributed. They lurk day and night to destabilize the spirit and will of the good Jew and must be tirelessly fought. It is no exaggeration to say that after fighting and overcoming "evil inclinations," observant Jews undergo a reorganization of the spirit that allows them to continue a way of life in which little or nothing remains outside the "Halakhic program."

Furthermore, I find Asad's approach (1987; 1988) as fruitful because, as compared to the Freudian theory of religious rituals, it enables a more precise understanding of the phenomenon of ritual density in Orthodox Judaism. Freud sees religious rituals as "collective neuroses," and obsessive-compulsive behaviors as an individual form of religious ritual (Freud 1959). Despite the parallelism observed between both types of behavior, Freud points to four similarities and four fundamental differences between them. At this point, it seems enough to mention that, unlike religious rituals, obsessive behaviors seem to lack meaning, even for the patient, although they have a logic of their own that psychoanalysis is capable of interpreting. In contrast, religious rituals have a meaning that, although not always transparent to the observant person, is transparent to institutions and their religious leaders. This is not to minimize the relevance of Freudian analysis of the religious phenomenon, but to point out that it is valid for different religious forms and manifestations, while Asad's (1987, 171) restricted approach is more fruitful for our understanding of the mitzvot system that governs the daily life of Orthodox Jews. Asad reminds us that rather than a program that acts through the mechanical repression of prohibited behaviors, the disciplinary program that he studies governs external behavior and internal motivations, intertwining them in an inextricable way. Developing Christian virtues is the goal of the disciplinary program that takes as its exemplary model the saints of the church. Likewise,

> The things prescribed, including liturgical services, had a place in the overall scheme of training the Christian self. (Asad 1988, 80)

The predefined model of excellence to which Asad refers here reminds us of the a priori status that, according to Soloveitchik (1983, 20), Halakhah has for observant Jews. This means that Orthodox Jews decipher and relate to the world through the Torah as it reveals itself to them: as a body of precepts and laws that guide the Orthodox on the long journey of existence. Equipped with rules, judgments, and fundamental principles, pious Jews approach the world from the vantage point of a predefined relationship (Soloveitchik 1983). Thus,

> The essence of the Halakhahh, which was received from God, consists in creating an ideal world and cognizing the relationship between the ideal world and our concrete environment in all its visible manifestations and underlying structures. There is no phenomenon, entity or object in this concrete world which the a priori Halakhahh does not approach with its ideal standard." (Soloveitchik 1983, 19–20)

Soloveitchik's rationalist approach focuses on Halakhah as the model of conduct for observant Jews. Yet the history of Judaism has always had emblematic figures who, either because of their erudition—like Maimonides and the Gaon of Vilna—or because of their devotion and charisma, like the Great Hasidic Rabbis—acted and continue as a model to be followed by Orthodox Jews, eager to respect and fulfill the precepts of Halakhah in ways they consider most correct and genuine. At the same time, conceiving the ritual as a performative act makes it possible to understand the chumrot and the radicalization of Jewish orthodoxy from another angle.

In his articles on ultra-Orthodox Jews, Aran (2013a; 2013b) concludes that to approach extremist religious groups by prioritizing their internal rather than external relations—that is, focusing analysis on their relations with other members of the group and with other religious groups rather than contrasting them to modern and secular society[34]—is extremely fertile for a better understanding of the rigidity of their interpretations of canonical texts and of ritual and cultural practice.

With the purpose of justifying his argument, Aran argues that analysis of Jewish, Christian, and Muslim monotheisms shows that extremists see themselves as morally superior to other religious groups. Aran (2013a, 159) reminds us that it is common among Orthodox Jews to set standards of religiosity for themselves, their families, their neighbors, and other Orthodox communities. In turn, the term *itchazkut* (from Hebrew: "strengthening") is part of the vocabulary of Orthodox Jews and designates the current movement toward following precepts in the most stringent way. As an eminently performative orthopractic religion, strengthening turns more toward ritual practice than to faith or doctrine.

Another explicit term in the discourse of observant Jews used for measuring degrees of religiosity is *madregot* (from Hebrew: "ladder, scale"), used to establish distinctions between different levels of severity for compliance with commandments. The Orthodox distinguish between the men who devote themselves to full-time study—the *talmidim chachamim*—and for that reason gain prestige, and those at the base of the ladder, the men who do not study formally, known as simpletons or *amartzim*[35] (Aran 2013a, 159). Aran (2013a, 159–160) adds that from the Orthodox perspective there are several systems and subcategorizations to measure the degree of religiosity of individuals and families that sometimes overlap. The different levels of adherence to precepts are measured in all areas of life, including kashrut. As discussed in Chapter 3, categories such as kosher *le'mehadrin* or glatt kosher certification seals are examples of this phenomenon. In turn, the hierarchical classification of kosher foods is subject to constant change, controversy, and negotiation—and, as Aran (2013a, 161) reminds us, the quantification of religiosity can rarely be separated from issues such as prestige or financial and political considerations.

It is not my intention here to engage in extensive analysis of Gideon Aran's articles—the revealing insights of his empirical observations and theoretical reflections. Still, I believe it is important to point out that the type of competition that exists in Orthodox Jewish communities differs substantially from crusades or religious wars. It is characterized by a more subtle competition—between peers who share the same doctrine, who do not necessarily have disagreements in relation to the exegesis of the sacred books or nurture rivalries in relation to privileges or positions of prestige (Aran 2013a, 162).

In the historicization and analysis of Jewish orthodoxy, Aran (2013b: 395) draws attention to a phenomenon that in some way is one of our pivotal points: the radicalization of contemporary orthodoxy. One such example given by this Israeli anthropologist refers to the departure from moderation that characterizes the Shulchan Aruch as it is mobilized by a significant number of Orthodox leaders. Aran writes,

> In certain cases, supreme authority is attributed not to the written law, but to what they refer to as the "spirit of the law." This revolutionary concept is an expression of contemporary ultra-Orthodox rabbinical interpretation that has pretensions of awareness of the original intent of the ancient rabbis and of the semi-prophetic capability to uncover the hidden meaning of the Torah. (Aran 2013b, 395–396)

In both aforementioned articles, Gideon Aran emphasizes that the fact that it is performative makes Orthodox Judaism a religion in which the degree of religiosity of its members is easy to measure. In his view, the itchazkut, the madregot, and the kashrut certification seals are all mechanisms that are used as a means of competition between different groups and between individuals of the same group, whose goal it is to evaluate who complies with precepts most devoutly.

Interestingly, Kramer (2009, 160–172) has another take on similar mechanisms put into practice in the sphere of kashrut, results of the chumratization of Orthodox communities in recent decades and reflecting the Great Rabbis' desires to set new boundaries to distinguish authentic and good Jews from those who are not so good or not so authentic. It is, above all, a question of identity that can be summarized in the famous and problematic question "Who is a Jew?" I return to this topic in Chapter 5.

Lastly, regarding OCD and its possible connections to Rabbinical Judaism, it is worthwhile to note that warnings against unhealthy pointillism in mitzvot consummation could already be heard in the second century CE:

> [Upon removing bread from the home on the eve of Passover] One should not fear that a little housewife may have dragged [a crumb of bread] from a [still uncleaned] house to another [already cleaned] or from one place to another. For, in this case, could it not be from one patio to another, or one city to another? There would be no end to the matter![36] (*Mishna Pessachim* 1.2)

In the *Talmud*, we read that Rav Pappa[37] says,

> If feces are on the spot where they emerge from the body, one may not recite Shema. What is the case? If it is visible, this is obvious! If it is not visible, the Torah was not given to the ministering angels.[38]

In another treatise of the Talmud, Berachot 17b, in relation to personal restrictions in avoiding work in *Tishah b'Av*—where the community usually labors—we read, "Regarding a personal stringency to avoid work on Tishah b'Av, in a place where the community normally does work: Since everyone does work, and he does not do work, this will appear like self-righteous arrogance."[39] These verdicts and many others reflect the concerns of those who wrote the Talmud in creating limits to impede the Fence around the Torah from extending itself ad infinitum, in addition to offering capital importance to majority opinion. Today, however, it would seem that the Great Rabbis chose quite the opposite: to create a Fence around the Torah through laws that do not cease to multiply. They do while holding majority opinion in contempt, and—with similar innovativeness—undermining a seminal principle in Judaism: the union of the people of Israel.

In the thirteenth century, Nachmânides established the following principle in relation to the laws of the *chatziza*:[40]

> Among the laws of chatzitzah: It is not good to be overly strict, seeking doubts to disqualify her immersion for a light reason, for there would be no end to it. . . . One should not insert his head into serious, interminable doubts, such as whether she closed her eyes too much or pursed her lips too much or other doubts, for who could evaluate whether she closed them too much or not?

Centuries later, the rabbi Ysrael Kanievski (1899–1985) became known for his concern over mental problems affecting observant Jews, and in particular, disturbances coming from obsessive consummation of commandments.[41] In the article "Ultra-Orthodox Rabbinic Responses to Religious Obsessive-Compulsive Disorder," penned by Greenberg and Shefler (2008), several questions raised by observant Jews with OCD symptoms appear, alongside Rabbi Kanievski's respective answers. The orientation is always the same: not to provide specific explanations for the rabbi's decisions in relation to those who demonstrate some obsessive behavior, because such explanations will be used by the latter parties as reasons for rejecting the instructions they have received, a phenomenon also observed in Greenberg and Shefler's clinical offices. At the same time, Kanievski, based on Jewish sources, warns that religious acts should be distinguished from unhealthy behavior, and that respecting the precepts of Jewish Law should produce pleasure and joy rather than suffering (Greenberg and Shefler 2008, 186).

Nowadays, there are several perspectives from which the obsessive disorders of the Jewish Orthodox population are analyzed. As already shown, specialists in a variety of disciplines such as psychiatry, psychology, and ethnopsychiatry have developed research that establishes possible cause-effect relations between Jewish orthodoxy and OCD. Yet there are also rabbis who have entered this realm with the goal of identifying the religious dimensions in which OCD prevails. They attempt to determine what kind of behavior can be encouraged to improve the life of those who, in their eagerness to implement certain commandments to the letter, succumb to an unhealthy battle that is not exempt from suffering. The book written by the rabbi Avigdor Bonchek, *Religious Compulsions and Fears: A Guide to Treatment,* is a clear example of the recognition the problem is receiving in Orthodox communities. The work was prefaced by the renowned rabbi Abraham Twerski, recognized worldwide for his work as a psychiatrist specializing in patients who engage in substance abuse. In an interview given to the *Jerusalem Post* in 2009, Twerski offers a pertinent piece of information: over his forty-five years of psychiatric practice, he observed a "sharp increase" in the prevalence of OCD among his patients.[42] Nonetheless, he makes sure to emphasize that we cannot be certain whether this noted increase is due to greater awareness of the illness or a real rise in its incidence.

Bibliographical sources of an academic, rabbinical, or journalistic nature are many, and almost all of them emphasize initial difficulties in distinguishing between the behavior of an extremely pious Jew and that of an Orthodox Jew with OCD. Such difficulties constitute relevant empirical data and create a horizon for diverse inquiries. During the fieldwork that I carried out as part of the present research, I confess that I never heard direct complaints regarding the increasingly visible tendency toward chumratization within Orthodox communities. Rather, what I saw and heard was a passive obedience in relation to new rules, and the elaboration of complex mechanisms to respect them. Nonetheless, and although it was not a representative position, I find it pertinent to cite the comments on this topic that were made to me by an interlocutor during an interview in Beitar Illit:

> In my opinion, the tendency to *leachmir* [putting chumrah into practice] does not come from the place of man's relationship to the Creator, but the opposite. Chumrot happen precisely because there are people who do not have a relationship with the Creator. Because we need not only *irat ha'bore* (fear of the Creator), but *ahava la bore* (love of the Creator), and love for the Creator is very difficult because He is very distant and we have no relationship with Him, so people choose the chumrah path. This is a deviation in life, and instead of the Jew living with joy, he lives in fear all the time and thinks that if he offers God one chumrah after another, he will be more righteous than all others. This leads to distortions that are not good.

It is interesting that my interlocutor's analysis penetrates diverse and different characteristics of rabbinical Judaism, following the example set by ethical and historical monotheism, whose transcendent God is one with whom a relationship is not always easy. Thus, in the above-cited passage, eagerness to fulfill Divine will, compounded by the difficulties that Orthodox Jews have in their communication with the Creator, foster the development of extreme behavior. If we take into consideration that, for Rabbinical Judaism, what unites man and God, the finite and the infinite, are the mitzvot, it is not hard to fathom that severe practices constitute an attempt to get closer to him. However, there are more than a few dangers in these strategies, such as the development of obsessive behaviors among Orthodox Jews or undermining the unity of the people of Israel on the part of rabbis. I also believe that it is essential to consider my interlocutor's observation that it is important not only to be righteous but to be "more so than everyone else"; this confirms Aran's (2013a; 2013b) interpretation of the importance and meaning of demonstrating to co-religionists the zeal with which commandments are consummated, in a movement of intragroup competition.

Another interlocutor asserted that "with each passing Pesach, things get more difficult, and there is no way to keep the calm in the face of so much work, so many rules and so many changes in relation to certain foods." "It is very hard," she insisted, and "anxiety runs high." To scrutinize and clean off the most minute particle of leaven before Pesach begins, as described, is a frenetic race against time so that no tiny bit of chametz remains anywhere within the family home. Nonetheless, chametz is qualitatively different from foods considered nonkosher—such as the meat of impure animals, mixing meat and dairy, ingesting insects, and so forth.[43]

I am unaware of how conscious observant Jews are of the punishment that is meted out to those who consume leaven or make use of it during Passover. *Karet*, the punishment cited in the Torah for this transgression, implies excommunication, removal from the community. Yet although impossible to measure, the anxiety that hovers over Orthodox communities and the fear of committing and being punished for a transgression is part of observant Jews' everyday life. And it could not be otherwise within a group whose religion is based on the punishment of transgression and the blessing of those who follow the correct path. In the language that observant Jews use, the expressions *be'ezrat ha'Shem* (with God's help) and *Toda la El* (thank God) are mentioned in virtually every sentence, to the point that they seem to merge with the structure of language. The fear of God is as omnipresent as God himself; thus, it is no coincidence that, in Hebrew, the Orthodox Jews call themselves *charedim* (the fearful ones) or *ieiri shamaim* (the God-fearing).

The hypothesis of the existence of an obsessive component in Halakhah in general, and in kashrut in particular—a trait that purportedly is increasing in today's world—is not exclusive to nor obviously reflected in the preparations and celebration of the Jewish Passover. There are other dimensions in which chumrah has intensified, especially since the 1980s—most expressively in the redoubled care to eliminate insects, dead or alive, from the food consumed by Orthodox Jews. It could be said that nowadays, insects have become the stars of the kashrut stage. At the same time, other animals suitable for Jewish consumption, such as cattle and poultry, have not come similarly under the scrutiny of rabbis and kashrut supervisors. This has led to novel and complex situations, such as the circulation and consumption of nonkosher meat in Israel and in some diasporic communities. The purpose of the next chapter is to describe both scenarios, in an attempt to find an explanation for a paradox of such magnitude.

5

Insects, mammals, and birds: The crooked paths of kashrut

Blessed art thou, O Lord, our God, Ruler of everything, who makes us holy with His commandments and commands us concerning kosher slaughter.

Blessing recited as animals go to slaughter

The shechita process is very complex and involves several people. It all starts with the shochet knife. For this there is a professional called a bodek. He is a specialized shochet that constantly checks the blade of the knife. This knife must be at such a caliber that the person can cut himself and does not realize he has done so. It is not uncommon that when the shochet washes his hands to draw blood from the animal, he realizes that he too has cut himself. I've had this experience in my work, of cutting myself at least twice and not realizing it. Not knowing that the blood that was oozing was my own.

Ritual butcher in São Paulo

How did they do it before? I don't know, but this is important from a Halakha point of view. In my house, entire years would go by without us eating lettuce with the exception of the Pesach Seder. And to eat lettuce at the Pesach Seder, one would sit half day in the sun and check leaf by leaf to make sure it was clean. That was before. Today, Baruch HaShem, there are places that produce clean vegetables and fruits.

Kosher supervisor from the Eda Charedit

Although my contact with the Orthodox world in recent years cannot be characterized as typical fieldwork, it has not lost intensity. Rather, I have

The Sacred and the Impure in Judaism. Marta F. Topel, Oxford University Press. © Oxford University Press 2024.
DOI: 10.1093/oso/9780197677667.003.0005

continued to conduct in-depth interviews and have done considerable reading on various aspects of the Orthodox universe as well as of material read by the Orthodox public itself. I have watched documentaries on different communities of observant Jews and followed numerous websites of Orthodox currents (Brazilian, Israeli, Argentinian, and North American) with perseverance. Asking myself if there were clear limits to the addition of new rules and customs to Halakhah, I came across data and analysis that led me to a negative response: at present there seem to be no limits to the creation of new rules and customs. Just where the layperson's imagination might erect a barrier or perceive a dead end—that is, the limits of legislating on a certain topic—Orthodox rabbis encounter new problems, whether as a consequence of the incorporation of technology in everyday life, the perception of a constant threat to the structure of Halakhah, or even because those who are devoted full time to a certain occupation are expected to demonstrate results.[1] The uninterrupted creation of new rules may be a way to maintain a population that increasingly depends on rabbinical authorities for its modus vivendi, within a situation of continuous threat and uncertainty. And this involves not only religious dimensions but also other arenas, such as political choices or options regarding which city to live in, what to name a child, to which yeshivot to send children who excel in their studies and where to send those who don't. The expansion of Halakhah to areas beyond the strictly religious is a moot point among diverse researchers of orthodoxy (Aran 2013a; Dan 1997; Silber 1992; Friedman 1991; Liebmann 1983). With this in mind, some of the questions guiding my research were: Which type of person aims to build Halakhah, or which type of person seeks it out: the "holy man" or the "common man," with all the flaws and limitations of "common men"? And not more importantly, what type of person is developed because of the expansion and radicalization of Halakhah?

One of the singularities of kashrut that attracted my attention, which constitutes an important part of this research, is the existence of a dimension of the dietary laws that escapes the chumrah, that is, the most stringent fulfillment of precepts and customs. Furthermore, the leniency that characterizes it, although not a complete novelty in the Orthodox universe, has suffered dramatic changes in recent decades because of the way technology itself is incorporated into the process of production of animal protein. I refer specifically to the circulation of meat that is considered *treif* (not fit for Jewish consumption), within Orthodox communities in Israel and within the diaspora. Curiously, this situation showed me how much I still had to learn about the views of the Orthodox world. This realization came as a great surprise, yet I discovered that the phenomenon is known by not a few people in the Orthodox communities.[2] Even so, my own amazement and surprise continued to grow until I managed to conjure the reasons underlying the two phenomena: the circulation of treif meat and the blind eye that rabbinical leaders turned to it.

As a secular Jew and a daughter, granddaughter, and great-granddaughter of secular Jews, I knew little or nothing about dietary law before I began my research on Orthodox Jewry. Yet there was one thing I did know: pork, in addition to forbidden, was a symbol of all other dietary prohibitions, and the consumption of kosher meat is usually the last rule to be relinquished by those Jews who, little by little, begin to give up religious practices.

Over the following pages I analyze the reasons for which industrialized production of kosher meat has as its correlate the impossibility of following the precise and detailed Halakhah rules for the slaughter of animals, which signifies infringing on the Jewish principle of *tzaar baalei chaim*.[3] According to this principle, causing unnecessary suffering to animals is forbidden. This runs up against the structural cruelty that is embedded in the current industrialized system of meat production and distribution.[4]

The objective behind rules for slaughter as prescribed by Halakhah is to avoid the suffering of animals as much as possible, quickly rendering them unconsciousness and insensitive to pain by beheading them alive (cutting their carotid arteries and jugular veins). For these purposes, a knife called a *chalaf* is used. It is close to half a meter long, is extremely sharp, and must be repeatedly checked by a *bodek* (knife checker). After slaughter, the lungs are inspected for the presence of adhesion. If not put into practice, the meat is considered treif.

But if the circulation of treif meat within the Orthodox communities of Israel and the diaspora is a long-standing phenomenon, other animal species are now the subject of such detailed scrutiny that the fact has aroused criticism within orthodoxy itself—which, as we have seen, increasingly privileges the chumrah path to fulfilling commandments. Tiny, multitudinous living beings with the ability to cause an observant Jew to transgress five mitzvot in one mouthful,[5] populate foods like vegetables, legumes, fruits, grains, vegetables, spices, jams, and a long list of other foods.

The Torah forbids the consumption of insects, worms, and other "creepy crawlers." There are specific prohibitions regarding those that live in rivers and lakes, those that crawl on the ground, and those that fly in the air. The prohibition against eating insects is so extensive that the Talmud (Makot 16b) notes that eating a one single insect whole can lead to multiple transgressions. According to some exegetes, the reason for this extraordinary combination of prohibitions is the ubiquity of insects and the resulting ease with which people may transgress this dictate.

The search for insects using high-precision technological instruments such as microscopes, or tools of lesser precision such as light boxes and magnifying glasses, has become a routine, both on farms producing vegetables and fruits for Orthodox communities and within Orthodox homes. Thus, in addition to specialized literature, the most varied technological resources are employed to allow the identification and eradication of insects from raw, cooked, and industrialized foods that are distributed in Orthodox communities. Experts in checking for insects labor arduously to learn all the tricks the little bugs are capable of devising to confuse good Jews. Rabbi Moshe Vaya, who holds the honorific title of *Posek Ha'dor* or Leading Halakhic Arbiter on Insects of Our Generation and with whom I had the privilege of speaking during my stay in Israel in 2015, remains steadfast in his role of ensuring a completely insect-free kosher diet, whether these creatures are dead or alive, whole or crushed.

In order to exemplify the growing importance that insects have acquired in relation to the kosher diet from the 1980s onward (Kramer 2009; Fishkoff 2010), I find it interesting to mention the existence of a vast bibliography and videos on the internet that provide advice on how to wash vegetables for food without committing transgressions. This topic has been incorporated into courses on Halakhah in general and on kashrut in particular. Simplified versions of Rabbi Moshe Vaya's books are available in several different languages, as are sociohistorical texts that analyze the phenomenon (Adams 2017).

The extreme rigidity in the search for insects in food, including in foods that had never been suspect, clashes with the leniency in relation to mammals and poultry. This paradox, which I was not aware of before starting my fieldwork, then became one of the most relevant issues of this research, and several questions have arisen in the process of finding a minimally plausible answer to explain such nonsense. Can the detailed verification of insects be interpreted as a supercategory that meshes with the superreligiosity analyzed in the previous chapter? More precisely, and based on Mary Douglas's work on biblical dietary laws, can it be said that the more detailed the classifications, the more the people of Israel are separated from other peoples of the world, thus granting greater holiness to those whose lifestyles incorporate these new classifications? Or perhaps Kramer's conclusion is more accurate, according to which obsessively checking for insects is a metaphor for the need to check again and again who is really a Jew, in times in which it has become impossible to be sure of what was once evidence? Hasty conversions, chozrim bi'teshuvah who in the thousands enter the supposedly closed Orthodox world, and Jews identified with the Conservative movement who, although in recent years have moved closer to orthodoxy, are still not considered Orthodox—these and other phenomena of the larger society and internal to the Orthodox communities are perceived as threats to a group that presents itself as the bearer of the one and only truth and authentic form of Judaism.

When I interviewed a middle-aged couple in Beitar Ilit and we spoke of rules regarding insects, it became clear that while the wife took this topic very seriously, even when it came to the vegetables coming from Gush Katif—distributed in closed plastic bags and planted with higher levels of pesticides than are usually employed in Israeli farming—her husband showed greater skepticism. As he put it,

> A part of this business of *chipus charakim* (the search for insects) is not so important for kashrut, but for the mental state of those who engage in it. There are many people for whom religion is an obsession. Maimonides wrote that many people who see themselves as religious study the kashrut obsessively. This is not what *Ha'Shem*[6] wants. People live in fear, which is not always a relationship with *Ha'Shem* or not a good relationship with Him.

As I have stated, it was by delving into the universe of the kashrut that I gained access to some facets of orthodoxy that I would never have imagined to exist. For an anthropological study, this is certainly a gain. But in this specific case, unlike earlier research,[7] my findings are paradoxical, not only from my anthropological perspective but from a secular Jewish one—and even for a fair number of groups within orthodoxy itself. Paradoxes, harsh contradictions, omissions, serious transgressions that are silenced: this is the reality of kashrut today. The existence of double standards in certifying which kosher foods may be infested with insects, on the one hand, and on the other, the meat that circulates within Orthodox communities—in particular, the large ones such Israel's—are revealing of expressive inconsistency.

The awareness that treif meat is sold as kosher in Israel has led a number of rabbis and members of the Orthodox community to stop eating the meat sold there. Yet there is one fact that draws attention: the very same people who refrain from ingesting animal protein in Israel consume it when they visit small diaspora communities. Based on these data, can we conclude that exile is more kosher than life in Israel, since complying with kosher commandments seems easier and more reliable outside it? Considering the problems that industrial production of meat has created for Orthodox communities, another interesting finding of mine comes to the forefront: the existence of two types of kosher diets. One, a strict kosher diet—possibly the le´mehadrin kosher—contains animal protein and is considered kosher by the majority of Orthodox rabbis and members of the orthodoxy. The other is a vegetarian or vegan kosher diet, advocated by smaller segments. Yet this finding is hugely important because it places the new and current functions of kashrut firmly onstage—such as separating not only Jews from Gentiles or observant Jews from secular ones but separating the Orthodox themselves into two major groups.

I remember that when I interviewed kashrut supervisors in Israel, five of them told me that they did not eat meat away from home. I was especially surprised when a supervisor whom I interviewed in the city of Betar Ilit, a specialist in supervising food for big events such as marriages and bar mitzvot, told me he never ate meat at such places. His justification, like that of other supervisors, was evasive, saying, "No one cooks meat the way my wife does, so that's why I only eat it at home."

Size isn't everything: The alleged ubiquity of insects

At present, the great concern of kashrut legislators focuses on the insects that can be found in fruit, vegetables, grains, and flours. This unease, which we could define as affliction, has created extreme vigilance around foods likely to be infested by insects among kashrut producers and supervisors, on the one hand, and among the Orthodox population as a whole, on the other.

During my stay in Israel, in 2015, I had the privilege of talking with Rabbi Moshe Vaya, bearer of the prestigious title of *Posek Ha'Dor* (Leading Halakhic Arbiter) on the theme of insects. My interview with him gave me privileged access to a worldview that, in the eyes of an outsider, looks like a universe of obsessive people who embody a religious current that is equally obsessive. But in the eyes of insiders, it is no more than the only way to be Jews, good Jews. "Good Jews" refers to those who follow Halakhah precepts or Jewish Law to the letter. And good Jews have priorities that are different from those of Jews who are not so good, or non-Jews.

Rabbi Vaya's receptivity was enormous, as was his generosity in responding to all my questions and doubts in greatest detail. On several occasions, the rabbi would pick up a copy of his book on insect-checking[8] to illustrate issues he wanted to be clear to a layperson. Usually, the rabbi would open the book to a page on which there were two photos: one of vegetables and fruits with tiny spots (insects invisible to the naked eye) and on the next, exponentially magnified reproductions of these same insects with a microscope. The photos were spooky, even repulsive renderings of large animals with huge legs, feelers, and wings, like the insects we see in horror movies.

During the two hours that I spent in his home,[9] Rabbi Vaya lamented that his assistant was not around to demonstrate the modus operandi of his laboratory, which is set up in the basement of the house. Nonetheless, after the interview concluded, he took me there. At the outside entrance to the laboratory was a box with vegetables and produce. According to Rabbi Vaya, someone had left the box there so that he could check the content which, most probably, contained "problematic" produce.[10]

What Rabbi Vaya refers to as his laboratory is a small and very disorganized room, home to several new copies of his trilogy on insect-checking, in Hebrew, and the abridged version, also new, in English. There were other books on kashrut sitting on tables and shelves. The desk the rabbi worked at was laden with piles of letters in their respective envelopes, some of which held powder or dark-colored particles. Rabbi Vaya told me that were letters from women who were consulting him on things that they had found in foods while they were cooking. They had been unable to determine whether these particles that were stuck to vegetables or fruits were simply dirt or were in fact insects. This was the "powder" that I had seen coming out of envelopes a few minutes earlier. In one of the sinks of the laboratory, the rabbi showed me an almost transparent filter, explaining that it was what he usually uses to wash the leaves of vegetables in his tenacious search for insects.

In an abridged Portuguese-language version of Rabbi Vaya's monumental trilogy, *Checking Foods according to the Torah*, we read the following instructions regarding romaine lettuce, a vegetable that, from an Orthodox perspective, is seen as especially problematic:

1. Do not use the outer leaves.
2. Separate the leaves and soak them for several minutes in a solution of water and detergent.
3. Gently rub a sponge moistened with soapy water over all parts of each leaf on both sides.
4. Rinse the leaves in running water (making sure that it reaches the hidden spots).
5. Hold the leaves to the light, removing any green aphids or yellow spots you may find.

Hydroponic lettuce is just as affected as ordinary lettuce.

Note 1: In Brazil you can find **lettuce packed in a vacuum-sealed plastic bag,** which is cleaner than common lettuce, as it is pre-washed. Although the checking process is the same, we will certainly find fewer worms and insects on it than on common lettuce. Make sure to check for white flies and yellowish tunnels. Something like grooves or stripes that an insect leaves on a fruit.

Note 2: In Israel and now in Brazil as well, one can find **specially-grown lettuce** that has no worms or insects. In these cases, it is enough to merely separate the leaves, letting them soak in a solution of water and detergent for several minutes and then wash them carefully. (Vaya 2011, 67—author's emphasis)

Care must be taken not to ingest insects, and there are numerous internet videos that show kashrut supervisors demonstrating how to wash vegetables considered problematic with the help of a light box, suggesting the viewer do the same at home.[11] Another recommendation, followed by most Orthodox families, is to stop eating vegetables that are considered problematic, such as romaine lettuce, broccoli, cauliflower, and strawberries. Lastly, and as has been mentioned already in this book, in Israel today there is a supplier of vegetables specifically for the Orthodox public: Gush Katif uses a greater quantity of pesticides in an attempt to ward off all possibility of insects infesting crops.[12]

In one of the Eda Charedit offices that I visited in Jerusalem, I first interviewed a kashrut supervisor and then visited the premises. In a small room, on two long tables, were test tubes containing samples of what I later found out were insects and larvae. When I asked the supervisor why these samples were being kept, The answer was quite to the point: "The working supervisors and the housewife need to know, need to see what they are looking for; if they don't know what they are looking for, they won't find anything." The supervisor immediately informed me that, after being analyzed by experts, these samples are photographed from different angles and published in different Eda Charedit media.

As for why there is now a need to check foods with a stringency unknown in the past, Rabbi Vaya explained the reasons for applying chumrah as follows:

> We live in very problematic times. Why? Because in the past, Jews lived in the diaspora, yet each group had been in the same place for hundreds or even thousands of years. The Yemenites, for example, had been in there for two thousand years. In Europe, in Poland, they had been there for eight hundred, nine hundred years. In Morocco, four hundred, five hundred years in the same place. So even if they were in the diaspora, they had been in the same place for hundreds of years. And the foods they ate were set, they had a food tradition and also a tradition regarding what had to be checked. They did not have much food! Today every country has food from all over the world. There is no food that is not transported from one country to others. We have no tradition and many new foods, not only new ones, but ones from all the other countries and together with their import and export, pests are imported and exported. And such is the problem: there is biological transmission.

In another part of the interview, the rabbi justified the extra care and use of technology in insect checking:

> The rule works this way: what the Torah prohibits is only that which the person can see. Yet at times, a minuscule insect appears to the naked eye as but a little dot. When an insect moves, no one would claim it is not a creature, but when it is dead it is hard to tell if it is an insect or not. So I use a magnifying glass just for things that we cannot see with our naked eyes and for which we would need a microscope. I sometimes also use a microscope to identify a green, very green thing. But in general terms, a magnifying glass is enough for clarification.

The long and detailed explanation given by Rabbi Vaya shows that kashrut innovation is the direct effect of the process of the chumratization of orthodoxy, which has included neutral foods (known as parve) that until two decades ago were not seen as a threat to the kosher diet, as a category similar to dairy and to meat and its derivatives. The term "parve," of unknown etymology, is relatively new and has been integrated within the kashrut system, even though it appears neither in the Hebrew Bible nor the Talmud (Tzuberi 2012, 171). In other words, fruits, vegetables, grains, and spices have become foods that deserve attention and represent a threat to the kosher diet, as they were not during other times in history.

Another innovation speaks to the legitimation of experts in insect checking who until a few decades ago were not subject to scrutiny. Since, as we have seen in Chapter 3, kashrut supervisors are usually men, women are left destitute of authority in a terrain in which, over the centuries, their knowledge prevailed. As in other dimensions of life,[13] the Orthodox Jewish housewife is no longer seen as someone who is capable of choosing what is best for herself and her family. Nowadays, the vegetables, fruits, dried fruits, and grains consumed by family members in observant households depend on expert knowledge; in this case, a male kashrut supervisor whom the housewife can and should call whenever she has questions.[14] If as Tzuberi claims (2012, 169), in the same way that the Great Priest served in the Temple (to which the author refers as "holy able'), the common Jew, largely represented by a female figure, serves "the common table," the fact that kashrut experts are men demotes Orthodox women from a role that is not secondary but rather paramount to religious life.

Rabbi Vaya's position, which legitimates and fosters the use of high-precision instruments such as the magnifying glass and the microscope for checking fruits, vegetables, produce, and flours has stirred controversy within the Orthodox universe, stimulating what is known as the "defamation of earlier generations"—the belief that the generations that came before us transgressed the law. From such a perspective, grandparents and great-grandparents committed major transgressions due to the lack of instruments needed to follow Halakhah to the letter, yet people today, aware of all existing threats because we have the technology for detailed—almost scientific—checking of what we eat, are obliged to do so.

With this conviction, there are, as already mentioned, different rabbis and Orthodox kashrut supervisors who teach housewives to clean vegetables, fruits, and produce considered problematic, paying attention to the most minute details. This material is disseminated by Orthodox institutions through lectures and courses and, in recent years, internet sites. In the latter, we see rabbis making use of the light box, special lamps, and magnifying glasses to wash fruits and vegetables or to examine grains, spices, and dried fruits.

Faced with such a situation, some voices within orthodoxy have contested the chumrah of Rabbi Vaya and his followers. Rabbi Moshe Feinstein, a US Posek Ha'Dor recognized worldwide for his expertise in Halakhah, has reiterated another view, replicated on several websites. According to Rabbi Feinstein, one should not question the behavior of previous generations by forbidding the consumption of certain fruits. Lenient positions can be taken to allow us to avoid spreading rumors about preceding generations that did not have the technology we have today. Rabbi Feinstein is emphatic when he says that what is invisible to the naked eye cannot be forbidden.[15]

A similar position was expressed by Rabbi Oren Duvdevani, kashrut supervisor for the Israeli NGO Hashgacha Pratit, in an interview that he granted in February 2018:

> I find the insect issue a bit exaggerated, that it is a problem to slander our grandparents. And this is a halakhic concept: "*leotzi laag al dorot ha'rishonim*" [to defame those who preceded us]. I'm better because I do things my grandparents didn't! Wait a minute, what didn't they do?!? A hundred years ago, did they not do right? Or did they not act according to Halakhah? That, for me, is very difficult to say, to assert, because I think Judaism was built around respect for those who came before you. That's your strength. When I ask myself why I should do these things, the answer is because my grandfather did them and my great-grandfathers did them.

Unlike the Orthodox establishment, Rabbi Oren Duvdevani is committed to the Halakhah and to its versatility, so that it can be adapted to our times as, in his view, it was adapted over the course of the centuries. I cite Rabbi Duvdevani in detail once again because his observations are extremely enlightening:

> The approach that claims that it is forbidden to eat something because it is impossible to clean it is one that does not exist in Halakhah. None, at least no one who I found in the sources, said, "Don't eat that because it is impossible to clean." There is talk of a better cleaning, or of not eating a certain

part of a fruit. . . . The only limit that exists regarding edible vegetables are related to the mitzvot of the Land of Israel: *shnat Shmitá,* that sort of thing. But there are limitations related to insects and we must face them. I think that my role as legislator is to solve problems and make it possible for people to follow Halakhah, not to do things that make it impossible to do so. There are two issues here. When a building is too high, it loses stability. The second is that now that we live in an industrialized world; many traditions have been forgotten. In the past, everyone knew how to slaughter an animal, how to salt meat, right? . . . But today, if you show up and say to people, "Just eat vegetables without insects that we clean for you," what will happen when the person has no one to ask? This means we are creating a situation in which people are ignorant, in which they are unaware, and even kashrut supervisors don't know everything, so they call out, "Forbidden!" Because they don't know what to do with this, don't know how to face it.

The image of the building to refer to Halakhah is inspiring, and also emphasizes another of its traits: one that is created through stages and surfaces that, like the bricks of great European cathedrals and churches, reflected the ways of thinking, values, and interests of each generation. Like an ancient cathedral in which different styles of architecture and artists contributed to buildings and frescos, the Halakhah is made up of different layers in which changes, contradictions, divergent ideas, and opposite conclusions have been compiled over the centuries, the product of phenomena both internal and external to Jewish communities.[16]

And here, once again, we can ask what type of person Orthodox Judaism aspires to construct at present. Is it one who studies, as Maimonides advocated, in order to fulfill precepts, or a person who has no autonomy and is dependent on rabbis and experts in order to carry out a life of religious observance?

Rabbi Duvdevani's considerations, in addition to pointing to the lack of knowledge on the part of many members of the Orthodox public regarding certain practical aspects of kashrut, serves as explicit confirmation of the excessive concern that exists in relation to accidental ingestion of insects, the consequence of current legislators' inability to deal with problems wrought by the industrialization and importation of foods. It seems that zeal and technology go hand in hand in the Orthodox communities of the twentieth and twenty-first centuries. This could lead us to suggest the hypothesis that technology, for Orthodox Jews (except for certain specific issues such as the use of electrical energy on Shabbat, through timers) does not represent a chance to overcome obstacles and make daily life easier. Rather, the increasing sophistication of technology has created complex situations leading to the creation of greater obstacles to be overcome in order to correctly comply with the mitzvot. Delving further into the multifaceted relationship of orthodoxy to technology goes beyond the limits of the present text, but it is nonetheless possible to argue that this complex and ambiguous relationship varies according to the arena of social life to which it pertains or is being applied.[17]

In the last chapter of his previously cited book *Jewish Eating and Identity through the Ages*, which bears the ironic title of "Bugs in the System (the Kashrut Wars)," Kramer (2009) points to the decade of the 1980s as a moment in which kashrut became an obsession within Orthodox communities, creating new situations and unleashing veritable wars between North American certifying agencies in a process that can easily be extrapolated to the Israeli context and other Jewish diaspora communities. The chapter begins with mention of a *New York Times* news item from June 1, 2004, alerting readers that, under the microscope, the city's water supply renders a significant quantity of copepods and zooplankton. The news stirred great concern among the city's Orthodox communities. Two decades earlier, the "vinegar scandal"[18] led several North American rabbis to raise the standards for production and distribution of foods that were considered parve (neutral), and different media sounded the alarm to alert members of Orthodox communities. The parallel that the president of the Orthodox institution Young Israel draws between the "vinegar scandal" and the Chernobyl nuclear tragedy is impressive, communicating the sense of threat that transgressing kashrut commandments represents for observant Jews (Kramer 2009, 149–150) and, in the case in point, revealing how the problem of insects has been rapidly incorporated by those who want to follow a strictly kosher diet.[19]

Fishkoff (2010), like other scholars of orthodoxy in other domains, sees the radicalization of laws related to kashrut as a result of the chumratization process that Orthodox communities undergo. In her view, the change in the Orthodox leadership's approach to kashrut can be found in the detailed search for insects in raw and frozen vegetables, and in dried fruits such as raisins. In the chapter devoted to insects, she discusses technological innovations to detect the most minuscule of them, in addition to the positions taken by diverse rabbis on the ramifications of this new threat.

In his analysis of the chumrah in kashrut that prevails today, Kramer (2009) wisely notes another variable at play: it is no longer enough for products to be very strictly kosher. It is now equally important that producers, supervisors, and sellers of kosher products are Orthodox Jews who follow the Jewish Law in the strictest manner. In this sense, the kosher seal has the function of informing consumers as to the origin of those who evaluate and approve a certain product, that is, to make known who is behind each seal, rather than referring to the kosherization process itself. In the United States, as mentioned earlier, seals from supervisors of the Conservative movement, which sometimes employ similar strategies and stringency in supervising kosher food, are prohibited a priori by Orthodox rabbis (Kramer 2009; Fishkoff 2010).

The industry of kosher certification is gigantic, both in Israel and the United States and in small diasporic communities such as in Brazil and has been significantly on the rise since its consolidation in the 1990s. In 2015, while doing my fieldwork, I found that in addition to the rabbinate's own kosher seal, there were twelve others in existence on the Israeli scene. It is worth noting, as already pointed out, that the term "kosher" has been monopolized by the Israeli rabbinate. This is a curious piece of information that reveals the importance of keeping under the rabbinate's wings a dimension of Jewish religious life apparently no less important than family law (births, marriages, divorces, and burials), over which it also maintains a monopoly.

Compassion for animals at the cutting edge

In a video produced and distributed by the Israeli NGO Anonymous,[20] titled *Rabbis Speak about the Meat Industry*, several Orthodox and ultra-Orthodox rabbis, as well as a ritual butcher[21] appear, condemning the current forms of animal slaughter employed in Israel. The video begins with the testimony of a rabbi whose name does not appear in the video credits but who is recognizable as a rabbi from some Hasidic current. His contribution is very brief: "all of us eat *nevelot u trefot*," which in a literal sense indicates the meat of animals that have not been slaughtered according to the rules of kashrut. He is followed by a rabbi identified as Rabbi Holand, who asserts that the principle of tzaar baalei chaim is not taken into consideration by poultry butchers in Israel, emphasizing that the cruelty they employ is unprecedented.

This same rabbi adds that all who partake of the chicken produced by the industry legitimate it. In turn, Rabbi Shabtai Rapaport warns that although the Orthodox population naively spends large sums of money on the purchase of an *etrog mehudar*[22] and le´mehadrin kosher meat, at some point it will come to the realization that these foods, seen as "superkosher," are not so relevant; rather, they have serious underlying problems. Rabbi Avi Zarki claims to have engaged in deep study on the topic of butchering, witnessing how much hens are made to suffer. He goes on to say that "the *Torah* forbids torturing an animal and then killing it so that it can be eaten." The video, which lasts two minutes and thirty seconds, ends with Rabbi Shalom Arusch's admonishment that "Animals also have a soul."[23]

Both the written Torah and the Talmud contain numerous references that demonstrate the importance of compassion, mostly for domestic animals but also regarding wildlife. Spector (2012, 4) claims that there are more references to animals in the Bible than there are to Shabbat. Evidence of the importance of the tzaar baalei chaim in the Hebrew Bible is that fact that it constitutes one of the seven laws of Noah[24]—commands that regulate the ethical conduct of gentiles; thus, not only Jews but all of humanity must show compassion for animals. Here follow several examples of biblical verses that express the importance of animals and demand specific treatment from humans: Deuteronomy (11:15): "I will also provide grass in the fields for your cattle—and thus you shall eat your fill"[25], a verse that says that animals must eat before their owners do; Deuteronomy (25:4): "You shall not muzzle an ox while it is threshing"[26]—the idea expressed by this commandment is that the ox provides a service to humans by providing them with food; it is therefore wrong to muzzle it so that it cannot graze. In other words, it is forbidden to make an animal suffer while it is working. Another verse from Deuteronomy (22:10) warns, "You shall not plow with an ox and an ass together,"[27] a commandment interpreted by Jewish legislators as a reminder that if a donkey is put to the plow alongside a stronger animal, it will be subjected to stress and suffering. Likewise, the ox will be frustrated at being held back and having to pull the donkey along with it. This specific rule is mentioned frequently in parables within the canonical books of Judaism.

Nonetheless, reference to animals and the statute of animals appears much earlier in the Bible. Thus, in the story of the creation of the world in Genesis (1:29),[28] God tells man that all the herbs and the trees will provide him food, a rule that indicates that humankind's nourishment in Eden came only from vegetable sources. Immediately thereafter (Genesis 1:30),[29] we read that animals too are herbivores. There is an agreement among Jewish exegetes of all times: in the age of paradise, in which there were neither laws of history nor laws of nature, humanity was vegetarian. It was only after the diluvium that

God allowed man to eat animals. Corrupted and corrupting the Earth, Noah's generation and their descendants were allowed to eat meat because God understood that humanity was not prepared for the ideal that today we would call vegetarian or vegan.[30] Antediluvian vegetarianism was interpreted by numerous rabbis and legislators from different times, sometimes highlighting its moral aspect and on other occasions, privileging materialist issues, such as the deteriorated quality of vegetables eaten by human beings after the flood or the impossibility of surviving on a vegetarian diet alone.

In an article that goes deeper into this topic, Yael Shemesh, researcher at the University of Bar-Ilan, states that there are different opinions as to why human beings were authorized to eat meat after the diluvium; some are complementary while others contradict each other. After careful analysis of the positions taken by the most important Jewish legislators, including nineteenth- and twentieth-century rabbis such as S. R. Hirsch and A. I. Kook, Shemesh (2006, 150–151) arrives at the following conclusions:

> In general, the Talmudic sages and traditional commentators took
> meat-eating for granted. None of them preach or recommend that
> their flock or readers switch to a vegetarian regimen.

There are those who emphasize that only after the diluvium, the moment of man's ascent to rational being (*medabber*), were humans permitted to eat meat, a license that, according to rabbinical perspective, also "benefits" the animals that are consumed. According to this eminently hierarchical reasoning, just as plants are benefitted by being ingested by animals, creatures superior to the elements of the vegetable world, animals are elevated by being consumed by humans, superior beings, the only species created in God's image and likeness.

Materialist and mystical interpretations can be found in different Judaic sources, attempting to reconcile the tension between the rules that oblige people to act compassionately toward animals and the need to slaughter animals for human consumption. According to an article from the Aish Ha′Torá congregation,[31] ten laws oblige Jews to treat animals with compassion:

a. It is prohibited to cause pain to animals—*tzaar ba'alei chaim*. (Talmud, Baba Metzia 32b, based on Exodus 23:5)
b. One is obligated to relieve an animal's suffering (i.e., unburden it), even if it belongs to your enemy. (Exodus 23:5)

c. If an animal depends on you for sustenance, it is forbidden to eat anything until feeding the animal first. (Talmud, Brachot 40a, based on Deuteronomy 11:15)

d. We are commanded to grant our animals a day of rest on Shabbat. (Exodus 20:10)

e. It is forbidden to use two different species to pull the same plow, since this is unfair to the weaker animal. (Deuteronomy 22:10)

f. It is a mitzvah to send away a mother bird before taking her young. (Deuteronomy 22:7)

g. It is forbidden to kill a cow and her calf on the same day. (Leviticus 22:28)

h. It is prohibited to sever and eat a limb off a live animal. (Genesis 9:4; this is one of the "Noahide" laws that apply to Jews and non-Jews alike.)

i. *Shechita* (ritual slaughter) must be done with a minimum of pain to the animal. The blade must be meticulously examined to assure the most painless form of death possible. ("Chinuch" 451; "Pri Megadim"— Introduction to Shechita Laws).

j. Hunting animals for sport is viewed with serious disapproval by our Sages. (Talmud, Avoda Zara 18b; "Noda BeYehuda" 2-YD 10)

In general terms, rabbis agree that the existence of a classifying scheme for animals that can and cannot be eaten by Jews, on the one hand, and rules for the ritual slaughter of animals, on the other, are factors that limit or encumber excessive meat consumption.

Yet if from the start Judaism had to confront the rules of tzaar baalei chaim and people's need or avid desire to eat meat, at present the challenge is greater, given the amount of violence and cruelty that characterizes the production of animal protein on modern farms and in today's slaughterhouses. In turn, ritual butchers from different diasporic communities are obliged to follow the local laws, making it difficult to implement injunctions regarding compassion for animals. In Brazil, for example, the principle of tzaar baalei chaim is violated, not only because the kashrut rules regarding ritual slaughter are not plausible in industrialized slaughterhouses, as we will soon see, but also because Brazilian law—as is probably the case in other countries of the diaspora—demand that certain protocol be followed. As a ritual butcher in São Paulo explained,

[Brazilian] legislation demands a twenty-four-hour period before the animal is taken from the farm to the slaughterhouse: food is cut off. Why?

So that its system is cleaned out. These are Health Department demands. The animal takes care of its physiological needs and eliminates excess food. Then, fasting, it is taken away, and at the slaughterhouse it waits between six and twelve hours before slaughter. It must go for that much time without food in order to clean its system out.

When I asked my interlocutor if fasting included water, I was told that according to the Halakhah, animals were allowed to drink water, something that Brazilian legislation prohibits. Nonetheless, the shochet was vehement in his argument that ritual slaughter according to Jewish law causes animals less suffering than the electric shocks or pneumatic pistols that are commonly used. He says,

> The issue of the *bedikah* of the razor[32] is so the razor's edge is sharp enough so that the animal doesn't even feel the razor and dies in a few seconds; since the trachea and carotids are cut simultaneously, neither oxygen nor blood are able to rise to the animal's brain. So it goes to sleep, sleeps before death. I want to explain to you how Halakhah is concerned with respect for animals. They are sacrificed but must not feel pain.

This assertion contradicts the explanations given by this very same butcher on the suffering that animals face before they go to slaughter. The accounts of another shochet, also Brazilian, were a detailed attempt to transmit the degree of suffering that animals underwent in the local poultry and beef industry slaughterhouses. In his view, Halakhic transgressions are many, but rabbis turn a deaf ear to the complaints of butchers and supervisors. Structural cruelty toward animals, and negligence and breaking of Brazilian laws led this butcher to photograph some scenes and forward them to the NGO PETA. When asked why he thought such an unusual situation prevailed—of rabbis who were unconcerned with systematic transgression of the Halakhah— he replied by shrugging his shoulders and saying that he did not know what the reason was. Yet a few minutes later, he asserted resolutely,

> I am a mashguiach in Brazilian society, and a mashguiach who tells a rabbi what he sees and says what he thinks is sabotaged by the rabbis in an absurd way. A mashguiach who appeared on TV to explain what kashrut is all about was vilified terribly. He was fired, he was mocked and humiliated. It's a very serious mafia. . . . Since you said you won't publish my name, I feel

safer, because it's a serious mafia, it's a tough mafia. There's a lot of money involved in all of this [in kashrut]. Very, very much.

The tension between essentialism and pragmatism in Halakhah can be clearly observed in the terrain of kashrut. In the case of meat, it could be argued that eating it is a necessary evil. To the extent that a society of vegetarians or vegans cannot be established, meat eating becomes a way of sublimating our aggressiveness.

Known for being a vegetarian and for having written on the subject, Rabbi Abraham Isaac Ha'kohen Kook (1865–1935) argued that it is inconceivable that the Creator had planned a world of harmony and perfection for man, discovering, thousands of years later, that this plan was wrong. According to Rabbi Kook, the ban on eating meat lapsed after the flood because humanity suffered a significant spiritual and ethical decline. In this context, it became necessary for people to maintain a positive self-image, superior to that of other beings, and to focus their efforts on improving their relationships with others. Permission to consume meat was then conceived by Rabbi Kook as a temporary dispensation until humanity, reaching a higher age, would return to vegetarianism (Kook 1983).

This reinforces the idea, widely disseminated among the Orthodox population, that opting for a vegan or a vegetarian lifestyle does not mean one is kosher. To be kosher is directly and intrinsically related to obeying God and following his commandment to the letter. Being kosher is not a matter of choice but the correct way to be a Jew.

In an article signed by Rabbi Eliezer Melamed,[33] which, curiously, has the title "*Dinei tzaar baalei chaim*" (Laws on compassion for animals), we encounter very extreme arguments that are used to justify meat eating. After summarizing the chronology of antediluvian vegetarianism, in a passage titled "We Should Not Educate for Vegetarianism," the rabbi insists that Genesis tells us that animals were created to be used by man, from which can be drawn the conclusion that their meat may be eaten. To show pity and compassion for animals would be detrimental to relationships between humans, amid whom there would always be the impious who, after appeasing their conscience by treating animals with kindness, would steal, oppress, and even kill other human beings to consume their meat with no moral qualms whatsoever. In their hearts, an even greater justification—love and compassion for animals—would reside. For these reasons, according to Rabbi Eliezer Melamed, the Torah instructed us not to abstain from eating meat.

Based on Rabbi Kook's perspective, Rabbi Eliezer Melamed's conclusions reveal a speciesist conception built on a rigid hierarchy: at the bottom, the inanimate, followed by the plant kingdom, the animal kingdom, and finally humanity. Placing animals on a plane equal or close to humans bears several perils: "If we pay attention to the issue of animal welfare, if we show exaggerated compassion toward animals, there is a danger that we will feel that what we have done is enough, enabling us to clearing our conscience and deny compassion for the poor, creating more misery for humanity."

I recall how some of my interlocutors, when I shared the early findings of the present research with them, tried to explain to me that tzaar baalei chaim is a principle rather than a law. They pointed to this fact as a justification for the persistent consumption of meat within Orthodox communities, notwithstanding the cruelty to which animals are subjected through industrial farming and slaughterhouses. Furthermore, a person stated that if there were technical problems in animal slaughter, Orthodox leadership would most certainly "take the necessary measures" to resolve them. Yet such explanations result in a common error, as within Judaism there is no principle that is not accompanied by a related mitzvah. In other words, rabbinical Judaism is not a religion of principles; rather, it is a normative religion based on practice, the quintessence of all orthopraxical religions.

Another video of the NGO Anonymous, which aired on Israeli television's channel 11 on October 18, 2017, is eloquent on this matter. It shows scenes of considerable violence and cruelty in the slaughterhouses where officials from the Israeli rabbinate and private kosher meat certification agencies work. In theory, these people are there precisely to make sure that the slaughtering processes—before, during, and after—are carried out following the guidelines and techniques prescribed by Jewish Law. Throughout the documentary, the viewer is confronted with situations that dramatically violate the principle of tzaar baalei chaim, such as the scene where two employees throw live chickens at one another several times, in what appears to be a prank. In other stretches it is possible to see injured chickens, hanging somewhere between life and death. Yet the video is not only intended to shock viewers by revealing the intrinsic cruelty in the way animals are treated at industrial farms and slaughterhouses. It is more ambitious: its main objective is to provide a platform for Orthodox figures to explain why poultry produced in Israel is not kosher, thus encouraging important segments of the public to stop consuming it. This goal is pursued by impressing viewers with harsh accounts given by Orthodox figures (rabbis, butchers, and kashrut supervisors) on the routines of Israeli slaughterhouses. Interviewees use the Jewish Law as a parameter to carry out evaluations and inquiry into the suitability of the animals that are slaughtered. Viewers learn of serious transgressions, such as the episode in which kashrut supervisors found horse meat from the Gaza Strip in an Israeli slaughterhouse, meat that was packaged with the kosher seal. Throughout the video, there are scenes of chickens hanging by their feet on a conveyor belt so that supervisors can inspect them and make sure that each of the animals is suitable for consumption by observant Jews.

One cannot help feeling shocked by what one sees and hears. As the documentary goes on, it becomes clearer and clearer that the pace of work at the slaughterhouses impedes the realization of pre-, during, and post-slaughter processes according to Jewish Law.[34]

In a voiceover, we hear again and again that the problems encountered in the Israeli system of production of meat and eggs go unquestioned within Orthodox communities; in fact, they are silenced. In the video, Rabbi Avi Zarki explains that according to Jewish Law, the shochet blade should be checked twelve times before butchering, yet this cannot possibly be carried out at the "murderous pace" of factory production. "How can I check eighty chickens per minute? Less than one second per bird!" Rabbi Zarki categorically insists that it is impossible.

Rabbi Oren Duvdevani, whom I interviewed in Jerusalem during my fieldwork, in addition to providing numbers on the slaughtering of chickens in Israel,[35] was adamant in his assertion that

> In slaughtering activities in Israel, there is a catastrophic problem, one which stems from the fact that slaughter according to Halakhah is bent on reducing meat consumption, while industrial slaughter is meant to do just the opposite. Production goals essentially contradict the laws of Halakhah, as reflected in the pace of slaughter and the way in that chickens are treated. I refer to an objective situation, an objective situation that is not good: a situation that does not follow the laws of Halakhah. That's why I don't eat chicken in Israel, I only eat chicken abroad. Abroad, as quantities are much smaller [because the demand is lower], the situation is much better, because there is not as much pressure.

Rabbi Oren Duvdevani's statement that he eats meat only when he is abroad, and not in Israel, enables us to suggest the hypothesis that for him, as perhaps for other Orthodox Jews who share his thinking, the diaspora proves more kosher than Israel. This thesis is of considerable interest for the present research. Yet it seems to me that the rabbi's assertion should be restricted to certain Orthodox communities, from which the Brazilian community should be excluded, and perhaps the Argentine and Paraguayan communities as well, since the three of them supply most of the beef that is eaten in Israel, coming from highly industrialized farms and slaughterhouses.

On this matter, when I asked the kashrut supervisor whom I interviewed in São Paulo if the pace of industrial production would tarnish its suitability, he provided a detailed response. And if from his perspective it may be inferred that in Brazil the slaughter of animals follows the rules of kashrut, what echoes in his words is quite the opposite:

A shochet slaughters *only* 2,300 chickens from seven a.m. to eleven-forty a.m., eleven-thirty a.m., noon, sometimes noon and ten. So you have an average of about five hours a day. Two thousand three hundred divided by five hours is 460 birds per hour. Four hundred sixty birds per hour divided into sixty minutes is 7 birds per minute, which is getting close to the ideal number. So this issue is properly observed here in Brazil. In Brazil this is done at the Mehadrin slaughterhouse, I had no experience at Leven, and Swift only works with beef, not chicken. In Rio there are also those who slaughter Chabad chickens. The numbers I gave you are from Mehadrin: 6.9 chickens per minute. But there are people with special abilities. I, in particular, met a shochet who is now in the United States and he has an unusual ability. He looks like a machine, he's super-fast, but you can trust what he does. He is a separate case. Now, [if it's] a person who doesn't have that natural ability but gets the job done faster, you're in a perilous situation. I can assure you that this is not the case in Mehadrin.[36]

In the slaughterhouses of the beef industry, problems are even greater, leading to greater violation of the rules of tzaar baalei chaim. Among the most blatant infractions is the treatment of animals prior to slaughter, because, in addition to the cruelty with which cows and oxen are raised on industrialized farms, a long and inhumane process takes place from the time the animal is selected on the farm to the moment it is sent to the slaughterhouse. The process of chaining and hoisting the animal to be slaughtered[37] is added to the numerous hours that the animal spends without food and water. A slaughterhouse supervisor whom I interviewed in São Paulo described the process for me:

The oxen to be slaughtered arrive at the slaughterhouse at five o'clock in the afternoon. They are put into place in a machine that makes them walk in circles. They walk in circles until the morning of the next day. No food and no water. This is so that they defecate before slaughter and can be taken inside with their system clean. They all go through the same process. Then they are moved through a narrow corridor, where two men come in with something that looks like a broom handle but transmits electric shocks. This forces the oxen into the aisle, where they are lined up one behind the other. It is a structure that pushes them inside, through shocks from doors and walls. . . . Then they are forced into a cage where they are slaughtered one by one. Once the chain carrying the cattle that had been slaughtered broke. Then everything froze, including the animal that was next in line to be slaughtered. And I went out to see what was happening on death row. . . . There is no doubt that this last animal and all the others were aware of what was happening, that they would be killed.

Pressure from Israeli civil society, through the work of its NGOs, has been able to win trigger changes in slaughterhouse practices.[38] Hence, Brazil and other Mercosul[39] countries, major exporters of beef to Israel, have also been pressured toward changes in the "shackle and hoist" system, to the cattle-rotating slaughter box that, according to those who defend it, causes less animal suffering.

In Israel, as I have mentioned, Rabbis Amnon Ytzchak and Assa Keisar engage intensely in the conscientization of the Orthodox public, attempting to convince them to abstain from eating meat. Rabbi Keisar's book[40]—as well as the videos and talks that he publicizes through his blog—provide numerous examples of what goes on in Israeli slaughterhouses, examples that are explained through the prism of Jewish Law and through analysis of Hebrew Bible verses, discussions of the Talmud, and the laws of medieval rabbinical legislators.

In the above-mentioned documentary aired on Israeli television, a religious journalist expounds a unique perspective on the failings, negligence, and frauds of Israeli kashrut, a wise vision that is of extreme interest. He explains that the situation that inheres on Israeli farms and in slaughterhouses is not a matter that is exclusive to Orthodox interest but a question of concern to the entire Jewish population. Although not all Jews care about the kosher seal, the vast majority of Israeli Jews eat kosher meat, probably due more to the desire to maintain tradition than to religious considerations per se. Thus, the journalist concludes, what is on our table is our culture itself: someone who cheats on me in what is so important to me "is literally eating me: he is sinking his teeth into my flesh."

The journalist's analysis, accompanied by catchy images, vehemently condemns incorrect practices and frauds that sabotage the underpinnings of a food tradition that is part of the Jewish cultural repertoire. The statement "My culture is there on my table" echoes the analyses of Douglas (1966) and Tzuberi (2012), who set up an analogy between altar and table, in the sense that after the destruction of the Temple, the holiness of the Jewish people began to express itself in other spaces, among which the most important were the dining table and the body. We should keep in mind that the animals that are forbidden as offerings in the Temple are the same as those that are proscribed in Jewish dietary laws, and the blessing recited by the Great Priest before an offering is the same blessing that a ritual butcher pronounces before killing an animal. In parallel, for centuries Jewish dietary law has had the role of marking out the boundaries between insiders and outsiders, Jews and non-Jews, strengthening the religious and cultural identity of the group.[41]

The importance of food in the construction of Jewish culture and identity is fundamental, and its functions are several. As a religion that is re-created primarily within the home, Judaism stipulates a series of rituals that include food and specific meals for each day of the calendar, and there are those who argue that the last link that assimilated Jews maintain with Judaism is food itself. In relation to the role that food plays within the Jewish cultural repertoire, Baumel Joseph (2002, 8) makes the following observations:

> Consider the way in which food provides the mechanism of preservation of tradition. This is more than mere nostalgia. Food contains the language of memory—fully embodied. . . . Eating enables simultaneous participation in the past and the present; it is a strong link between generations. As food is ingested the eater partakes of all its symbolism, becoming one in a tradition seemingly without effort. Engaging all the human senses, food establishes or confirms social groups and interpersonal guardianship.

Lastly, I draw attention to the fact that the documentary made by the NGO Anonymous ends with an interview with a staff person from the Kashrut Section of the Israeli rabbinate who recognizes that there are mishaps in the production and distribution of kosher meat in the country and states that the necessary measures will soon be taken.

The long kashrut history of kosher meat

When Rabbi Vaya, the Great Legislator of Our Generation on Insects, explains that kashrut supervisors at present are confronted with problems that did not exist several decades ago, he refers not only to globalization—which allows the inclusion of foods from other countries and continents in our diet—but also the direct and indirect technological advances related to food production. Regarding animal protein, over the last few decades the growing industrialization of meat—beef and poultry—has created a series of debates in Western societies that extrapolate from the professions of nutrition and medicine. Large-scale production and consumption of unprecedented quantities of animal protein have awoken different types of consciousness in relation to the systematic cruelty that has been exercised against animals, its incumbent environmental destruction, and the contamination of cattle through excessive and unregulated use of antibiotics and hormones, in addition to the exploitation of human workers who work on ranches or farms or in meatpacking places and slaughterhouses.

The Industrial Revolution has created new phenomena regarding food and eating. Among them are the increased and heightened diversity of foods, as well as new modes of production and transport and innovative modes of meal preparation. In agriculture, we observe rising productivity and the creation and improvement of conservation techniques that allow for a more comprehensive and lasting distribution. At the same time, as Pellarano (2017, 2) points out, over time, the food industry takes on, as given by consumers, responsibility for the food, from the processing of ingredients to the ready-made dish.

The elements that go into each industrialized food are so many, and our diet so varied, that we can speak of a veritable "food cacophony." Thus, it is not without good reason that Rabbi Vaya perceives unprecedented and constant challenges to the community of observant Jews that originate in industrialization and globalized production of foods. Bearing the title of the Great Legislator of Our Generation on Insects, the rabbi focuses attention on the difficulties arising within his particular sphere of action.

As I have already stated, the major goal of this chapter is to uncover the relationship—providing there is one—between the growing concern that orthodoxy has for the possible ingestion of insects, on the one hand, and the circulation and consumption of treif meat within Orthodox communities, on the other.

As I have found to be common among many Jews today, I had also believed, rather naively, that to buy meat at a kosher butcher's or, in some countries such as Israel and the United States, to purchase meat at a supermarket that sells products with a kosher seal, would be enough to consider this meat suitable for consumption by Orthodox Jews. Yet as I delved into the complex rules of kashrut—reading manuals, codifications, and recipe books; analyzing sites that explain that housewives ought to redouble care to maintain a kosher diet; talking with Orthodox women in Israel and Brazil and with kashrut supervisors in both countries—I soon realized that many questions are lacking a clear answer. I highlight several of them: Why, in communities increasingly radicalized in the observance of Jewish Law in general, and in the observance of the laws and customs of kashrut in particular, has an issue as important as the status of meat not become the target of the keen eye of supervisors, butchers, and rabbis? Why do hundreds of pages of manuals on kashrut not even mention the existence of serious problems related to the high probability that observant Jews unwittingly consume treif meat? Furthermore, why would a question like this be less important than the topics that fill kashrut manuals? Among such topics, I cite several examples: Iruy: liquid poured from a hot utensil," "The prohibition of dairy breads," "Dairy ingredients and equipment."[42] "Eating dairy products after eating meat"; "*Iruy*: Liquid spilled from a hot utensil"; "The problems of leaving utensils or food in the care of a non-Jew take double care"; or "Porcelain cups, glass cups"; "Blood in eggs"; "Summer fruit check"; "Peeling, beating, and crushing fruit"[43] and the detailed observations, cited in the previous pages, about the care to be taken when ingesting fruits, vegetables, and grains.

These issues become even more relevant if we keep in mind that dietary law or kashrut makes up a part of what we refer to as chukim (divine statutes) which, by definition and unlike other commandments, are imperative, yet have remained immune to any attempts at explanation. Furthermore, and as we saw in Chapter 3, the notion of the sacredness—more precisely, the holiness and singularity—of the Jewish people is inseparable from kashrut.

This glaring omission, as I have shown, not only caused me great surprise but was met with astonishment and indignation on the part of secular and observant Jews with whom I shared the findings of my research. If we take into consideration that traditionalist Jews, even if they follow only a portion of the mitzvot, largely choose to consume kosher meat, we could say that we are facing a veritable conundrum. On the one hand, there is the importance of kosher meat within conscience, religious memory, and Jewish tradition, while on the other, the hard-to-understand circulation and consumption of treif meat that bears the kosher seal of Orthodox communities with the rabbis' consent.

Yet if the existence of this reality caused surprise among my Orthodox and secular Jewish friends in Brazil and Israel, there have been serious problems regarding the kashrut of meat consumed by Orthodox Jews since the late nineteenth and early twentieth centuries, which has been recorded in different sources. Mark A. Berman, in his exhaustive article on kosher meat frauds in the United States (1992), pulls up a quantity of interesting data on the matter and on how it rearranged certain dynamics within North American Orthodox communities. He also shows how numerous cases of fraud were taken to court. In his argument, despite the discrepancies among different currents of Judaism regarding a clear definition of the meaning of kosher meat,[44] bad faith and hunger for profit were, in the last analysis, the causes that led different certifying organs and sellers of kosher meat to engage in fraud. Starting from the premise that the sale of kosher meat is a business in which profit is the main goal, on the second page of his extensive article Berman asserts,

As is true of most businesses, there is money to be made in the kosher food industry by cutting corners. Since the price of many kosher foods includes a premium to cover the added costs of kosher preparation, profits can increase sharply if a non-kosher product is sold as kosher, at the kosher food price. This is especially so in the kosher meat industry where, because of the labor-intensive nature of kosher slaughter, premiums are at their highest. (Berman 1992, 2)

Although the purpose of Berman's text is to demonstrate how the kosher meat fraud statutes violate the First Amendment of the US Constitution, which stipulates strict separation of church and state, his work becomes a compendium of court cases that reveal rich data on the shortcuts taken by US supervisors and certifying agencies to sell treif meat as kosher within the country's Orthodox communities. Intense conflicts between different rabbis and supervisors reveal that what is seen as a mitzvah—the slaughter of animals for the consumption of observant Jews[45]-—is in fact an activity intersected by different variables such as costs and conflicts in relation to the rabbis who are involved in it. The production and circulation of kosher meat thus emerge as a terrain that is overloaded with conflicts, taking on the appearance of veritable warfare.

In the Middle Ages, local Jewish communities applied kashrut rules that controlled the ritual butchers through a mixed system of moral persuasion and punishment. Concerns with one's own reputation led butchers to exercise their labor assiduously. Traditional ways of regulating kosher slaughter depended on centralized community authority, and those who were caught perpetuating fraud had limited opportunities to survive through their trade. They were forced to leave the community and start their lives elsewhere. These conditions of control over all of those who were involved in the production of kosher meat were hard, if not impossible, to replicate in modern and contemporary societies (Lytton 2013b, 11).

A reading of literature on kosher meat frauds reveals that they are so ancient that even Rashi (1040–1105), a Jewish exegete of great influence among Orthodox Jews of all times, concluded that the ritual slaughterer is a "friend of Amalek,"[46] explaining this sentence from the Mishnah as follows: if in most professions people have the potential to cause physical harm to others through financial deceit, the harm produced by the shochet is infinitely greater since, as stated in the Talmud, consuming treif meat reduces people's degree of spirituality and their ability to feel the Divine Presence and Divine Providence.[47] This certainly renders a seller of such meat a "friend of Amalek."

Centuries later, albeit before the modernization of beef ranching and poultry farms and their conversion into veritable industries of animal protein, a rabbi from New York City described, in 1887, the state of supervision of kosher meat in the following way:

> So great is the scandal in this great city, that thousands of honest families who fear and tremble at the thought of straying into one tiny prohibition or sin never suspect that they are eating all kinds of unkosher meat. (Lytton 2013b, 10)

According to Berman (1992), in addition to the cases that took place in New York City and in New Jersey during the second half of the twentieth century, twenty-two states in a variety of cities around the country took accusations of fraud in the kosher meat market to the courts, winning statutes against them at different levels of the judiciary. The goal of the US courts is to ensure that consumers of products sold under particular seals comply with the premises that the latter stipulate. Nonetheless, because they reflect disputes over issues that are often highly detailed from a religious point of view, and therefore incomprehensible for state judges, civil courts prove incapable of ensuring compliance with religious standards. Thus, it is no coincidence that Lytton (2013b, 10) refrains from euphemism in describing the situation in the US kosher meat market from the mid-nineteenth to the mid-twentieth centuries:

> Slaughterhouse owners and butchers regularly sold non-kosher meat and poultry as kosher while supervising rabbis whom they employed turned a blind eye. Trade associations and unions engaged in illegal price-fixing schemes and extortion, enforcing their demands through intimidation, physical violence, and even murder. (Lytton 2013b, 10)

According to Lytton (2013b), despite efforts on the part of certain Jewish institutions to contain them, frauds in the kosher meat industry have not only continued but multiplied. It is important to note that the author does not deal with isolated cases but analyzes the structural problem of kosher meat supply in the United States in general, and in New York in particular.[48]

Although problems regarding the production, distribution, and sales of kosher meat are many, we must distinguish between frauds and the technical and logistic difficulties that plague the production, slaughter, and sale of kosher meat leading to the circulation of treif meat within Orthodox communities. In parallel, although there have been problems with the certification of kosher meat since time immemorial, the industrial production of animal protein has noticeably affected the kosher meat market, creating new phenomena. Among them, we would like to emphasize two in particular: the demarcation of new boundaries within the Orthodox population and the creation of unprecedented ways of conceiving Orthodox Judaism or, more precisely, what some groups have named "putting Jewish ethics into practice." In this context, the struggle of secular NGOs within broader society[49] has played a fundamental role. The Postville scandal stands out as emblematic.

The Postville scandal is an episode that reveals the multiple variables that are at stake in kashrut today. It involved the Agriprocessors factory, the target of police involvement in actions that shook up the city of Postville. Agriprocessors, the largest kosher meat processing factory in the United States, was founded and managed by the Rubashkin family, members of the Chabad-Lubavitch movement. In 2004 the NGO PETA filed a complaint against Agriprocessors for systematic mistreatment of animals; in 2006, a wide range of reports in the US press incriminated the company for exploiting its employees, depriving them of basic rights.[50] Both events had negative repercussions on the North American Jewish communities, producing a confrontation, initially, between liberal and Orthodox rabbis, and later among different Orthodox streams. At the core of the discussion, as reported in detail by Hornstein (2013), was the dilemma of what should be prioritized: respect for a millenary Jewish ritual, a divine commandment, or Jewish ethics?[51] The issue emerges in reference to the systematic exploitation of Agriprocessors workers.

The data that I have brought out here should not be met with surprise because, in a certain sense, over the course of the centuries a number of controversies have arisen among different currents of Judaism—the more or less religious, the Ashkenazis and the Sephardic, the religious and the traditionalists—with regard to what can be eaten and how foods must be prepared if they are to be considered kosher. However, today's debates seem to have intensified, generating constant negotiation among different groups in a process that has significant impact on Jewish identities, as well as demonstrating how boundaries between groups have been realigned. Thus, in the Israeli case, we find vegans and animal rights activists—that is, Jews who are largely secular—joining forces with Orthodox figures such as Rabbis Amnon Ytzchak and Assa Keisar, in their efforts in defense of a Jewish ethic that prioritizes the relations between humans and animals, in contrast to a focus on preserving rituals. In the United States, some organized Orthodox groups and rabbis join forces in defense of a Jewish ethics that privileges the relationship between human beings rather than concentrating attention exclusively on ritualistic aspects. In a broader sense, these examples show how binary oppositions, whether of Orthodox versus liberal Judaism, or Orthodox versus secular Judaism, no longer fit the bill. Hornstein (2013, 7–8) summarizes the dilemmas emerging from the Postville scandal:

> The ensuing clashes surrounding dietary ritual and ethics were not, however, dichotomous ones between pre-existing "liberal" Jewish groups and their "Orthodox" counterparts. Rather than forcing Jews into one of two camps, the debate spurred by Postville compelled participating individuals, groups and institutions to continuously negotiate their identity

in relationship to each other. These tensions reflected, reinforced and complicated communal boundaries as the debate over contemporary liberal ethics' connection to *kashrut* escalated.

From an anthropological point of view, kashrut becomes an object revealing of new identity configurations and of how the phenomena of larger society contain the potential to trigger new processes within orthodoxy. The Israeli NGO Ashgacha Pratit, whose objective—as mentioned earlier—is to contest the rabbinate's monopoly over kashrut supervision in that country, in another elucidative example of this new scenario. Directed by an Orthodox rabbi and employing mostly women to work as kashrut supervisors, Hashgacha Pratit is gaining ground in Jerusalem and expanding to other Israeli cities. It is important to emphasize the goodwill with which its initiative is met on the part of traditionalist and secular sectors of Israeli society. At the same time, the celebrated and popular Rabbi Amnon Ytzchak, whose sermons and lectures draw throngs of eastern Orthodox and traditionalist Jews, has created a gap between his view of what foods make up a kosher diet and the Israeli Orthodox establishment's conception of it. The videos and book by Rabbi Assa Keisar, a fervent advocate of a vegan lifestyle, have also marked a new position within orthodoxy as to how Jews should position themselves in relation to meat eating, when such meat comes from slaughterhouses in which, despite the existence of kashrut supervisors, the animals are kept in inadequate conditions and in constant suffering.[52] In this regard, Rabbi Assa Keisar also brings innovation to current definitions of the kosher diet.

In the United States, another situation prevails. Hornstein discusses this in relation to the Orthodox group Uri L'Tzedek, critics of Agriprocessors and of the rabbis and Orthodox institutions of the establishment. The group aspires to incorporating ethical values that have been abandoned or are considered less important within the circles of established Orthodox leadership and their communities. In Hornstein's words (2013, 59),

Uri L' Tzedek's motivation is not to gain acceptance within the ultra-Orthodox community. They admit that they operate separately from the ultra-Orthodox world. Rather, they are trying to create a new kind of space where it is acceptable to espouse progressive political views while unambiguously identifying as Orthodox.[53]

Jewish sources and kosher meat: Some data

It is common lore, among both Jews and Gentiles, to comment on the typical feasts of the holidays of the Jewish calendar. Gefilte fish[54] and chicken soup with *kneidalach*[55] are an inseparable part of the Ashkenazi Jewish festivities. And if each and every one of the celebrations can be characterized by typical foods, whose symbology goes back centuries— such as honey and foods made with honey for the New Year, dairy products at Shavuot[56] and matzah and its derivatives on Passover—these delicacies do not substitute the main dish which, for both Ashkenazi and Sephardic Jews is meat-based.[57]

The obligation to eat meat on the Sabbath and on the holidays of the Jewish calendar come from the premise that eating meat is a pleasure, and that on Shabbat one must be cheerful.[58] At the same time, Jewish exegetes agree that, although in antediluvian times eating meat was forbidden, the prohibition was dropped in its aftermath. Paradoxically, the deluge created a breach of Jewish tradition. The ethical and spiritual descent of humankind showed that laws were necessary to improve relations between human beings and allow them to perform acts of kindness and justice and, thus, to work for *tikkun olam*.[59] Following this tradition, only after the messianic era would eating meat again be forbidden. It is interesting that, as in other places within Judaism, in the realm of kashrut, the mythical past and the messianic future have a qualitative relationship to one another.

At the same time, the disapproval of eating animals can also be attributed to a God who, portrayed in the Bible as the creator of all life, places priority on its maintenance. Hence, it is from him that come the dietary restrictions placed on the people of Israel. It is important to re-member that one of the prohibitions of kashrut refers to ingesting blood, as blood symbolizes life.

Nonetheless, although over the last few decades vegetarianism has be-come the object of debate within some Orthodox communities, generating more than a few controversies, there is still far from any consensus on the matter. Debates have multiplied because of the influence of worldviews that are alien and external to orthodoxy, such as those of vegans and animal rights activists, as well as those that are internal to orthodoxy, such as the reports and criticisms of slaughterers and those who supervise farms and slaughterhouses.

Within this new scenario, internet sites and rabbinical conferences for the purpose of establishing objective criteria on the obligation to eat meat on holidays have also multiplied. They are meant to clarify doubts and answer questions raised by people who fear transgression of Halakhah precepts through disregard for the principle of tzaar baalei chaim, or by not eating meat on Shabbat and the holidays of the Jewish calendar, if they have adopted a vegetarian or vegan lifestyle. Rabbis' positions on these issues are varied and contradictory. Thus, within the same text, titled "The Significance of Eating Meat,"[60] Rabbi Eliezer Melamed argues vehemently that vegetarianism is not an option for Jews because of concern over the suffering of animals. According to Melamed, until the coming of the Messiah, Jews should continue to eat meat on Shabbat and at holiday festivities. Yet in a text that can be accessed on the Chabad site, penned by Rabbi Moshe Goldman and titled "Do I Have to Eat Meat on Shabbat?" opposite conclusions are drawn. Based on the Shulchan Aruch, Rabbi Goldman answers, "There is no obligation to eat meat or drink wine on Shabbat. Rather, since it is assumed that most people take more pleasure in eating meat than in other foods, and in drinking wine more than other drinks, therefore they should increase in [consuming] meat and wine according to their means."[61] Nonetheless, Goldman argues that those who are vegan or vegetarian and do not take pleasure in eating meat should then avoid it on Shabbat and holidays as well.

Despite the contradictions among different rabbinical authorities, we may come to the following conclusions: there is in the Talmud a mention of the precept that on holidays (Yom Tov), one should be cheerful (*simchah*). At the Shabbat meal, cheer is directly related to the consumption of meat and wine. Nonetheless, commentators demand that meat be consumed within the specific context of the sacrifices (*Korbanot*) enacted in the Temple, meaning that there is no obligation to eat meat at present. Regarding Shabbat, the Talmud recommends eating meat for another reason—not cheer, but delight.[62] In this case, although the suggestion is very personal and subjective, over the centuries it translated into the custom of having meat at Shabbat dinner.[63]

Although the texts contradict each other, and over the last few decades, vegetarians and vegans have developed different interpretations of biblical laws and rabbinical tradition, their voices remain marginal, and the majority of Orthodox Jewry continues to eat meat not only on Shabbat but almost on a daily basis, both in Israel and within diasporic communities.[64]

Mammals and birds versus insects: Unraveling the charade

In recent decades, meat and insects have come to represent a problem within Orthodox communities, albeit for different reasons and in different ways. Thus, if as of the mid- 1980s insects became the major threat to keeping kosher, as we have seen, meat—a basic ingredient of the Orthodox kosher diet—has also had its issues. I have tried here to map out the underlying reasons for these two phenomena, as well as how they are experienced and explained by Orthodox authorities and experts, whether rabbis, supervisors, or ritual butchers. The explanations I have shared with the reader separate prescriptions and proscriptions regarding the ingestion of insects from those related to meat consumption. This way of presenting data is neither personal choice nor pedagogical strategy; rather, it results from the fact that none of those whom I interviewed nor the sources I consulted drew a relationship between the two. This brings us face to face with two dimensions of kashrut that seem to bear no relationship to one another: insects, on the one hand, and mammals and birds, on the other.

A book perhaps forgotten by anthropologists, Nick Fiddes's *Meat as a Natural Symbol*, brings important contributions to our understanding of why, despite the existence of serious problems in the production of kosher meat, it was not banned from the diet of observant Jews, as were various other types of food that in theory pose less threat to the rules of kashrut, such as vegetables and industrialized and semi-industrialized foods. Fiddes (1991, 5) begins his book with a statement meant to provoke his readers, arguing that while it is easy for people to agree that vegetarianism is an ideological or even a political position, it seems difficult for them to see meat eating in the same light. Yet, he goes on, since eating habits differ over time and space, meat eating demands interpretation and explanation just as vegetarianism does. He proceeds to share a finding with readers: while the bibliography on the vegetarian and vegan movements dates from the eighteenth century and in recent decades has proliferated, social science research on the importance of meat in the Western menu is on the sparse side, and tends to be very superficial. Furthermore, investigations into sectarian and fundamentalist religious movements reveal that the imposition of strict diets that dictate what is mandatory to eat, what is forbidden to eat, and when and how food should be eaten constitutes a strategy of social control over group members. At the same time, the imperative to follow certain diets is one of the surest ways to build the loyalty of group members.

As I have reiterated here, if we can consider Orthodox communities as groups whose members depend on the verdicts of rabbinical authority both on what is most and what is least important, we can understand kashrut as one of the most effective strategies for social control of the Orthodox population, in addition to the other functions of kashrut already mentioned. Nonetheless, and paradoxically, this strategy of social control reveals more than a few fragilities and inconsistencies that become clearer when we try to answer the following question: what would happen if the Great Rabbis who today shape the directives of Orthodox doctrine decided to forbid their followers from eating meat, based on its high probability of not being kosher?

Given the characteristics of contemporary orthodoxy, for which one of its pillars is the reduction of individual autonomy, a first answer might be that just as in other areas of social life, Orthodox Jews obey interdictions coming from the Great Rabbis. This position flows from the premise that obedience to the *Daat Torah* is unquestionable. Today, as we have seen, and notwithstanding all the complaints against the farms and meatpacking plants that produce and distribute treif meat, no prohibition has come—not even an alert, in fact—from rabbinical leadership in relation to the consumption of animal protein. Only a few rabbis have taken up the banner of vegetarianism and veganism, guided by the goal of avoiding noncompliance with Halakhah through the consumption of meat that is likely not to be kosher.

Given this scenario, is it not strange that the Great Rabbis, and Orthodox rabbis as a whole, have been so remiss in the face of a phenomenon that would openly lead hundreds of thousands of Orthodox Jews to violate Jewish Law? How to explain this phenomenon for a group that constantly disseminates, through different media (internet, pashkavelim, lectures, courses, books, handouts) new prohibitions on laws and customs related to the most diverse dimensions of life? We must not forget that Orthodox Judaism is an orthopractic religion and ritual determines its uniqueness as a religious system. The second fundamental question that I have repeatedly mentioned is the following: How can we explain the leniency in relation to eating problematic meat vis-à-vis the prohibitions and redoubled efforts to avoid the unintentional consumption of insects?

When I asked the first question to informants over the course of my fieldwork, I received the following replies: "The Orthodox public won't listen to the rabbis on the meat issue"; "The Orthodox will not stop eating meat"; "There may be problems, but they are always solved"; "I was told there is a *moshav*[65] that does kosher slaughter for groups who have these concerns."

This last response, in fact, referred to the only group that could solve the problem, a service restricted to small numbers of persons with a certain amount of buying power. The response before it was a clear attempt to avoid the issue. The two that were the most interesting were the first ones, which confront the issue of the Orthodox community and their relationship to their leadership. If we recall—and this is a fundamental point—that the kashrut rules are considered chukim, that is, unquestionable holy commandments, the scenario takes on further complexity. It is no longer a matter of massively disobeying the rabbis around a custom, as was the case with the refusal of women to stop wearing wigs (despite the ban and admonition of several highly prestigious rabbis) nor of voting for a candidate different from the one the rabbi endorses. The possibility that the Orthodox public not heed the warnings and prohibitions of their rabbis on such an important issue as violating a mitzvah could easily be interpreted as an act of insubordination.

Amid my efforts to find an answer to such questions, it may be necessary to pause for a brief analysis of the meaning and value of meat in Western societies, since the issues at stake here—or more precisely, the impossibility, refusal, or the difficulties involved in giving up meat—concern issues that go beyond Jewish orthodoxy.

Several studies reveal that eating meat is an indicator of prosperity and prestige and, above all, a way of showing ourselves that we dominate the wilderness and the environment that lies outside or beyond the civilized world (Leroy and Praet, 2017; Willard 2003; Fiddes 1991). Fiddes (1991, 14–15) explores widespread legal and academic concepts that start from the premise that meat is food par excellence, sometimes even considered a synonym of the latter. Based on this observation, the British anthropologist coined the expression "meat hunger" to indicate situations in which a diet free of animal protein leaves people feeling unsatiated; in other words, depriving themselves of meat is equivalent to starvation for most individuals and groups in Western societies. Yet although this idea is partly common sense, Fiddes does not restrict his analysis to this way of understanding the world, but offers us examples from Lévi-Strauss and Edmond Leach, two anthropologists for whom, in different ways, food and meat are equivalent. Thus, the former defended the thesis that in the human passage from nature to culture, what differentiates us from animals is the fact that we cook food; meat, to a large extent, becomes the main reference for the cooked.[66] Regarding Leach's approach, Fiddes (1991, 15) argues:

> In his analysis of 'Animal categories and verbal abuse' (1964) [Leach] per-
> sistently talks about 'food values and 'food names' whilst his discussion
> revolves around animals and flesh foods to a degree utterly dispropor-
> tionate to their role in the diet, measured by monetary value, nutritional
> value, or bulk.

In light of these observations, Fiddes's conclusions (1991, 15) go right to the
point: the fact that meat and food are considered synonymous reflects meat's
preeminence, not only in the Western diet but in Western thought.

On the other hand, although the consumption of meat in Western
societies has fluctuated—showing peaks, such as in the High Middle Ages
and the eighteenth century, because of innovations in agriculture—a meat
diet continued to be the privilege of the aristocratic classes and the more
affluent. Until the beginning of the Second World War, meat consumption
among the poorest sectors of the population remained very low, and even the
Industrial Revolution did not inject more animal protein into workers' diets
(Fiddes 1991).

It is still necessary to point out that the choice of what we eat is not just a
matter of preferences, but an act imbued with social meaning, cultural practice, and political ideology (Willard 2003, 105). Barthes (1975, 47) goes further and states that there are several sources beyond appetite that we draw
upon for inspiration when we choose what we eat, such as culture, family
tradition, politics, and the rhetoric of food and nutrition. Food is a communication system, a collection of images, and a cultural set of conventions for
different situations.

There is also a gender issue in meat eating. The historical narrative and
rhetoric that accompanied meat consumption masculinized it by asserting
that it provided physical strength and endurance. Assuming that physical
power is historically associated with masculinity and virility, it is possible
to conclude that meat has been perceived as male, or as an object for men
(Willard 2003, 112). In turn, from a perspective similar to Fiddes's, Rifkin
(1992, 244) states that the identification of raw meat with power, male dom-
ination, and privileges is one of the oldest and most archaic cultural symbols
still visible in contemporary civilization.

It is not my purpose to go further here into a topic that I return to in the
conclusion of this book. At this point, I merely highlight its relevance in order
to begin to answer the two questions mentioned earlier, as follows: Why don't
the Great Rabbis and the Orthodox rabbis prohibit the consumption of meat

despite the doubts surrounding their kashrut? Why, in an Orthodox society in which rumor is a structural component, has news about the unsuitability of meat consumed by the population not spread as would be expected? Both issues are directly related to the predictable hypothesis that the Orthodox public does not want to give up meat consumption, neither daily nor festive. It might be said that the prestige and prosperity of a meal that includes meat as a main dish, as well as the phenomenon of meat hunger are introjected values that are hard to give up.

Regarding excessive care in insect checking, two hypotheses are possible. The first is presented by Kramer (2009, 160) in his rigorous analysis of the last chapter of his book. There, Kramer adds to the puzzle that insects represent, a question regarding whether the Orthodox need to live in a state of permanent alert. The radicalization of the postwar orthodoxy again becomes part of the answer. Based on a famous article by Soloveitchik (1994), Kramer argues that the new practices, as well as contemporary chumrah, come from a recent orthodoxy whose practices have emerged not from observation and imitation but from readings of the Law as it was recorded in the books. The new orthodoxy, or post-Holocaust orthodoxy, is submersed in relentless battle not only with Zionist, secular, Reform, and Conservative Judaism and with modernity as a whole but also, and above all, within itself. Internal struggles between Orthodox currents use food and its regulation as a battleground (Kramer 2009, 160). The competition between different kashrut seals is an indicator that there are several legitimate authorities that decide which foods are kosher and which are not.

The chumrah that has become the common practice of contemporary Orthodox communities, and of which the meticulous and persevering search for insects is an important component, expresses the conditions of identity in present-day Judaism. And although modernity has given rise to various ways of re-creating Judaism, making Jewish identity a more complex issue, confrontations at present have become more aggressive and the Jewishness of individuals more suspect. Hyphenated identities, patrilineal Jews, intermarriage, and chozrim bi'teshuvah become a constant threat to the integrity of Judaism as orthodoxy conceives it. To know for sure who is a Jew, relentless checking and detailed questioning are needed. Based on these data and analyses, Kramer (2009) concludes that the insects' key position within today's kashrut constitutes a metaphor (although Kramer does not use this precise term) for what is going on within contemporary Orthodox Judaism. In this sense, vegetables, fruits, produce, and nuts that present themselves as kosher must also be checked again and again: appearances are deceiving and may be misleading. Somehow, the seemingly invisible insect has contaminating, destructive power.

If, over the centuries, kashrut rules have served to separate Jews from non-Jews, today they become a source of separation among different groups of observant Jews. Nowadays it is not enough for the food to be kosher; it becomes equally important that the supervisor and, in the case of meat, the ritual slaughterer, be Orthodox Jews who follow Halakhah strictly. Products sold under the seal of the Conservative movement, although produced in the same way as those bearing the seal of Orthodox certification agencies, are no longer considered kosher by Orthodox rabbis.

The exaggerated concern for insects observed in recent years demonstrates that the Orthodox public must always be on the alert and act according to strict guidelines, constantly watched over not only by God but also by the rabbis. If food is an important dimension that allows rabbis to control the members of their communities, it is possible to conclude, once again, following Asad's (1987; 1988) approach to ritual, that the Orthodox body is governed by a disciplinary program from whose gaze nothing escapes.

Lastly, if we consider that over the centuries raw vegetables and fruits were the only food Jews could share with their non-Jewish neighbors, a major change in Halakhah has taken place in recent decades: observant Jews can now not even share vegetables and fruits with other Jews—or if they do, it is done with much more than a little mistrust—a more than curious phenomenon for a community whose leaders represent it as a group that was, is, and will always be the same: Judaism as authentic, immutable, and true.

Rabbinical leaders of the different Orthodox currents make few concessions to interpretations coming from liberal currents. In this context, only rabbis identified with modern orthodoxy may actually seek dialogue with rabbis of the Masorti movement. Orthodox leaders' steadfast defense of orthodoxy as the only correct and true way of practicing Judaism is justified, among other ways, by the fact that Orthodox Judaism followed in the footsteps of historical Judaism, the Judaism of Rabbi Gamaliel, Ravi Akiva, Maimonides, Yosef of Karo, and the Gaón of Vilna, as well as more recent figures such as Rabbis Chatam Sofer and Chazon Ish. No less important in this genealogy are great-grandfathers and grandfathers. Although this historical lineage is quite controversial, this is nonetheless how Orthodox logic works.

But to what extent is there a real identity linking generations separated by millennia and centuries? Such an identity is anchored in the notion that the people of Israel were God's chosen people, a status that, from an Orthodox perspective, defines the singularity of the Jewish people, a people of priests who sanctify themselves through mitzvot. This historical continuity, as the Great Orthodox rabbis claim, is distinguished by the rigid performance of biblical commandments, later compiled in the Talmud and in medieval and modern codifications. Yet this long path is not exempt of obstacles and difficulties, manifesting themselves in a number of problems. The most important one that I identified in this research was the systematic violation of several commandments with the consent of Orthodox leaders. Among such transgressions I have highlighted is the violation of the principle of tzaar baalei chaim and the consumption of treif meat in Orthodox communities, whether due to meat certification fraud or technical difficulties arising from the industrialized processes of animal protein production.

6

Some answers, some findings, and some questions: Kashrut as both stage for and reflection of tensions within Orthodox Judaism

Speak to the whole Israelite community and say to them: You shall be holy, for I, your God, am holy.

Leviticus 19:2

And you shall eat your fill
And praise the name of the LORD *your God*
Who dealt so wondrously with you—
My people shall be shamed no more.

Joel 2:26

When the Holy Temple was in existence, the Altar atoned for Israel;
today, a person's table atones for him.

Talmud, Berachot 55a

Kashrut and the sacred

Eating is part of daily life. We cannot survive without food. Yet eating is so much more than a matter of survival: we cannot celebrate extraordinary events without including food, whether as protagonist (as it is in certain celebrations) or in a supporting role. Matzah is a requirement in the celebration of Jewish Passover, as well as other foods (charoset,[1] boiled egg, and bitter herbs), symbols of the different values and moments of the Jewish people on their journey toward freedom. Shabbat is not Shabbat without its three prescribed meals, known as *shalosh seudot Shabbat*; they are not an

The Sacred and the Impure in Judaism. Marta F. Topel, Oxford University Press. © Oxford University Press 2024.
DOI: 10.1093/oso/9780197677667.003.0006

addendum to Shabbat but its constitutive parts. Hanukkah, the Festival of Lights, wouldn't be Hanukkah without the foods fried in oil that are part of it,[2] nor could Rosh Hashanah, the Jewish New Year, be celebrated without honey—and the cakes and sweets made with it.

Among some ethnic and religious groups, certain foods are carefully kept for religious celebrations; others are considered taboo and cannot be consumed by the group or by some of its members. Food prohibitions and prescriptions are common to all cultures.

In modern secular society, eating is also ordered and organized: we eat certain foods according to predetermined schedules, we avoid those that cause us revulsion, demonstrate special interest in those that are considered delicacies, and try to maintain a healthy diet. Over the last few decades, a wide range of diets has been created to help us lose weight, become more agile, return to traditions, collaborate with the sustainability of the planet, and understand that we are also animals— that is, a category that includes both humans and nonhumans in a similar moral status that should encourage us toward a vegan diet. No less important is the fact that food involves moral, economic, and social aspects.

On the other hand, and as Mintz (2001, 31) points out, habits and behaviors around food are related to our sense of ourselves and thereby influence our social identity. Our attitude toward food is formed in childhood and usually inculcated by adults who have authority over us, thereby endowing our habits and behaviors with affective and potentially enduring traits. Another aspect that Mintz points to (2001, 34) is that foods are associated with national groups, a phenomenon that inevitably leads to the identity dimensions of food. On the other hand, in the globalized world in which the circulation of food is increasing and diversified, our attitudes toward our own food and that of others are linked to behaviors that are at the same time conservative and flexible. More precisely, we do not give up "our" food, but become curious experimenters of the foods of other cultures. From another angle, it is worth remembering that it is through memory that dishes and recipes are transmitted from generation to generation (Woortmann 2016). When people distance themselves from their roots, the emergence of groups that aspire to re-create the original recipes of community or region, in a movement in search of authenticity, are not uncommon.

Food has received considerable attention in classic ethnography, serving as an instrument to understand the different values of the societies that are studied. Food can thus reveal what is considered sacred and what is taboo or how relations of inequality are expressed; it can also be taken as an indicator of a group's form of social organization (hunter-gatherers, nomads, farmers, fishermen). In recent years, foods—or some foods—have been recognized by UNESCO as immaterial heritage, understood as arrangements of inherited activities that are passed from generation to generation, as a collective element that is claimed by a community—or even a state. Heritage must have social, symbolic, and affective force (Garcia Parpet 2016).

The transmission of certain values and customs from generation to generation should perhaps be relativized within the current context in which numerous re-ethnicization movements have emerged. The latter, seeking roots in a past they turn to for its traditions, brings gaps between different generations to the surface. In the case of Judaism, two phenomena are worthy of emphasis. The first is that Jewish food—understood here as food prepared according to Jewish Law, strictly following the commandments and customs of Halakhah—is not about flavor, shape, and aesthetics. The influences of the different habitats in which the Jews and their neighbors lived are clear and are reflected in the typical foods of the Jewish ethnic subgroups, such as the food of the German Ashkenazi Jews and the Ashkenazi Jews of Poland, or the typical food of the Moroccan, Iraqi, or Syrian communities. Nothing that is characteristic of the foods of each of these communities would be familiar to Jews who do not belong to those groups. Thus, a Jewish meal—as it has been defined and analyzed throughout this book—has much less to do with the folkloric aspect of ethnic foods than with strict religious rules for its preparation. In other words, kosher foods are those that are prepared considering the prohibitions and prescriptions contained in Halakhah and other Jewish codifications; interest in flavors, shapes, and aesthetics is mere commentary.[3]

Also worthy of emphasis is the fact that tradition has been "evaporated," if I may say so, by decades of short circuiting or distance between the oldest and the youngest, or both. Tradition is now being reclaimed by different types of mediators whose efforts are directed toward the preservation of specific practices—whether a typical food, dance, or the clothing of specific groups. As far as food is concerned, "ethnic" cookbooks are a clear example of how gastronomic heritage is reclaimed.

In the case of Orthodox Jews, kosher cookbooks, in addition to attempting to reclaim a tradition—or an alleged gastronomic tradition—also have another function. Based on the insights of Barbara Kirshenblatt Gimblett, Stolow (2006, 16) states,

Through recipes, commentary, prefaces, illustrations—and where they exist, photographs—cookbooks reproduce the "traditional" while at the same time extend the repertoire of legitimately "Jewish" food into new domains, through the incorporation of new technologies and techniques, ingredients, styles, and dietary principles, inspiring both novices and culinary virtuosi to expand their repertoires. On these terms, cookbooks also register changing relationships between author and reader, where neither faith nor locally acquired knowledge provide a sufficient basis for the successful (re)production of Jewish food.

Stolow's assertions reflect another area in which the traditions of diverse Jewish communities have been replaced by a movement toward standardization, one that has been in effect for a number of decades or perhaps for even more than a century. The replacement of the books of customs (*sifrei minhag*) of medieval communities by texts that follow the *Daat Torah* to the letter is the emblematic example of this pattern. And as we have seen, the authority of the *Daat Torah* is unquestionable, in addition to expressing the strictest version of commandment fulfillment.

Perhaps Soloveitchik (1994) was the first to describe this tendency toward polarization in terms of broader social change: from a mimetic mode to a textual and pedagogical one. The knowledge and practices acquired by parents, friends, and neighbors was codified and standardized in print books, which at the same time went through a process of textual abstraction and a demand for ever increasing precision and rigidity in the interpretation of rabbinical law. The strict conduct observed in Orthodox Jewish communities is, thus, linked to the ever more prevalent experience of conceiving of practicing Judaism "by the book." Lastly, when taking a middle ground is seen as an unfair concession, extremes may become more palatable (Soloveitchik 1994, 72).

At another level, we cannot forget that food is one of the most important means to link an individual to the social body, unstably situated between sustainability and pollution, desire and taboo, and governed by complex norms of taste, commensality, and etiquette (Stolow 2006, 15). Eating is much more than eating, or to put it another way, a particular type of food brings with it multiple meanings and functions.

Within Judaism, eating is considered an intentional activity to the extent that all food that is ingested (liquid or solid) possesses a specific blessing, and prayers are recited before and after meals. These prayers serve to promote a system that recognizes divine action in the creation and production of foods. Kramer (2009, 75) explains that by instituting prayers for each food, Jewish tradition removes the act of eating from the sphere of the mundane and turns it into an act in which God and his designs are present. The prayers turn the act of eating into a sacred one. In parallel, the fact that the prayers are recited in the present tense has as a correlate the invocation of God as the creator of the food that is to be consumed. Since there are no references in the prayers to times past, in which God created natural cycles, the reference is to a God who creates food continuously. The underlying idea is that God is the master of the universe and therefore requires human beings to recognize the source and master of creation before partaking of it. Finally, there is the aspect of distinction that is expressed in the fact that the Jew who observes the ritual and recites the required prayers before eating will be ever aware of the active presence of God in his life, thus distinguishing himself from his Gentile, apparently less sensitive, neighbor (Kramer 2009, 76–77).[4]

Rabbi Daniel Sperber (2019, 56) corroborates, to some extent, these characteristics of food within Judaism, stating that,

> The complexity of life, the fusion of physical matter and spiritual energy that is expressed in food, is a remarkable wonder worthy of our amazement. As we come to appreciate this gift, we open our eyes to the possibility of eating in the presence of God. Like a sacrifice on the altar, our consumption of food is a sacral moment.

Before probing more deeply into the meanings of holiness and purity inherent to the Jewish tradition as expressed in kashrut laws, it is time to answer a few questions this research has raised.

The twists and turns of technology and carnal sin

Part of this research has been devoted to understanding a dissonance that I found extremely revealing: the rigidity in the search for insects vis-à-vis lenience in relation to the consumption of meat that is dubiously kosher. I refer to the certain condescension present in the checking of kosher meat that coexists with the severe prohibitions, public warnings, and admonishments on matters supposedly less important from the point of view of the Halakhah.[5] Examples of this are the ideal length of the sleeves and necklines of the dresses that Orthodox women wear, the ban on Orthodox women frequenting certain public spaces or the ban on drinking mineral water without the "kosher for Passover" seal during Passover. It is essential to point out that hundreds of other prescriptions and proscriptions are the subject of intense dissemination, meant to prevent the type of gaps or blind spots in the enunciation of rules that could lead individuals to transgress a law or a custom. We took a detailed look at how Halakhah works today in relation to the Passover, and some of the requirements needed to have a kosher kitchen. It is not in vain that Rabbi Assa Keisar asks himself why it is forbidden to consume chametz on Passover and why meat and meat products are allowed to reach our tables after serious violations of the principle of tzaar baalei chaim and rules related to techniques of slaughter (Keisar 2017/8, 18).

From this observation, which seems almost a riddle, two conclusions can be reached. The first is that most of the Great Rabbis are aware of the situation of the farms and slaughterhouses from which treif meat certified as kosher comes, or meat whose kashrut is suspect because of its butchers and supervisors, but about which the latter neither share information with their followers nor impose sanctions on meatpackers. A confrontation with the meat industry is out of the question, given the industry's evident economic power. The second conclusion regards the intense and comprehensive dissemination of what goes on in the meat industry, in which the industrial breeding and slaughter of animals violates not only the principle of tzaar baalei chaim but also eminently technical issues found in Jewish Law. In the latter case, banning the consumption of meat that, despite its kosher seal, is not suitable for consumption by observant Jews could trigger adverse reactions in the Orthodox public, difficult for the rabbis to control.

We may even consider the possibility of disobedience on the part of sectors of the Orthodox population that are not willing to do without meat on their menu. As I have already emphasized, eating meat—not only on the feasts of the Jewish calendar and on Shabbat but also in everyday life—is a very ingrained custom in current Orthodox communities, in particular, and in Western society as a whole.

The possibility that significant segments within the Orthodox population disobey laws stipulated by rabbis is not a new phenomenon. Furthermore, such a situation also resembles many others in which religious leadership is contested from below. The reticence and refusal of a significant number of Israeli Orthodox women to stop wearing wigs, after repeated public admonitions by Great Rabbis, among them Great Rabbi Ovadia Yosef, shows that the authority of rabbis is not always able to triumph.[6]

In his scholarly and thought-provoking book *The Shabbes Goy*, Katz discusses varied historical dynamics that have emerged around the creation of the mitzvah. He emphasizes the influence of social, economic, political, and cultural contexts. Faced with new conditions of life, the halakhic decisions that are found in the Talmud may no longer be relevant precedents. In such cases, solutions can come from two sources: as a spontaneous popular approach or from rabbinical authority. There is always a possibility that a custom takes root in the community before it is introduced to Halachic authorities. When this happens, as Katz explains (1992, 19), authorities are confronted with several dilemmas.

In the case that concerns us, a not insignificant problem concerns how the rabbis and the Orthodox population would face the fact that for years kashrut laws were being transgressed. And how would people react, feeling betrayed by rabbis, supervisors, and ritual slaughterers who, aware of the situation, did not warn them about the dangers of consuming such meat? A clue can be found in Grandin's account (1980, 383) of the reaction of a group of US Orthodox women when they discovered that a kosher cattle slaughterhouse used the method of shackling and hoisting animals:

> Most Orthodox Jews in the United States have not witnessed slaughter operations. This is especially true of the younger generation. . . . If Jewish consumers were made aware of how their sacred ritual has been corrupted in some plants, they would demand a stop to it. One large kosher slaughterhouse stopped shackling and hoisting and installed two ASPCA restraining pens because housewives picketed the grocery stores which owned the plant.

Another clue, perhaps a little fanciful, but no less inspiring, appears in the short story "Blood" from the book *Brief Friday* by Isaac Bashevis Singer ([1963] 1978). In this tale, upon learning that the meat sold by the farm of owner Risha and ritual butcher Reuben was treif, the Jews of the town, enraged and wanting revenge, went off in search of the two, planning to kill them.

> [The women, in turn,] ran out onto the streets, pounding their heads with their fists, crying, and cursing themselves. By all indications, the population

had been eating unclean meat for years. Healthy housewives took their crockery to the market and smashed it to pieces. Sick and pregnant women fainted. Devout men tore their robes, covered their heads with ashes, and sat down to mourn. A mob rushed to the butchers to punish those selling the meat that Risha provided.[7]

The search for insects using magnifying glasses, special lights, and light boxes shows that technology has entered Orthodox communities as a complicator rather than as a facilitator of life—or perhaps technology has paved the way for following Jewish Law more strictly than in the past. In the sphere of meat and processed meat production, technology has collided head-on with Halakhah, given its pace and its objective of maximizing results. The act of shackling and hoisting animals for kosher slaughter represents a clash between an ancient ritual—which sought to reduce the suffering caused to animals—and the coldness and need for efficiency that characterize modern technology.[8]

In short, technology, despite its status as almost the only dimension of modernity that observant Jews accept, has been incorporated through a fluctuating movement in which conflicts and contradictions stand out.[9] It is possible to argue that technology entered the Orthodox world because in our times no other options exist—examples of the impossibility of controlling technology's encroachment on the day-to-day life of Orthodox families are processed foods, public transportation, cash machines, and the intrusive and threatening internet. Such innovations, which in secular society were meant to make daily life more pleasant, in Orthodox communities had the opposite effect, creating new situations that in the eyes of the Orthodox elite became threatening. In relation to kashrut, as I have stressed throughout these pages, the incorporation of technology brought new problems in food certification and, as one of its correlates, the emergence and institutionalization of new professionals: kashrut experts.

Both phenomena allow us to consider the following equation: the more technology is available, the greater the problems and complications. Yet what surprises me is the fact that technology is applied to matters that are alien to it. Thus, insects have always existed, but only today is technology used to check whether foods contain them or not. In this case, the "complication" is a matter of choice, and the choice that is made leads to chumrah.

In another vein, I believe that one of the most interesting—and surprising— issues regarding the tzaar baalei chaim principle in our times is how it has revealed an exceptionally progressive worldview among Jewish legislators, when compared to both non-Jewish philosophers of the same period and with contemporary philosophers and social scientists. It conceives of sentience—although this precise term is, obviously, absent from Jewish sources—as a parameter for governing human behavior in relation to other animals. The examples are many.

Thus, medieval lawmakers like Maimonides (1138–1204) warned that people should not crowd their respective chickens together when they take them to the ritual slaughterhouse, as allowing one chicken to watch another one being killed causes undue suffering. A contemporary Brazilian shochet stated that this principle is respected by one of the local certification agencies, explaining that "Mehadrin's chickens are slaughtered in twos, in a separate place. The rest do not even see. They are stuffed into a bag in such a way that they don't see the shochet coming with his knife and don't see the chickens that have already died."

I am reminded of the prohibition of separating calves from their mothers before the seventh day postpartum. Maimonides, the famous exegete and philosopher, explained why the ban was important:

> There is no difference in this case between the pain of man and the pain of other living beings, since the love and tenderness of the mother for her young ones is not produced by reasoning, but by imagination, and this faculty exists not only in man but in most living beings.[10]

A similar argument is made by Nachmanides (1194–1270), who stated,

> This is also an explanatory commandment of the prohibition "Ye shall not kill [the dam] and its young both in one day" (Leviticus 22:28) because the reason for [both] commandments is that we should not have a cruel heart and be discompassionate or it may be that the Scripture does not permit us to destroy a species altogether although it permits slaughter [for food] within that group.[11]

The polemic that unfolds between the two exegetes emerges exclusively in relation to the *taam ha´mitzva* (the bases for the precept) and not with regard to animals' capacity to suffer: while Maimonides believes that the purpose of the mitzvah is to avoid causing animals to suffer, Nachmanides claims that its purpose is to guide Jews along a straight path and to extirpate the cruelty that exists within them.

Contemporary utilitarian philosophers such as Peter Singer (2010) suggest that it is not morally justifiable to exclude nonhumans or nonpersons from moral considerations, since they clearly have the capacity to suffer. Any being that shows an interest in not suffering deserves that interest to be taken into account, and a nonhuman animal who acts to avoid suffering has precisely that interest. Singer drew largely on Jeremy Bentham's book *An Introduction to the Principles of Morals and Legislation*, in which the philosopher rejects the widely held view in Western thought that humans can treat animals as things without any moral obligation toward them, because animals are not rational beings and do not have the ability to communicate through language.

The last two decades have been prolific in research on the moral and juridical status of animals (Singer 2010; Regan 2004; Francione 2013), and the current tendency is to consider speciesism as an obsolete paradigm in which ethical and epistemological errors abound. Taking into consideration this reality vis-à-vis the positions of medieval Jewish legislators, there is no room for doubt: they were centuries ahead of others in terms of conceiving sentience as a parameter for reducing cruelty toward nonhuman animals, emphasizing the similarity between the suffering of human beings and that of nonhuman animals.

* * *

During my last stay in Israel, I was astonished by the number of technological devices used by Orthodox Jews to avoid transgressing the Halakhah. One example was when I interviewed an Orthodox rabbi and, upon entering his office, noticed a small device that had been placed in an upper corner of a door. It was meant to avoid the *ichud* (meaning "union" in Hebrew) and in practice serves as a strategy to reinforce (and at the same time, soften) the ban against a man and a woman being together in a closed room. The artifact was designed to allow the door to be opened without having to use the handle, which, from the perspective of the new legislators, is equivalent to an open door.[12]

Orthodox Jews use this artifice, known as *shinui* (literally, "change" or "modification") to reach a goal, despite a particular ban in relation to it. There are many examples of the use of a strategy of this sort, particularly to carry out activities that are forbidden during Shabbat. The ban on driving can be circumvented if someone has fallen ill and their life is at risk.[13] However, right-handed drivers must turn on the motor with their left hand, and vice versa for the left-handed.[14]

The reassertion of a system of religious precepts through the use of subterfuges that transgress them was the object of Monique Augras's (2011) reflections on the *quizilas* in Candomblé *terreiros* in Grande Rio. Quizila, according to Augras, is the delicate lattice of precepts and prohibitions linked to the idiosyncrasies of the "owner of the head" of each initiate. Public violation of the precepts, including by the Pais de Santo,[15] is a constant in the *terreiros*. On dietary laws, the following example illustrates how subterfuges work in other religious groups—in this case, in Afro-Brazilian religions:

> Calling pumpkin "red yam," or a forbidden type of crab by the name of another becomes a way of getting around situations. But the ban remains. The infraction, while jokingly emptied of transgressive meaning, paradoxically seems to highlight the intangibility of the law. (Augras 2011, 158)

Equipped with a solid theoretical framework—while noting the scant research that has been done on the dynamics of transgression in religious groups—Augras concludes that the way limits are established through their transgression produces a paradoxical type of knowledge that cannot be restricted to the correction of that which has been violated. Another issue that she analyzes and illustrates with numerous examples throughout the article is the impossibility of studying prohibition and transgression separately, as they form a dialectically articulated unit (Augras 2011, 159).

Although Augras's analyses (2011) constitute a useful counterpoint for reflections on social control and subterfuge in Orthodox Judaism, there are significant differences between it and Candomblé. First, in Candomblé the quizilas are commonly violated and there is even an incentive to do so. Second, the diversity of *quizilas* varies considerably from one *terreiro* to another and have no written explanation, meaning that the initiate must learn them through trial and error. Third, the quizilas differ and depend on who the *orixá do filho de santo*[16] is; they are not stable but change according to the status of the initiate (Augras 2011, 178). Fourth, only the initiated must submit to the regime of prohibitions, which do not apply to the entire community.

In the case of Orthodox Judaism, the violation of commandments is not encouraged. In spite of the variation in the details of enactment among different Orthodox currents, rituals possess written codes that, in a very similar manner—such as the Shulchan Aruch and the Mishna Berura—are followed by all Jews who are defined as Orthodox. Nonetheless, and as mentioned earlier, subterfuges are a part of the legal system, most probably because, as Cohen put it, a modicum of transgression, minimized rather than repressed, may function as a "safety valve" against discontent and providing some relief from the tensions of the legitimate order (1968, 24).

The sacred, once again

In Chapter 3, I introduced the theoretical approaches that analyze the biblical laws about clean and unclean animals, putting emphasis on Leviticus. Clean animals must have two basic traits: they must "chew their cud" and have split hooves. According to Mary Douglas (1966; 1993/4) animals that have only one of the two characteristics are "out of place": their ambiguity makes them more dangerous than animals that are completely outside prohibited the classification boundaries.

Rabbi Nathan Cardozo (2019, 11) comes to a similar conclusion regarding ambiguous animals, reminding us of the Torah's admonition that animals that possess only one of the required traits are not purer than those that possess neither; rather, animals with a single "kosher" trait are even more impure. He explains this in the following manner:

Because animals with only one kosher sign represent a negative character trait—namely, hypocrisy. The camel, the rock badger, the hare and the swine all give the appearance of being kosher. The first three can demonstrate their "kashrut" by emphasizing that they do, after all, chew their cud. The swine, too, can show its cloven hooves in order to "prove" its virtue. They all, therefore, have the ability to hide their true natures behind a façade of purity. Only upon close inspection do we realize that these animals are unclean.

Cardozo (2019, 11) affirms the Torah's warning that animals having only one of the required traits are not purer than those that have both traits, as one might speculate. On the contrary, animals with a single "kosher" trait are actually more unclean; possessing only one kosher sign evinces a negative character trait—namely, hypocrisy:

The camel, because it chews the cud but does not part the hoof, it is unclean to you. And the rock badger, because it chews the cud but does not part the hoof, it is unclean to you. And the hare, because it chews the cud but does not part the hoof, it is unclean to you. And the swine, because it parts the hoof and is cloven-footed, but does not chew the cud, it is unclean to you. (2019, 150n26)

The biblical classification of animals into ritually clean and unclean is relatively simple, and some approaches emphasize that an overwhelming majority of animals apt for consumption are herbivores. This reinforces the thesis that there is an embryonic seed of the vegetarian ideal in the Jewish tradition, extrapolating from the antediluvian era.

Although Orthodox Jews claim to follow biblical precepts strictly and in accordance with the way the Great Rabbis have interpreted them over the course of the centuries, there are substantive differences between the kashrut that emerges from the biblical text and that which is practiced today. This is an obvious observation; it is worth analyzing whether, as a correlate of the countless changes that the Jewish diet has undergone over time, notions of clean, sacred, and unclean have remained identical or if there have been significant changes in the conception of which foods are clean and which are not.

Spector (2012) raises an interesting but not unproblematic issue regarding the way particular present-day behaviors implemented in relation to permitted animals disobey biblical classifications that distinguish between clean and unclean animals. This has to do with problems found on modern farms. An example is the fact that calves are separated from their mothers after birth and immediately placed in small pens that prevent them from moving. Not only are they extremely weak but may also be fed with industrialized feeds as they begin to grow. This situation also obliges farmers to bottle- feed calves until they are taken to slaughter, approximately in their third month of life. Thus, the modus operandi of modern farms directly violates one of the laws of the tzaar baalei chaim, according to which it is forbidden to separate the calf from the mother within the first seven days after birth. Furthermore—a point that is extremely relevant for our discussion— as a consequence of this practice, the veal calves that are usually part of the festive dinners in observant Jewish homes cannot be considered kosher: despite their cloven hooves, they have been deprived of the opportunity to chew their cud. In other words, anatomically they are ruminant animals, but in practice have never done so.

Although Spector's (2012) insights regarding ruminant animals are controversial, it is evident that there is a significant difference between the Bible and the Talmud, on the one hand, and the laws of kashrut, on the other. The Bible and Talmud place emphasis on the treatment of animals during life and death; kashrut laws focus only on the treatment of the animal at the time of its slaughter and the way in which the meat is handled in the aftermath. As a result of this division of topics in Jewish legislation, philosophical reflections and ethical principles give way in the face of pressure or the need to eat meat, and pragmatism prevails over essential principle.

This finding can be taken as a strong clue to understanding why Orthodox leadership tolerates violation of tzaar baalei chaim. To it we add another variable that is extremely relevant from the point of view of kashrut experts and rabbis. As a Brazilian shochet explained to me,

> In the end, what happens on the farms is not the responsibility of either the ritual butchers or the rabbis: our work, the work of the Jews, begins at the slaughterhouse, in the preparations for the slaughter of animals. Strictly and legally speaking, this is where our responsibility toward animals begins.

In the words of the shochet, the justification of the Orthodox establishment regarding the violations of the tzaar baalei chaim is expressed: they are actions of others, not the actions of Jews. If we consider the Israeli case, this "we" refers to butchers, the rabbinate, and the Orthodox certifying agencies that begin their work once animals have been received from farms owned by "them": secular Jews.

* * *

The structure and logic of Judaism, understood as a normative religious system based on practice, tends to escape anthropological analyses of ritual that, as we discussed in Chapter 4, are usually analyzed as extraordinary moments that break with group routines, whether to strengthen group cohesion, communicate certain messages, or provoke a catharsis. The hyperritualization of daily life in a normative way for the whole group—and not just for a caste, an elite, or a specific age group—is uncommon. This has resulted in the scarcity of research attempting to understand the phenomena I examine here. However, Asad's (1987; 1988) approach has proved crucial to our understanding of some aspects of the ritual density that characterizes Orthodox Judaism and the daily life of Jewish Orthodox communities. The objective of the monastic discipline imposed by medieval Benedictine orders—put into practice through a program of multiple and rigorous religious rituals, as well as practices considered mundane—comes close to the Jewish desideratum: to create subjects whose greatest aspiration is obedience, considered a skill and a potentiality, and the greatest of virtues.

In Judaism, the hyperritualization of everyday life has a clear objective: to sacralize the Jewish people. Understanding the meaning of the holiness (or sacredness) required of the people of Israel is a task still at hand. We have seen several sources claim that the Jewish home, the Jewish table, and the Jewish body take the place of the Temple altar in Jerusalem, awarding the laws of kashrut a pivotal role in achieving holiness.

Over all these years of research on orthodoxy, being with Orthodox Jews as they shared with me their modus vivendi, I asked myself on more than one occasion what is—*if* there is—profane time in the life of observant Jews, a time free from divine demands, free from mitzvot? I remember asking this question to a Chabad rabbi, upon which I was told that there is no time in the life of an observant Jew when God is not present: Jews consecrate themselves by respecting Shabbat in the same way they do when they zealously wash a cauliflower with water in order to check for the presence of insects, when they fast on Yom Kippur, or when they repeat blessings for each food they eat. In fact, the Bible tells us that the Jewish people are a people of priests: "And ye shall be to Me a kingdom of priests and a holy people" (Exodus 19:6).

The holiness of the people of Israel is based on the notion of serving God by following his path, expressing what may be considered the quintessence of the theocentric view that characterizes Judaism. Furthermore, as Chwarts (2012, 144) states,

> The people are sanctified to the extent that they serve their God, as a priest does, observing precepts and rules, aligning himself to divinity through ritual. The pragmatic character of this idea is clear.

In another passage, Chwarts (2010, 147) goes even further, arguing that in the Hebrew Bible, respecting precepts nullifies the sphere of the profane—which would be the dichotomous opposite of sacred—and the people of Israel are allowed only a sanctified life, leaving no other possibilities. What sanctifies the people of Israel is their contact with God and the covenant instituted on Mount Sinai, in which the election of Israel consecrated them as a chosen people, a people of priests.

But if in Judaism, the sacred and profane are not an antinomy, as the one that Durkheim (1996) and Eliade (1999) established, some spheres and moments are more sacred than others, as well as different levels of purity and of impurity.[17] Spaces, moments, utensils, and foods that do not conform to the rules of purity then distance Israel from holiness.

Some key terms can help us understand the unique dynamics of what is pure and what is impure in Rabbinic Judaism, and what the meanings and goals of purity are. It is important to remember, however, that the Hebrew Bible does not constitute a coherent whole and that the interpretations of exegetes over the course of the centuries have modified certain concepts, adapting them to the reality of their time.

In *The Elementary Forms of Religious Life*, Durkheim points out that the distinction between sacred and profane is harsher than the distinction between good and evil, as the latter two belong to the same sphere, that of morality (1996, 22). The sacred and the profane are, in his view, of a profoundly different nature and separated within the human mind as two opposing categories. Thus, the sacred and the profane have always and everywhere been conceived by the human mind as separate genera, as two worlds between which nothing exists in common. The energies manifested in one are not simply those found in the other, with a few degrees more; rather, they are of a different nature (Durkheim 1996, 22).

According to Durkheim, the forms of contrast between the sacred and the profane are varied, that is, they can be embodied in different elements of the physical universe. Yet the contrast itself is universal (Durkheim 1996, 22). In turn, the sacred and the profane are contradictory opposites that cannot be conceived of separately. Neither can they come close to one another without losing their singular nature. For Durkheim, sacred things are those that the prohibitions isolate and protect; profane are the things to which such interdictions are applied. The passage from the sacred to the profane exists but is not automatic: there are rituals for this passage that, in the words of the French sociologist, imply a "veritable metamorphosis" (Durkheim 1996, 22). At the end of this work, Durkheim (1996, 450) argues for the centrality of these polar opposites in religious life, and states that all religious life gravitates around two contrary poles, between which reigns the same opposition between the pure and the impure, the saintly and the sacrilegious, the divine and the diabolic.

Although Durkheim did not define sacred and profane in any other way than through their interrelation, it appears that the profane is that which is ritually dirty, which corrupts, which desacralizes. This is where the idea of contagion emerges, a matter of fundamental importance for understanding the issues highlighted at different moments of this research. It can be summarized in the following question: if dietary laws aim at sacralizing the people of Israel, what is the meaning and purpose of Israel as a holy people?

Durkheim saw contagion as the result of contact between radically different kinds of things—things that followers of a religion classify as sacred versus things profane. Surprisingly, for the French sociologist, it is not only the profane that tarnishes the sacred; the sacred also has a great ability to contaminate the profane.

As mentioned earlier, Judaism does not fit into Durkheimian theory, as there is a whole spectrum within which different concepts interact, signaling different types of holiness and purity, of the profane and the impure. Thus, "kadosh" becomes a synonym of the holy, the sacred, and is an adjective used for God and the people of Israel. As we saw in Chapter 2, kadosh also means to separate, and in this context we infer that just as God separates himself from his creation, the people of Israel must separate themselves from other nations.[18] *Tahor* (pure) is the antonym of *tameh* (impure), yet the word "tahor" is never used in reference to God. Insects and pork are "tameh." According to the Even Shoshan dictionary,[19] a person with leprosy, a menstruating woman, and an animal that cannot be eaten belong to the category of tameh. It can be said that tameh is the impure, defined as that thing or element in which the sacred does not penetrate.

Another concept that is directly related to dietary laws is treif, a term that applies to a food that is not inherently impure, as is pork. Rather, a slaughtered animal whose meat has been handled without following kashrut rules, becomes impure. Thus, for example, beef is allowed, it is not intrinsically impure, but becomes treif if the Halakhah has been violated in the animal's slaughter or in its aftermath. Even Shoshan (2000) includes utensils that have mixed milk and meat as tameh.

There is also the intentional fabrication of the impure. Chametz (yeast) is an emblematic example. In this case, we are dealing with an ingredient that is consumed throughout the year, except for the eight days of Pesach, a period in which it becomes impure, an impure whose ability to contaminate seems extremely powerful, if we remember the rigid rules to eliminate even the last morsel of chametz from the homes of Orthodox Jews during Passover. Thus, chametz is not related to the concept of *tumah* (ritual impurity). We could say that there are specific laws that "create" chametz on Passover. It is an interdiction that has to do with the nature of time, the calendar, and Passover rules, rather than with the nature of a food or substance. In other words, wheat can be eaten unproblematically in other periods (excepting Passover) and thus chametz can be understood as an ontologically distinct category, unlike other forbidden foods, and thus revealing the complexity of the system.

Another seminal matter within Judaism is the fact that impurity corresponds to a condition and there is always a route—a ritual—that allows for the purification of the impure, relocating it within the system. If someone has transgressed unwittingly, such as eating a forbidden food, they may recite a prayer; entering a state of impurity is not a necessary consequence of a voluntary or unconscious action. Thus, a woman who is menstruating or has just given birth, considered persons with some level of tumah,[20] may undertake a purification ritual and with this be able to return to marital life.[21]

The only impurity, the most impure of impurities, is death, known as *avi avot ha'tumah* (the principle of all impurities, the *prime* impurity). The reason that death contains the highest level of impurity might be because after death, Jews cannot fulfill the mission for which they were created: serving God. Lastly, *toavah* (abomination, aberration, excrescence) expresses the idea of repulsion, indicating that we are facing something that taints and contaminates at significant levels. Nonetheless, toavah is a concept that is only applicable within the sphere of morality.

At this point, I believe it is important to signal that ritual and morality come together within the Jewish worldview, despite its orthopraxical nature that many believe led Rabbinical Judaism, instead of focusing its attention on morality, to privilege or—even drowned itself in—ritual. Nonetheless, as Maccoby (1999, viii) states,

> The proliferation of ritual rules in Judaism, especially in the area of ritual purity, tends to obscure the fact that ritual in Judaism is ultimately subordinate to morality, or, more accurately, exists as the self-identifying code of a dedicated group whose main purpose is ethical.

Like Douglas (1993/4), Maccoby (1999) attempts to come up with an explanation for the fact that Leviticus 19 is devoted to basic moral principles,[22] as it is in Leviticus that the laws of purity—and among them, the laws of kashrut—are introduced and described in detail. Maccoby has no doubt that in Leviticus and its rabbinical interpretation a relationship is drawn between ritual and morality. In his view, although purity rituals are concerned with holiness, at a next level they are related to morality, since holiness exists for the sake of morality. According to Maccoby (1999, 205), the rituals found in

Leviticus mark the people of Israel as a holy people, who distinction implies superior moral status. And although the author probes the kashrut laws no further, he suggests that they are an insignia that distinguish the people of Israel as a people with a moral mission.

In his book *Jewish Eating and Identity through the Ages*, Kramer (2009) presents other functions and meanings for the kashrut laws, based on the scholarly works of Milgrom (1991), Eilberg-Schwartz (1990), and Douglas (1966), among others. Milgrom (1991), in his attempt to explain the separation of animals into categories of clean and unclean, asserts that the purpose was to limit the Israelites' access to an excessive number of animals, reducing meat consumption and its respective ingestion of blood. Both restrictions would thus have taught the people of Israel a reverence for life. As we have seen in Chapter 2, for Milgrom (1993), the God of Israel is a God who worships life, the God of life. However, for Kramer (2009, 18), this explanation fails, since meat consumption was very low in Ancient Israel.[23] For the same reason, Kramer (2009, 18) concludes that the Levitical code (which is continued in Deuteronomy) expresses the perspective of the priests, the only ones who consumed meat regularly. Yet Kramer (2009) and Eilberg-Schwartz (1990) also defend the idea that the interpretations of Mary Douglas (1993/4) and Jacob Milgrom (1993) would make no sense and would sound bizarre to the people of Israel. Once again, the argument is made that in ancient Israel, the meaning of the law was only understood by the priests.

Having ruled out the possibility that the Levitical codes of law served as teachings for the people of Israel, Eilberg-Schwartz (1990, 125) concludes that clean and unclean animals should be seen as metaphors. Thus, ruminant animals with cloven hooves, such as sheep and deer, would be used as a metaphor for Israel, in contrast to predators, such as vultures and eagles, which symbolized other peoples. Kramer (2009, 20), however, believes that the Eilberg-Schwartz scheme should be modified and that clean and unclean animals do not necessarily serve as metaphors for Israel and the peoples, respectively, but as metaphors for positive and negative personality traits. The author recalls that the books of the prophets include many examples of animals that embody either positive or negative characteristics.

Drawing to the end of his account of theoretical approaches that attempt to produce an understanding of Jewish dietary laws, Kramer comes to two conclusions that are (pardon the pun) unorthodox. First, given the fact that, excepting the priests, the people of Israel ate meat only rarely, dietary laws did not have the function of separating Israelites from other peoples. Most of the people of Israel probably fraternized with neighbors, sharing seeds, bread, fruits, and vegetables. The second conclusion points to the importance of kashrut laws for the cohesion of the people of Israel and for the crystallization of their identity:

> It is noteworthy that the only times Israel would commonly have consumed meat were festive days—holidays, more modestly on sabbaths and, less frequently, clan or family celebrations. On these occasions, Israel was celebrating her identity in multiple and various ways. What has not before been noticed is that one of the ways she was celebrating that identity was in what she ate. In fact, in light or what we said above, she was not only celebrating, but also eating, her national identity. (Kramer 2009, 22)

To exclude separation from other peoples from the functions of dietary laws seems a bit risky. Although in antiquity the Israelites may have fraternized with foreigners and with members of other peoples, sharing meatless foods, the truth is that as history progresses and the Israelites live in exile, rabbinical codes come into play. Jews increasingly separate themselves from those who are seen as a threat to their cultural identity, and this separation was strengthened by the laws of kashrut that made it impossible to share a meal with a Gentile. Furthermore, if—as I assume—for centuries one of the functions of dietary laws was to separate Jews, the chosen people, from non-Jews, modernity brought about a significant transformation in this premise. From this moment on, food makes it difficult for observant Jews to share the table with their liberal and secular counterparts. In other words, this function of separating groups, which I consider fundamental to dietary laws, from modernity onward, also separates different types of Jews. As I have shown in previous research,[24] the phenomena of chazara bi´teshuvah[25] made it difficult even for members of the same family to share meals. At the same time, even within orthodoxy different phenomena come together so that members of a particular current not consider the foods eaten by the followers of another rabbi as "kosher enough" for their own purposes, since each current buys food from different certifying agencies. Even in a small diasporic community such as the Brazilian one, there is a separation between the rabbis that certify meat and meat products through the *Leven* agency and those that resort to Mehadrin. Neither one of them considers its competitor's meat as kosher. As has already been mentioned, in the last chapter of his book, Kramer (2009) himself hypothesizes that, in times of uncertainty and doubt about who is a Jew, the obsessive search for insects serves a metaphor for a thorough investigation into who is really a "true" Jew, separating those who claim to be but, in the sharp, alert, and demanding gaze of the Orthodoxy, fall short.

And finally...

Two questions guided this research. The first emerged from my desire to find an explanation for a phenomenon that, although apparently contradictory, is also common in Orthodox communities: the leniency of religious leaders in the supervision of meat eaten by members of their own congregation, in contrast to the detail and stringency they apply to the search for the insects that may be hidden in other foods. Although over this long journey I have suggested that it may be a paradox for which there is no explanation, I believe that the different attempts to answer this question that have been made allow us to abandon this conclusion. The second question was to figure out whether we can speak of an obsessive component within contemporary Jewish orthodoxy.

Kashrut is a complex system, part of a gigantic textual and cultural compendium, if I may say so, that includes the Hebrew Bible, the Talmud, medieval codes, and the codifications and manuals of our own times. Within this compendium we find the norms that govern, or are supposed to govern, the conduct of Orthodox Jews. According to the characteristics of this research that, as I explained in the Introduction, is not an ethnography *stricto sensu*, I am unable to answer the question about the extent to which Orthodox Jews follow precepts and rules to avoid insects with extreme stringency, or how carefully—or obsessively—Orthodox women devote themselves to deep cleaning so that their families can enjoy their Passover without even the smallest particle of chametz in their abode. Nonetheless, contemporary Halachot books, analyzed here in Chapter 3, as well as material on the same subjects available on the internet or through the pashkevilim that are common in Orthodox Israeli cities, show that the chumrah of Orthodox Jewish communities is a fact. They also suggest that a large number of Orthodox Jews follow or attempt to stringently adhere to the new Halachot on insect checking. We must not forget that the chumratization of life is an uncontested phenomenon within Orthodox communities and has been researched by a considerable number of scholars.

Another already mentioned fact that corroborates this conclusion is the establishment in the 1980s of an Israeli farm that produces fruits and vegetables in special greenhouses, using a greater amount of pesticides to avoid any possibility of insect infestation. Gush Katif's products are distributed in Israeli markets, in outlets whose main audience is Orthodox.

With regard to Passover, we should not neglect the recognition and concern that emerge within the ranks of the orthodoxy, for all the emotional turmoil that preparations for festivities generate in a nonnegligible number of Orthodox women.

In parallel, there is a consensus among those who research Orthodox communities that chumrah is the mark of contemporary orthodoxy (Aran 2013a; 2013b; Brown 2011; Dan 1997; Soloveitchik 1994; Silber 1992; Friedman 1991; Liebman 1983), in addition to the fact that segments of modern Orthodoxy have let themselves be captivated by this tendency. No less illuminating of chumrah tendencies is the academic research on the incidence of OCD within Orthodox Jewish communities (Greenberg and Shefler 2008; Huppert, Siev, and Kushner 2007; Pirutinsky, Rosmarin, and Pargament 2007; Zohar et al. 2005; Greenberg and Witztum 2001; Burt and Rudolph 2000; Greenberg 1984). To them we add the warnings of certain Orthodox psychiatrists, such as Rabbi Abraham Twerski and Rabbi Avigdor Bonchek, that excessive zeal in complying with certain precepts, as well as damaging from a psychiatric point of view, also threatens to disrupt the spirit of Halakhah, violating other commandments through the rigorous devotion to just one of them.

The fixation, if I may say so, with following the strictest path in the consummation of a mitzvah has led some scholars of Orthodox Judaism to envision a new form of orthodoxy whose traditionalism collides with tradition. In fact, tradition is pushed aside or obliterated in favor of a vision of Judaism that celebrates extremes, something that was unknown or very rare in the past. And while Rabbi Oren Duvdevani, whom I interviewed in Israel, was annoyed by what is known as *laag la'dorot* (contempt for those who precede us), it seems to be a hallmark of contemporary orthodoxy. Stolow's words (2006, 9) illustrate this phenomenon:

The tendency among recent haredim has been to criticize community standards as "too lenient"—even at the risk of broaching the traditionally guarded respect for elders, or the proscription against la'az al ha-'avot [slander of the progenitors]—in order to establish themselves as a more authentic, faithful, pious, and competent religious vanguard and to clarify the inadequate or compromised character of customs and practices known to Jewish communities throughout the world, including many which claim to adhere strictly to "tradition."

The delegitimating of religious tradition in favor of a purism that is, in the best hypothesis, an invention, and in the worst, an imposition of new forms of interpretation of Rabbinical Judaism, constitutes one of the traits of religious fundamentalisms. Nonetheless, there is still one remaining doubt: do the generations of post-Shoah observant Jews who, according to their leaders, reconstruct an orthodoxy they have inherited from premodern times aspire to being "equal to" or "better than" the generations that came before them?

The traditional rabbinical conception has always respected the principle of *ieridat ha´dorot* (decline of the generations), according to which the generations that were witness to the revelation on Mount Sinai are, from an intellectual and spiritual point of view, superior to those that followed. The chumratization of orthodoxy, however, violates this principle and establishes the following paradox: although the level of orthodoxy in modern times is relatively inferior to what it was in the past, the last two generations have created pretensions of greater religiosity (Aran 2013a, 184).

In these last pages, I would like to record some of the questions I have asked myself over the years spent researching kashrut, the most important result of which is this book. If the meat consumed today by Orthodox Jews from Israel and from large Jewish communities such as the North American is treif, as many Orthodox rabbis—among them, Assa Keisar and Amnon Ytzchak—claim, can we thus infer that the diet of the vast majority of observant Jews is not really kosher? If this is the case, should we conclude that observant Jews who eat meat do not meet the principles of purity required of the people of Israel if they are to be considered holy, that is, a people of priests whose mission is to serve God through the commandments? Such a conclusion, if correct, would imply that we are facing the abandonment of Jewish ideology created millennia ago and crystallized over centuries. In short, by eating treif meat, Orthodox Jews would be committing a serious transgression that distances them from their original mission: to be holy as God is holy. Just as interesting and just as new would be the fact that the diaspora, the exile, is more kosher than Israel. I raise this hypothesis by recalling that several Israeli rabbis and ritual butchers told me that they do not eat meat in Israel, but do so when they visit small diaspora communities, where the low demand allows kashrut experts to carry out their work in accordance with all the halachic rules on the slaughter of animals and the principle of the tzaar baalei chaim.

Another consequence of the analysis is the existence of two large groups of Orthodox Jews, one purer—and holier—than the other due to dietetic choices. According to Jewish tradition, forbidden foods taint the heart and spirit; divine holiness thus departs and distances itself from human beings. Furthermore, when people eat nonkosher foods, they weaken their ability to connect with the sublime. Their ability to delve into the depths of the Torah and to feel what is spiritual diminishes. "It is far more difficult for his soul to soar heavenward on the wings of Torah study and prayer" (Forst 2013, xxxi).

On the other hand, it is interesting to note that, although it is a fundamental pillar of rabbinical Judaism, kashrut does not have its own treatise within the Talmud, but permeates other treatises to a greater or lesser extent. I infer from this fact that kashrut is of redoubled, rather than secondary importance.

Finally, the question remains: does the hyperritualization and hypercategorization that characterize contemporary Orthodox Judaism signal the exhaustion of a religious system or express its yearning to separate even more from those who are not Jews in order to get closer to God? I do not yet have an answer to this question, but do not doubt that, unlike premodern orthodoxy, contemporary orthodoxy—instead of privileging a core principle in the Jewish worldview, the union of Israel (*achdut Israel*)—places emphasis on controlling its members. Multiple consequences emerge from this position. Kashrut, as we have seen, is one of the major sites where such control is exercised, contributing forcefully with the re-demarcation of boundaries and the creation of new divisions among Orthodox Jewry.

Notes

Introduction

1. Topel 2005; 2011.
2. *Halakhah*, in Hebrew: "path": A compendium of laws and precepts that observant Jews respect and comply with in their daily lives. The corpus of Halakhah was compiled in the High Middle Ages; however, as a result of the emergence of new social arrangements, on the one hand, and technological advances on the other, new rules are constantly being added to the 613 commandments that it comprises, known as *Halakhot*.
3. Fence around the Torah: A way of legislating that opts for strict compliance of the commandments. In Deuteronomy 22:8 it is claimed that when someone builds a house, a fence should be built around the roof, in order to avoid blame if someone falls from it. This verse was interpreted by Jewish legislators as a demand to "build a house around the Torah," replete with new norms to protect the mitzvot.
4. Chumratization, a word derived from Hebrew *chumrah*: "strictness," in reference to a strict path in the consummation of precepts. It means the choice to follow precepts in ways that go beyond basic Halakhah requirements. Those who impose chumrah on themselves are referred to as *machmirim*.
5. *Shulchan Aruch*, from Hebrew: "a set table." It is the name for the Code of Jewish Law compiled by the sixteenth-century rabbi Iosef of Karo. The laws and verdicts found in this text are unanimously accepted by all currents of Orthodox Judaism. Unlike the Talmud, the Shulchan Aruch is a monosemic work.
6. *Shabbat*, from Hebrew: "Sabbath" (Saturday), holy day, day of rest. During Shabbat, observant Jews must respect a long list of interdictions in addition to complying with a series of precepts.
7. This fact was widely verified in my research on the *chozrim bi´teshuvah*, in which the women told me that they call their rabbis in case of any doubts regarding the laws of family purity.
8. In Chapter 3, I examine this NGO, stressing its role in the kashrut market in Israel. Hashgacha Pratit is an Orthodox social activism NGO formed in 2012. Its aim is to challenge the Central Rabbinate of Israel's monopoly on food certification and supervision. The NGO provides alternative kashrut supervision services. The expression "Hashgacha Pratit" contains a pun as it means "divine providence" but can also be translated as "private supervision."
9. Throughout this book, I use the term "legislator" to refer to the Grand Rabbis who are responsible for analyzing all matters of daily life, codifying them, and defining the rules and laws that identify eating behavior as complying with the Halakha or not.

As we will see later, there are Great Legislators who are specialized in subtle nuances, such as insect checking. These legislators (who may also be referred to as *coders*) put together complex manuals that in practice must be followed as a legal code that serves as reference for the community.

10. Eda Charedit: one of the ways of referring to ultra-Orthodox Jews in Israel, and responsible for the name that is given to their certifying agency.

11. *Charedi*, plural *charedim*, from Hebrew: "fearful" in reference to "God-fearing," as the ultra-Orthodox refer to themselves.

Chapter 1

1. Bund: Jewish workers' party active in Russia between 1897 and 1920. The Bund had important ramifications in Poland and in the United States.

2. Haskalah: A movement originating in central Europe at the end of the eighteenth century whose basic premise was the modernization of Judaism, from ideological and institutional points of view. The Haskalah wrought a revolution within Rabbinical Judaism by modernizing religion and education, creating the possibility for new forms of Jewish identity, such as the Reform movement, Zionism, and secular Judaism.

3. *Maskilim*, plural of *maskil*, from Hebrew: creators and followers of Haskalah.

4. Torah, from Hebrew: Pentateuch, or the Hebrew Bible.

5. Translated here from Portuguese.

6. Gentile (in Hebrew, *goy* or *goi*): A term used among Jews to refer to non-Jewish individuals or peoples.

7. Chatam Sofer (1762–1839) was one of the major rabbis of Orthodox Judaism during the first half of the nineteenth century. A fierce opponent of the Reform movement, he established a yeshiva in Pozsony that became famous because it was there that the future leaders of Hungary's Jewish Orthodox did their studies.

8. *Yeshivot*, plural of *yeshiva*, from Hebrew: school of rabbinical studies.

9. *Kolelim*, plural of *kolel*: school of rabbinical studies for men as of age thirteen, and in particular, for married men.

10. The Nazis, in addition to annihilating two-thirds of European Jewry, destroyed communities of observant Jews, each with its own singular characteristics and customs and under the leadership of rabbis who were recognized for their scholarly knowledge.

11. An important principle in Judaism is known as *achdut Israel* (the uniting of the Jewish people) that has reigned throughout obscure times and over centuries.

12. From Hebrew, which literally means "knowledge of the Torah," in reference to the learned knowledge of the Great Rabbis. This expression is used by Orthodox Jews to refer to the scholarly knowledge of the Great Rabbis, which is considered basically "infallible." The Daat Torah is an innovation within Orthodox Judaism. Thus, when a Halakhic opinion requires legal justification from recognized sources, the simple

Daat Torah is considered to be more subtle and requiring no legal justification nor explicit reference to earlier sources. In other words, to evoke Daat Torah as a justification is to defend one's own understanding of it.

13. This is the meaning given to the assertion that Halakha is democratic—rich and poor, ignorant and scholarly, young and old are all bound to fulfilling its precepts.

14. Matzah: unleavened bread. One of the mitzvot of Passover is to eat a piece of matzoh on each of the eight days of festivities.

15. The role and importance of this publisher in standardizing and radicalizing orthodoxy is analyzed here in Chapters 5 and 6.

Chapter 2

1. This book uses various transliterated spellings of kashrut/cashrut. I have done this in order to preserve the forms used in the works and websites that were my sources.

2. *Shomer mitzvot*, from Hebrew, which can be translated literally as "one who respects the commandments"—in reference to orthodox Jews.

3. That which characterizes mitzvot defined as *chukim* (laws) is that their logical basis remains hidden from man. This contrasts with *mishpatim* (judgments), whose meaning and raison d'être can be deciphered by human beings, who are also able to appreciate their positive impacts on society and in the individual.

4. Chabad or Chabad-Lubavitch: name of the Orthodox Hasidic current founded in the eighteenth century that had a preponderant role in bringing secular and liberal Jews closer to orthodoxy. In more recent years, it was led by the charismatic figure of the Rebbe of Lubavitch, Menachem Mendel Schneerson.

5. A moment of biblical epiphany in which God sealed a covenant with the people of Israel.

6. Well-known verse in the Torah (Exodus 24:7) that expresses the people of Israel's obedience to their God. The rabbinical interpretation conceives of it as a warning that we can only understand Judaism upon complying with its precepts.

7. Brazilian publisher of Judaic books, many of which are devoted to Orthodox Jews.

8. I alternate, according to the situation, on the spelling of kasher/kosher (the latter is a Yiddish expression for the same term, frequently employed in English-language texts), in order to remain faithful to the spelling that is used in brand names and quality seals, as well as in bibliographical references and websites that I have consulted.

9. See Beit Chabad do Brasil, "A 'dieta' judaica na teoria e na prática, O que é cashrut?," accessed February 11, 2020, http://www.chabad.org.br/mitsvot/cashrut/princi pal_cashrut/index1.html.

10. From Hebrew, plural of midrash: an allegoric interpretation of Bible verses found in the Talmud.

11. Translated here from the Hebrew.

12. Freely translated from the Hebrew.

13. *Chozrot bi'teshuvah*: women who chose orthodoxy as adults—a movement of "return" to Jewish roots, in reference to secular and liberal Jews who chose orthodoxy in the adult stage of life.

14. *Kavana*, from Hebrew: "intention," in reference to the feeling and reflectiveness that are supposed to be present in prayer.

15. Freely translated from Hebrew.

16. Gush Katif: Israeli company that markets supposedly insect-free vegetables for Orthodox consumers. However, there is some controversy surrounding the company's production process. While its website claims that its results are the consequence of the entire production process being carried out in specially designed greenhouses, many important rabbis and agronomists claim that their success in eliminating insects, worms, and larvae is due to the use of a greater amount of pesticides.

17. From the term "kosher," to indicate making kitchen utensils and furniture ideal for use by Orthodox Jews.

18. Capsules usually include animal ingredients, coming most frequently from pigs.

19. Mishnaic Hebrew: Hebrew spoken between the first century BCE and the fifth century CE. The Talmud was written in Mishnaic Hebrew.

20. From Hebrew *leitchazek*: "to acquire spiritual strength." Orthodox Jews use this term in reference to spiritual fortitude—that is, stringent compliance with the mitzvot.

21. For these verses, see https://www.sefaria.org/Leviticus.11?ven=The_Contemporary_Torah,_Jewish_Publication_Society,_2006&vhe=Miqra_according_to_the_Masorah&lang=bi&aliyot=0 (accessed August 3, 2022).

22. In Alter 1979, 47–48.

23. https://www.sefaria.org/Leviticus.17.14?lang=bi&with=all&lang2=en (accessed September 2, 2022).

Chapter 3

1. "Problematic" is a term used in books on kashrut to designate foods whose aptness is hard to determine. We could say that the term has in fact become a kashrut category.

2. *Pashkevil*, plural *pashkevilim*: signs or posters that are pasted or hung out on the streets of Orthodox neighborhoods in Israel, providing warnings, advertisement, news, or messages from rabbis and other Orthodox leaders. The pashkevilim are a cheap and efficient way for rabbis to communicate with their followers.

3. One of the Halakhah precepts prohibits the ingestion of insects. Difficulties surrounding the verification of insects are analyzed further in Chapter 4.

4. According to Fishkoff (2010, 5), in recent years the US market for kosher products has grown twice that of nonkosher foods.

5. Data from the United States and Brazil suggest that most consumers of kosher-seal foods are not observant Jews. Rather, a significant group of consumers are Muslim, and there are also people who believe that kosher products are healthier than other processed foods, as well as consumers who are unaware that they have chosen products with the kosher seal.

6. The *teshuvah* movement refers to secular or liberal Jews who opt for orthodoxy as adults. The movement was born in the United States in the decade of 1970s and

expanded to Israel during that same decade, reaching smaller diasporic communities as of the 1980s, when the movement planted roots in Brazil.

7. The Central Rabbinate of Israel, a state institution, is responsible for kashrut, which in turn endows it with major political and economic power. Nonetheless, there are kosher seals belonging to Orthodox Jewish communities that question the rabbinate's levels of stringency.

8. This phenomenon, after the creation of the State of Israel, rapidly covered the food sector as a whole: from production to commerce. Even today, most establishments that sell food products in the country, from butcher shops to greengrocers, including supermarkets, restaurants, kiosks, and hotels, sell only kosher foods.

9. *Mehadrin* indicates that the product is kosher, that all processes and elements that go into it were analyzed, and that there are no issues regarding purity.

10. Information obtained from ritual butchers.

11. In Israel, hotels and other establishments that work on Shabbat are not considered kosher, yet this has nothing to do with the kashrut quality of the food they offer.

12. *Mashguiach*: kashrut supervisor.

13. Bar mitzvah: ceremony marking the passage from boyhood to adult age.

14. In Brazil, there are three kosher meat seals available, as well as half a dozen certifying agencies that depend upon specific rabbis.

15. Parve: a category of foods that are considered neutral—that is, foods that can be consumed with either meat or milk, since they belong to neither one of those categories.

16. Over the eight days of Passover, Jews must refrain from consuming yeast or other leavening agents in any of its forms, nor may they use utensils that have touched the ingredient throughout the year. To avoid problems, it is recommended that families have special sets of pots, plates, and cutlery for Passover. Those who cannot afford this expense especially kosherize the utensils they will use at the holiday. Throughout this book I use the term "leavening agent" to refer to all types of fermentation.

17. The Orthodox Union is the oldest North American certifying agency, which supervises and certifies close to five hundred thousand products in over ninety countries. The Orthodox Union began to standardize kashrut in the 1920s (Fischer 2015, 1).

18. See Demirhan, Ulca, and Zenyuva (2012).

19. As I was correcting the proofs of this book, the Israeli government, headed by Naftali Bennett (2021–2022), implemented important changes in the modus operandi of the Central Rabbinate regarding kashrut.

20. The Sabbatical Year of the Land demands fulfillment of a long list of commandments, but only in the Land of Israel. Thus, the Jewish people of the diaspora are exempted from them.

21. Translation from Hebrew original.

22. Soldiers from the Israeli Army escorted Eda Charedit kashrut supervisors through regions of Palestinian autonomy to facilitate their passage through checkpoints and because the region is considered a danger zone for Israeli Jews.

23. *Shabbos goy*, from Yiddish: "the Sabbath Gentile," in reference to the Gentiles who help the Jews by doing chores from which they are prohibited over the Sabbath—such as starting a fire, dishwashing, using money if necessary, as well as numerous other

tasks. For a sociohistorical analysis of the polemics surrounding the establishment of the shabbos goy, see Katz (1992).

24. Using the services of a shabbos goy remains within the realm of choice, while not eating agricultural products planted in the Land of Israel during the Sabbath Year is a biblical interdiction.

25. The NGO has grown and diversified in 2021, changed its name, and begun to officiate religious weddings according to Orthodox tradition, but independently of the rabbinate.

26. In fact, no rule in Halakhah prohibits women from officiating as kashrut supervisors.

27. At present, Hashgacha Pratit is dedicated to the consummation of Jewish marriages, an attitude that also defies the rabbinate's obstacles to the marriage of people who, for some reason according to Halakhah, are not fit to marry, such as non-Jews and people whose Judaism is not recognized by the rabbinate, among others. We should keep in mind that in Israel there is no civil marriage.

28. *Shuk*, from Hebrew: "market," refers to the major open-air market in the center of Jerusalem where meats, fruits and vegetables are sold. It is a tourist attraction and right in the hub of the city.

29. Throughout his book, Fishkoff (2010) provides interesting data on the various forms of kashrut fraud, from selling nonkosher meat as if it were kosher to forging kashrut seals. See also Lytton (2013b, 16); Hornstein (2013). However, fraud is often the result of employees' negligence toward certification agencies.

30. Author's translation from Hebrew.

Chapter 4

1. Hasidism: a stream that emerged in eastern Europe in the eighteenth century. Hasidic Jews continue to be an important stream within Orthodox Judaism. They are characterized by their more stringent fulfillment of precepts and greater resistance in adopting the values of modernity.

2. In the Israeli kibbutzim (collective farms), Passover was celebrated emphasizing its calendar-related dimension, that is, the coming of springtime.

3. From Hebrew, in which it literally means "order," in reference to the sequence of rituals and songs that should be performed on the first and second nights of Pesach.

4. Haggadah: Book of liturgy used in Pesach celebrations.

5. Karo (1968, 151–152).

6. The sections are as follows: I: The month of Nisan; II: The search for leaven; III: Passover eve; IV: Seder preparation (program for the nights of Passover); and V: Seder on the night of Passover (1968, 151–161). Translated from Spanish.

7. If unable to rid themselves of all the leavening that is to be found on a particular property, some people and businesses sign a symbolic contract in which they sell all the leaven that is in their possession to a Gentile.

8. Religious Jews often have special Passover crockery, cutlery, pots, and pans. The poorest among them take kitchen utensils used throughout the year to Orthodox

synagogues, where they undergo a special kosherization process, through boiling, to completely remove any vestiges of yeast or leavening.

9. Ganzfried ([1864] 1968, 151–152).

10. Due to the increasing complexity of life and constant changes and innovations, the Great Rabbis have periodically written new encodings. At the end of the nineteenth century, the Chafetz Chaim, Rabbi Israel Meir Kagan of Radin, wrote the Mishnah Berurah, a commentary on the Shulchan Aruch that, among others, brought up contemporary themes while providing a compilation on previous legislators. Like the Shulchan Aruch, it is a universally accepted book.

11. Purim: a Jewish holiday that commemorates how the Persian Jews were saved from Haman's plan to exterminate them, as narrated in the book of Esther. Purim is also known as the "Jewish carnival" because of the joyous nature of the festivities and the use of costumes.

12. *Aish Ha´Torah,* from Hebrew, with the literal meaning "the fire of the Torah." It is an Orthodox Yeshiva whose most important mission is to bring liberal and secular Jews closer to orthodoxy.

13. Scheinberg ([5770] 2009).

14. Reb Nachman of Bratslav (1772–1810), great-grandson of Baal Shem Tov, revived the Hasidic movement combining esoteric secrets of the Kaballah with systematic study of the Torah. Over the course of his lifetime, the rabbi attracted thousands of followers, and his influence over Hasidic movements the world over persists until today.

15. Hillel's maxim "Do not distance yourself from the congregation" resonates in the words of the Rabbi of Bretslav.

16. Lindell (2018).

17. Lindell (2020).

18. The questioning of strict rabbinical rulings is not uncommon on Orthodox Jewish forums. Throughout my research, I saw how active these forums are and how, from the base, there is a questioning of the positions of Orthodox leaders on different issues, from demands that fathers who are at the head of their families be allowed to work to issues related to certain commandments and the most correct way to fulfill/perform them.

19. *Ke'zait,* from the Hebrew, in which it literally means, "like an olive," a measurement used in the Talmud to indicate, for example, the amount of matzoh that should be partaken when the Passover Seder begins. When discussions among legislators increase the amount that is considered to be ke´zait, the mitzvah becomes more difficult to fulfill on the part of people who, for diverse reasons, have issues with matzoh consumption.

20. The complex relations between orthodoxy and technology will be analyzed in Chapter 5.

21. Translated from Hebrew.

22. Translated from Hebrew.

23. In this case, stores whose owners are observant Jews.

24. Items that may contain yeast, such as medications, as well as others that may be considered dubious, are placed in a room within the house in which no member of the family is allowed to enter during the entire eight days of celebration.

25. Halakhah considers the fact that some of the holidays on the Hebrew calendar fall on Shabbat, providing advice as to how to proceed in each case. However, explaining halakhic solutions to these issues falls outside the scope of the present work.

26. See Kapferer (2004); Turner (1974); Gluckman (1954).

27. Rabbi Noah Weinberg was one of the founders of the *Yeshiva Aish Ha'Torah* in Jerusalem, whose mission is to bring secular and liberal Jews closer to orthodoxy.

28. There is a prohibition against men praying in the bathroom, or upon leaving the bathroom, if their bodies are not completely free of feces.

29. This observation is repeated in Greenberg (1984).

30. On the other hand, intentional exposure to situations considered to trigger compulsive behaviors among patients with OCD, known as desensitization—a necessary step in alleviating symptoms that cognitive and cognitive-behavioral therapies use—proves to be difficult to operate in the case of Orthodox people. The reason is that their objective is to encourage patients to develop a tolerance for risk, ambiguity, and uncertainty that allows them to better deal with compulsions. In the case of Orthodox Jews, the fear of undergoing experiences that could trigger religious transgression rules out the possibility of desensitization exercises, thus restricting the opportunities that cognitive therapists would have in helping to cure OCD among Orthodox Jews.

31. Although still studied in the yeshivot to—among other reasons—be consulted in the creation of new rules, the Shulchan Aruch is not what Orthodox families resort to when in doubt about a particular mitzvah or custom. Rather, they consult contemporary manuals or their rabbi.

32. There are laws relating to grains and others relating to legumes. For Pesach, in turn, one must know whether chia and quinoa ferment and if they can be ingested during festivities.

33. Asad (1987, 171) argues that while capital sin is the primary concern, surveillance of everyday sin is also a function of the program.

34. Aran refers to the extensive bibliography on religious fundamentalisms that focus their attention on the relationship between these groups and modern society.

35. Thus we see that for observant Jews, devotion to studies is directly proportional to level of religiosity.

36. Torczyner (2014).

37. Torczyner (2014).

38. Torczyner (2014).

39. Torczyner (2014).

40. Nachmanides, *Laws of Niddah* 9.25, in reference to the barriers that prevent a woman's entire body from being purified by the water of the mikve (ritual bathhouse), such as rings, bracelets, nail polish and a long list of other objects. During bathing, a woman is not supposed to close her hands or mouth, which would allegedly prevent the water from purifying these parts of the body. According to the laws of family purity,

a couple can only resume their sexual life after the woman has purified herself in the mikve, once her menstrual cycle is over.

41. Rabbi Kanievski's writings follow the "response" genre (interpretive response in the form of letters).

42. Siegel-Itzkovich (2009).

43. This issue is analyzed in the following chapter.

Chapter 5

1. Here it is important to take into account the huge number of Orthodox men who study full-time in the *kolelim* (religious studies academies for adult men, usually married). These are spaces in which, as several scholars have stated, the famous Talmudic discussions are no longer taught and practiced, since the focus is placed on Halakhah, that is, on the laws. We can presume that the existence of tens of thousands of men dedicated to the study of Halakhah for decades led to the creation of more and more manuals on laws, rules, and customs.

2. It is, however, a minority, made up of people who have a special interest in the type of foods that they themselves consume, such as vegetarian or vegan individuals or specific rabbis who in recent years have taken up the vegan or vegetarian cause, such as Rabbis Isaac Keisar and Amnon Ytzchak.

3. *Tzaar baaei chaim*: from Hebrew (literally): "the suffering of animals"—in reference to the biblical principle that prohibits causing suffering to animals.

4. In recent years, controversy over the greater or lesser cruelty of slaughter of animals according to Jewish prescriptions has intensified. See Melo Mendoniça and Oliviera Caetano (2017).

5. According to Rabbi Vaya, Leading Halakhic Arbiter of On Insects of Our Generation, "We are all aware of the Torah prohibition on eating pork. We would like to emphasize that this prohibition is equivalent to just one transgression, while the one regarding the ingestion of *tolaim* [insects] is equal to six transgressions, that is, as if we ate six *kezait* [portions] of pork" (Vaya [2011, 23]).

6. One of the names of God, much used among the Orthodox.

7. Topel (2005; 2011).

8. Vaya (2010).

9. I spoke to Rabbi Vaya several more times over the two weeks that I took his course on complex aspects of kashrut for young women.

10. There is every indication that this is a common practice rather than an extraordinary occurrence.

11. Among the numerous videos that are available are the following: Blue Apron (2015), Enlace Judío (2017) , OU Kosher (n.d.), Stak-K Kosher (2014), and Veja São Paulo (2009). Dozens of English-language sites explain the most up-to-date procedures used to wash vegetables, fruits, and problematic produce. There are also sites in other languages.

12. In Brazil, some kosher food businesses and Orthodox families buy their vegetables from the business that supplies McDonald's, as it purportedly sells vegetables without insects.

13. Other examples of recent forms of discrimination against observant Jewish women are related to the laws of family purity (Topel [2005]). In the article "Get Out of Our uteruses!" Ben-Shachar analyzes the exploitation of women's bodies by rabbis connected to the Puah Institute, and the latter's clear tendency toward chumrah. It reports on a new phenomenon: the training of Israeli nurses to carry out exams to ensure that a woman is fit to reinitiate her marital life. Thus, in order to fulfill a precept for which, in principle, only the woman is responsible because no one knows her body better than she, the Orthodox woman now needs the help of an expert. In an act of rebellion, Ben-Schachar, who identifies as Orthodox and feminist, vents, "Women also lose the benefits of keeping *Halachah* and tradition. If every time I clean rice or sift flour someone is standing by my side and watching over me, soon I'll have to stop doing that" (Ben-Shachar [2020]).

14. It is common currency that in Orthodox talks, courses, articles, books, and internet websites on different halakhic questions, rabbis reiterate the layperson's need to call them and consult them in if they have doubts. This reinforces the idea that ordinary people are not capable of making decisions. The rabbis often keep a special telephone for such purposes.

15. Feinstein in Adams (2017, 117).

16. To understand how rabbinic culture in general and Halachah in particular changed from the seventeenth century onward as a consequence of the invention of the printing press, unprecedented advances in scientific knowledge, the emergence of humanistic philosophies, and the seventeenth-century commercial revolution, see Berkovitz (2017, 349–377). For a sociohistorical analysis of how Halakhah is influenced by external phenomena that produce significant changes in it, see Katz (1992).

17. In addition to incorporating different technological devices in everyday life and creating the Zomet Institute in Israel, Orthodox Jews have important high-tech companies both in Israel and in the United States. For more on this matter, see Deutsch (2009).

18. A scandal that took place in the 1980s in the United States when Rabbi Eliyahu Shuman, of the Star-K certification agency, discovered that herring packed in vinegar supervised by the OK Kosher certification agency were sold as kosher during the Jewish Passover, yet vinegar made from corn or wheat, subject to fermentation, is forbidden at Passover. See Kramer (2007, 149).

19. For a chronological analysis of the importance of insects in Judaic sources, see Adams (2017). Another indicator of the importance that insect checking has acquired in recent decades is reflected in Rabbi Yoel Friedman's article "Waiter! There's a Bug in My Salad" (http://kosherpoint.passroads.com/waiter-theres-a-bug-in-my-salad), in which all the possibilities of insect infestation of vegetables and greens are mentioned, followed by the different opinions of Great Rabbis— from the strictest, such as Rabbi Moshe Vaya, to the most lenient, such as Rabbi Shlomo Amar (former Sephardic

Chief Rabbi of Israel). The extensive list of bibliographic references in this article, on the other hand, is an indication of how much knowledge has been accumulated in recent years on the topic of insects in maintaining a kosher diet.

20. The ONG Anonymous changed its name to Animals Now, according to information on the site https://animals-now.org/en/.

21. Rabbis Noam Bachur, Amnon Ytzchak, Gideon Holand, Shalom Arush Avi Zarki, and Shabtai Rapaport took part in the video.

22. In reference to a sweet and aromatic fruit used in a ritual of Sukkot, the feast of tabernacles. The etrog must be kosher, and the more beautiful it is, the more honor it concedes to those who acquire it. The *mehudar etrog*, that is, the embellished etrog, is often rare and very expensive.

23. Jewish tradition recognizes three levels of immateriality: *nefesh, ruach*, and *neshamah. Nefesh* corresponds to the vital soul, which gives life, and is common to humans and animals. *Ruach* is the spirit, which exists only in the human being; *neshamah,* the highest soul, which also exists only in humans, is our divine spark. This tripartite phenomenon is not clearly elucidated in the Hebrew Bible, emerging as a later offshoot of Jewish thought, especially within the Kabbalah.

24. Noah's laws were dictated to him and his family after the flood, as ethical rules for all humankind. From a Jewish perspective, Gentiles must follow the noetic laws, and Jews, the 613 precepts. Noah's sixth law (Hebrew: *ever min ha-chai*) forbids mistreating animals and is interpreted as permission to only kill animals for food.

25. www.sefaria.org, accessed on September 3, 2022.

26. www.sefaria.org, accessed on September 3, 2022.

27. www.sefaria.org, accessed on September 3, 2022.

28. Genesis 1:29: "God said, 'See, I give you every seed-bearing plant that is upon all the earth, and every tree that has seed-bearing fruit; they shall be yours for food.'" www.sefaria.org, accessed on September 3, 2022.

29. Genesis 1:30: "And to all the animals on land, to all the birds of the sky, and to everything that creeps on earth, in which there is the breath of life, [I give] all the green plants for food. And it was so." www.sefaria.org, accessed on September 3, 2022.

30. Genesis 9:3. "Every creature that lives shall be yours to eat; as with the green grasses, I give you all these." www.sefaria.org, accessed on September 3, 2022.

31. See Aish (n.d.)

32. *Bedikah*, from Hebrew: "supervision" or "checking"—in reference to the rules the ritual butcher must abide by regarding the blade used for slaughter.

33. Rabbi Eliezer Melamed is the son of Rabbi Zalman Baruch Melamed, disciple of Rabino Zvi Yehuda Kook. He has a column on the Torah World Gateway website, aligned with the ideology of the Israeli nationalist Orthodox movement. Available at https://www.yeshiva.co/ . Accessed on June 26, 2021.

34. Ritual slaughter is called *schechitah* and includes stages prior to butchering that are related to requirements regarding the place where slaughter will be carried out. Before the animal is slaughtered, a specific prayer should be spoken.

35. Rabbi Duvdevani also cited numbers to demonstrate the impossibility of kosher slaughter at present. He put it this way: "We are saying that in Israel a shochet has to

slaughter between twelve and fourteen chickens in a minute, while the ideal rate is seven or eight chickens per minute. It means that we find ourselves in a situation that is excessive, abnormal, and the pace of slaughter ends up influencing everything. It influences all the other stages: checking the chickens, salting and slaughtering them, and it also influences the previous stages, such as transporting live chickens from the farms to the slaughterhouses."

36. Emphasis added. The Mehadrin is a Brazilian producer and certifier of Kosher meat, founded in 1976, and known as the first kosher butcher in the country. As of the 1990s the firm grew and diversified, acquiring distribution points in several states throughout the country, in addition to its own poultry farm and slaughterhouses. https://www.mehadrin.com.br/.

37. Temple Grandin (1980) wrote an article that provides a detailed account of the process of chaining and hoisting oxen and sheep in the United States, questioning, from her research data, the kashrut of the meat consumed by North Americans.

38. According to the article "Keeping Kosher Update" (Farm Forward [2014]), the Central Rabbinate of Israel committed to refrain from certifying as kosher animals that were slaughtered used the painful shackle-and-hoist system, which nonetheless remains a practice in South American slaughterhouses.

39. The Southern Common Market, commonly known by Portuguese abbreviation Mercosul, is a South American trade bloc established in the 1990s.

40. Keisar (2017/8).

41. With the onset of modernity, kashrut began to separate Orthodox Jews from liberal and secular ones. New ways of drawing the boundaries have emerged in recent decades and are analyzed in Chapter 6.

42. Examples taken from Rabbi Forst's (2013) book on kosher cuisine. Translated from Hebrew.

43. Examples taken from Rabbi Fuks's (2002) book on kosher cuisine. Translated from Hebrew.

44. Berman (1992) refers to a single definition that is accepted by all streams of orthodoxy and can be taken into consideration by the US courts in case histories and recurrent litigation around fraud in the production and distribution of kosher meat. Existing differences between Orthodox streams make the work of North American judges harder.

45. According to Halakhah, ritual slaughter must be performed by an observant and pious Jew, knowledgeable in the laws of slaughter and experienced in its practice. It is the prevailing custom for the shochet to receive written authorization from a recognized rabbinical authority attesting to the qualifications mentioned earlier. By performing an activity necessary for the community, the work of the shochet is seen as fulfilling a mission.

46. According to Jewish tradition, Amalek was an ancient biblical nation that lived near the land of Canaan. The Amalekites were the first nation to attack the Jewish people after their exodus from Egypt. For this reason, they are taken as the example of the enemy of the Jews.

47. The analogy between the ritual slaughterer and "the friend of Amalek" can be found in a passage from the Mishnah in which derogatory phrases about various professions follow one another, such as the one declaring that the best of all doctors end up in hell. It is important to consider that this is a literary passage and not a legal judgment. See Kiddushin 82a (available at https://www.sefaria.org/Kiddushin.82a?lang=bi, accessed on June 18, 2021).

48. Lytton (2013b,10) provides a detailed account of cases against butchers and kashrut supervisors that reached the civil courts, stating that in 1925 the New York City Department of Markets estimated the volume of nonkosher meat sold in the city as kosher at 40 percent, while community associations and industrialists calculated that the percentage was much higher, reaching 65 percent.

49. In Israel, the most influential of them is the NGO Anonymous, while in the United States, PETA stands out.

50. The exploitation and mistreatment of ritual butchers and kashrut supervisors from slaughterhouses include long working hours without proper breaks, informal labor, and low wages, in addition to precarious workplace conditions. This complaint was repeated throughout the interviews, among Israeli supervisors and butchers and among Brazilians. A Brazilian interlocutor made sure to point out that the fear of being fired is part of the routine of slaughterhouse workers, since rabbis "don't really care if a masghiach or a shochet gets sick or has a problem. You miss a day and are replaced by someone else without anyone asking you what happened to you that day." To this must be added the psychological tension and physical difficulties to which those who work slaughtering poultry or cattle are subjected.

51. Creating an opposition between Jewish rituals and ethics is common among Jewish Orthodox groups, a phenomenon that initially might seem to suggest that Jewish ethics are not a fundamental part of Jewish precepts. I explore this issue in the next chapter.

52. The following and emblematic affirmation was made by Rabbi Keisar in one of the videos uploaded to his website: "Today, the greatest cruelty that is done to animals lives in the way that they live, not the way that they die."

53. Of significance is that the biggest criticism of Israel's farms and meatpacking plants resides in the cruelty with which the animals are treated; in the United States, however, although there have been complaints by PETA about animal abuse in the Rubashkin family's slaughterhouse in Postville, the issue that provoked the clashes between the different groups was the exploitation of their employees.

54. Stuffed fish, typical dish served at Ashkenazi festivities.

55. Balls made from *matzoh* flour, a typical Passover dish within Ashkenazi cuisine.

56. From the Hebrew for "weeks," it is also known as the Festival of Harvest or Festival of Ingathering.

57. Unless specified, I use the term "meat" to refer generically to beef and poultry.

58. In his article "The Significance of Eating Meat," Rabbi Eliezer Melamed (2014) leaves no doubt regarding the obligation to eat meat on Shabbat: "Since after the flood there is no ethical problem in eating meat, consequently, at meals in which it is a mitzvah to be happy, it is also a mitzvah to eat meat."

59. *Tikkun olam*, from Hebrew: "repair the world"—a concept that is interpreted by Orthodox Judaism as the perspective of overcoming all forms of idol worship. Liberal Jewish currents interpret it as the aspiration to behavior and action that are constructive and beneficial for the building of a world that is more just.

60. Melamed (2014).

61. Goldman (n.d.). https://www.chabad.org/library/article_cdo/aid/880198/jewish/Do-I-Have-to-Eat-Meat-on-Shabbat.htm

62. Not until the fifteenth century did meat bec0me a more frequent part of the Jewish menu. It is thus unremarkable that a food that is both scarce and rich in protein came to be used as part of holiday celebration (Kramer [2009, 93]).

63. I owe this interpretation to Rabbi Saul Paves.

64. In books on kashrut and in the homes of Orthodox people that I visited, the places where foods containing meat are kept and cooked, such as the refrigerator and the stove, are larger than those used for dairy products and foods containing them.

65. A type of Israel cooperative community. Many *moshavim* are devoted to agricultural activities.

66. What leads Fiddes to this conclusion is the fact that Lévi-Strauss points to actions such as smoking, charring, and roasting, processes that are primarily part of meat preparation.

Chapter 6

1. Paste made from apples and walnuts or dates and walnuts. It represents the putty that bricklayers used in the Egyptian constructions that were built with the labor of enslaved Israelites.

2. Oil-fried foods are a reminder of the oil that burned for eight days in the candelabrum of the Temple of Jerusalem during the Maccabean revolt against the Roman invasion.

3. Obviously, on Jewish holidays, especially among secular and liberal Jews, the typical foods of the group and the family add flavor to the celebrations—but from a strictly religious point of view, this is mere detail.

4. Rabbi Daniel Sperber begins his text "Eating as a Sacrament—The Eating Table and the Coffin" in the following manner, "Eating in traditional Jewish thought is a sacrament: a strict and pious endeavor. There are a variety of benedictions made before and after eating and drinking different kinds of food and drink, which reflect the understanding that God's sovereignty over all that is in this world; we acknowledge his beneficence for granting us of the fruits of his creation" (Sperber [2019, 43]).

5. Despite this, more and more manifestations are popping up, here and there, of Orthodox rabbis who oppose certain practices that violate the principle of the tzaar baalei chaim. A recent example is the petition of sixty Israeli Orthodox rabbis who condemn the practice of sending live animals to Israel for slaughter (Times of Israel 2018).

6. See Galahar (2010).

7. Free translation into English from the Portuguese-language version.

8. When the ritual was established, animals were obviously not treated according to the principles and practices of industrial society (Grandin [1980, 383]).

9. Even so, as I mentioned early in this volume, there are apps designed especially for the Orthodox public in order to make their lives easier. Examples of this use of technology are kosher cell phones, computer programs that filter content deemed inappropriate, Shabbat apps, and the creation of cutting-edge technology to produce apps and programs that facilitate, or in theory facilitate, the daily lives of observant Jews. The technology is incorporated and used by them, often in spheres that are exclusive to them, such as apps to let women know if they are pure or impure regarding having sex with their husbands, apps that tell tourists where the closest synagogues are, and apps that help you find out if a food in a restaurant is kosher, among many other possibilities.

10. Maimonides (n.d.).

11. Nachmanides commentaries on Deuteronomy, https://www.sefaria.org/, accessed June 20, 2021.

12. Home automation so as not to desecrate the Sabbath is relatively common among Orthodox families. The timer is the most used item, and is employed during Shabbat to turn lights and electric ovens on and off without human interference at preestablished times.

13. There is a principle in Rabbinic Judaism known as *kipuach nefesh* (salvation of [a] human life), according to which it is not only possible but a duty to transgress the commandments in order to save a human life.

14. Alan Dundes's book *The Shabbat Elevator and Other Sabbath Subterfuges* (2002) is a wonderful piece of anthropological research that provides in-depth understanding of the subterfuges that are created by Orthodox elites to assist observant Jews in daily life.

15. Term used for the male priests of Afro-Brazilian religions.

16. Term used for lesser divinities in Afro-Brazilian religions.

17. This statement does not endorse sacredness as purity, but serves as a heuristic element in our attempt to understand the notion of the sacred within the Jewish cosmovision.

18. In "The Abominations of Leviticus," Mary Douglas analyzes the term *kadosh,* placing emphasis on this meaning. See Douglas (1993/4).

19. Even Shoshan A. Ha´Milon Ha´chadash be Tesha Prakim. Jerusalem: Am Oved (Hebrew).

20. From the Hebrew, noun form of *tameh.*

21. In the case of the unclean woman, the term is *nidah*, and ritual purification culminates in a ritual bath, known as the mikve.

22. In Leviticus we find the injunctions not to lie, not to steal, and not to deceive (Leviticus 19:11); not to curse the deaf nor to put obstacles in the way of the blind (Leviticus 19:14); not to dishonor one's daughter, turning her into a harlot (Leviticus 19:29); and finally the injunction, "Do not seek revenge or bear a grudge against one of your people, but love your neighbor as love yourself. I am the LORD (Leviticus 19:18).

23. Kramer (2009, 17): "In the judgment of John Cooper, the common diet of the ancient Israelite consisted of 'barely bread, vegetables, and fruits, supplemented by mild products and honey.'"
24. See Topel (2005).
25. Movement of "return" to Jewish roots, in reference to the liberal and secular Jews who take up orthodoxy as adults.

Glossary

Aish Ha 'Torah: Orthodox yeshiva whose most important mission is to bring liberal and secular Jews closer to orthodoxy.

Bar mitzvah: Coming-of-age rites performed when a boy reaches the age of thirteen. The bar mitzvah is a moment of joy and celebration.

Bodek: Refers to someone who has the role of verifying, awarding proof. In ritual slaughter, the *bodek* checks to make sure the knife to be used has been properly sharpened.

Bund: Jewish workers' party that was active in Russia from 1897 to 1920. It had important ramifications in Poland and the United States.

Chabad or *Chabad-Lubavitch:* Name of the Hasidic Orthodox stream founded in the eighteenth century in Russia by Rabbi Schneur Zalman of Liadi, who played a leading role in bringing secular and liberal Jews closer to orthodoxy. In the 1970s the movement, now based in New York and under the leadership of the charismatic Lubavitch Rebbe, Menachem Mendel Schneerson, took shape as the transnational empire that it continues to be today.

Chametz: Any type of leaven or yeast. During the eight days of the Jewish Passover, Jews are not allowed to consume or keep any kind of leavening in the home.

Charedim: A word that can be translated as "the fearful," in reference to the God-fearing. One of the terms that is used to refer to ultra-orthodox Jews.

Charoset: A pasty food that symbolizes the clay used to make the heavy bricks that the Jews carried when they were enslaved in Egypt. Usually made from apples and walnuts or dates and walnuts, charoset varies greatly according to the ethnic origin of each family.

Chatzitza: "Thing that separates two surfaces," a term used specially to designate objects or surfaces that come between ritual bathwater and the body, such as rings and nail polish.

Chozer b'teshuva: Expression used to designate "women who opted for orthodoxy as adults." Movement of "return" to Jewish roots, in reference to secular and liberal Jews who become Orthodox as adults.

Chukim: Plural of *chok* (law), in reference to the kashrut laws, whose meanings and motives are deemed incomprehensible, in contrast to other commandments that have, over the centuries, been the subject of diverse interpretations.

Chumrah: "Strictness" or "stringency." In Rabbinic Judaism, *chumrah* refers to the choice of the most stringent ways of fulfilling the commandments. It is the choice to comply with them in a way that goes beyond the basic requirements of Halakhah (Jewish Law). Those who at some point impose *chumrah* on themselves become *machmir*. See also: *Fence around the Torah.*

Chumratization: Neologism that refers to chumrah—a process of radicalization of Jewish orthodoxy, initiated in Europe by Rabbi Chatam Sofer. A widespread phenomenon among the Orthodox Jews of last hundred years, it represents the will to follow the commandments as stringently as possible.

Daat Torah: "Knowledge of the Torah." Expression used by Orthodox Jews to refer to the learning of the Great Rabbis, which is considered basically "infallible." The *Daat Torah* is an innovation within Orthodox Judaism. Thus, while a halakhic opinion requires legal justification from recognized sources, *Daat Torah* is of a more subtle nature and does not require any clear legal justification, nor proof of explicit connection to earlier sources. This means that whoever invokes *Daat Torah* as justification does so based on their own understanding.

Eda Charedit: One of the names given to ultra-Orthodox Jews in Israel, and as a corollary, to their certifying agency.

Fence around the Torah: Process of legislating/codifying based on stringency in fulfilling the commandments. It represents an interpretation of Deuteronomy (22:8) in which it is stated that when a house is being built, its roof must be fenced off, to avoid blame in the event that someone were to fall from it. This verse was interpreted by Jewish legislators as a requirement to "build a fence around the Torah," with new norms that protect *mitzvot*.

Gefiltefish: (From Yiddish) "Stuffed fish," a typical Ashkenazi holiday dish.

Glatt kosher: A seal attesting to stringent compliance of kosher laws, a sort of "super kosher" guarantee.

Gush Katif: Israeli firm that produces allegedly insect-free vegetables, greens, and vegetables for the Orthodox public. There are controversies surrounding the company's production process. Thus, while the website claims that results are obtained through the implementation of specially designed greenhouses, many important rabbis and agronomists argue that it is the greater use of pesticides that enables them to produce insect-, larvae-, and egg-free produce.

Haggadah: Liturgy book used in the celebration of Passover.

Halakhah: Compendium of laws and commandments that observant Jews must respect. The Halakhic corpus was compiled in the High Middle Ages. However, due to the emergence of new forms of social organization, on the one hand, and technological advances, on the other, new rules are constantly being added to its initial 613 commandments, known as *halakhot*.

Hashgacha Pratit: Israeli nongovernmental organization created in 2012 that competes with the rabbinate in supervising food services in the country's restaurants, kiosks, and hotels. The expression *Hashgacha Pratit* is a double entendre that can mean both "divine providence" and "private supervision."

Haskalah: Jewish Enlightenment. A movement originating in Central Europe at the end of the eighteenth century, its central tenets were the modernization of Judaism, from both ideological and institutional points of view. By modernizing religion and education, Haskalah ushered in a revolution in Rabbinic Judaism, making way for new forms of Jewish identity, such as the Reform movement, Zionism, and cultural Judaism.

Hasidism: Stream of Judaism that came about in eighteenth-century Eastern Europe. Hasidic Jews are an important segment of Orthodox Jewry. They are characterized by their stricter adhesion to Jewish commandments and are more reluctant to adapt to the values of modernity.

Ieridat ha'dorot: "Decline of generations"—a rabbinical principle according to which the generations that witnessed the revelation on Mount Sinai are intellectually and spiritually superior to those that follow.

Itchazkut: "Strengthening," in reference to the strengthening of faith through extreme stringency in fulfilling the commandments.

Kosherize: Refers to methods for making kitchen utensils and furniture appropriate for use by Orthodox Jews.

Kneidalach: (From Yiddish) Matzah flour dumplings, a typical Passover dish in Ashkenazi cuisine.

Madregot: "Ladder" or "scale," in reference to different levels of stringency in fulfilling the commandments.

Maror: Bitter herb, used in the Jewish Passover supper as a symbol of the hardships that the Jews bore when they were slaves in Egypt.

Mashguiach: Supervisor.

Matza: The unleavened bread that must be eaten at Passover.

Mehadrin: "Embellished" or "prettier." The term is used to indicate more stringent levels of kosher food supervision.

Midrash (plural: *midrashim*): Allegorical interpretation of biblical verses found in the Talmud.

Mikve: Ritual bathhouse, where women purify themselves at the end of the menstrual cycle or before marriage; and men, before Yom Kippur and other holy days.

Mishnah: One of the main works of Rabbinic Judaism. It is the first major transcription of the Jewish oral tradition or oral Torah.

Mitzva (plural: *mitzvot*): "Precept" or "commandment". Observant Jews follow strictly the 613 commandments codified by Maimonides, based on the laws of the Torah (Pentateuch).

Moshav (plural: *moshavim*): Type of Israeli cooperative community. Many *moshavim* engage in farming.

Nidah: Period in which a woman is considered impure and therefore obliged to abstain from sexual intercourse.

Parve: Foods considered neutral, that is, which can be mixed with meat or milk, as they themselves do not belong to either category.

Pashkevil (plural: *pashkevilim*): Posters or announcements put up on the streets of Orthodox neighborhoods in Israel with warnings, information, news, or messages from the rabbis. Pashkevilim are an efficient and inexpensive way for rabbis to communicate with their followers.

Pikuach nefesh: "Salvation of a soul"; principle that proclaims the duty to transgress any other commandments in order to save the life of a human being.

Purim: A Jewish festival that commemorates the salvation of the Persian Jews from Haman's plan to exterminate them, as recorded in the Book of Esther. Purim is also known as the Jewish carnival, because of its joyous festivities and use of costumes.

Reb Nachman (1772–1810): Great-grandson of the Baal Shem Tov, Nachman revitalized the Hasidic movement by combining the esoteric secrets of Kabbalah with systematic Torah study. He attracted thousands of followers during his lifetime, and his influence continues today through many Hasidic movements around the world.

Schochet: Ritual butcher who follows all the Halakhic guidelines for the slaughter of animals, as well as stages that precede and follow it (such as meat salting).

Seder: "Order," in reference to a sequence of rituals that govern the Passover dinner.

Shabbat: "Sabbath," day of rest, holy day. During Shabbat, observant Jews must abide by a long list of prohibitions as well as obey a number of commandments.

Shomer mitzvot: "One who follows the commandments"; refers to Orthodox Jews.

Shuk Mahané Yeshuda (shuk): "Market," in this case, in reference to the large open-air meat, fruit, and vegetable market in the center of Jerusalem. It is a major tourist attraction, lying at the very heart of the city.

Shulchan Aruch: "The set table." Name for the codification of Jewish Law, compiled by Rabbi Yosef de Karo in the sixteenth century. The laws and judgments contained in this text are unanimously accepted by all streams of Orthodox Judaism.

Tahor: Pure.

Talmid chacham (plural: *talmidim chachamim*): A man whose life is devoted entirely to the study of the canonical texts of Judaism. *Chachamim talmidim* are the most venerated members of Orthodox communities.

Talmud: Also known as *Guemarah* and the oral law, a collection of canonical books of Judaism that include rabbinic discussions concerning law, ethics, rituals, and customs. It is a seminal text of Rabbinic Judaism. *Halakhah* is concerned with the legal dimensions compiled in the *Talmud*.

Taref (or *treif*): "Ruined meat," prohibited as unsuitable for consumption by observant Jews.

Teshuvah (Teshuvah movement): Refers to secular or liberal Jews who opted for orthodoxy as adults.

Tikun olam: "Reparation of the world," a Jewish concept interpreted by Orthodox Judaism as the perspective that overcomes all forms of idolatry. Liberal Jewish streams interpret it as the aspiration to behave and act in a constructive and beneficial way, based on the desire to build a more just world.

Torah: Pentateuch—by extension, the Hebrew Bible.

Tumah (adjective, *tameh*): Situation of ritual impurity.

Tzaar baaei chaim: "The suffering of animals," in reference to the biblical principle that forbids causing animals to suffer.

Yeshiva (**plural:** *yeshivot*): School of rabbinic/religious studies for boys over age thirteen.

*Yshuv (**Old Yshuv**):* Jewish settlement in Palestine prior to the establishment of the State of Israel.

References

Ackerman, A. (2002). "Judging the Sinner Favorably: R. Hayyim Hirschensohn on the Need for Leniency in Halakhic Decision-Making." *Modern Judaism* 22(3): 261–280.

Adams, S. (2017). "The Scientific Revolution and Modern Bedikat Tola'im Trend." *Akirah: The Flatbush Journal of Jewish Law and Thought* 22: 93–124.

Alter, R. (1979). "A New Theory of Kashrut." *Commentary.* Aug. 1.

Appleby, R.S.; Marty, M.E. (2002). "Fundamentalism." *Foreign Policy* 128: 16–22.

Aran, G. (2013a). "On Religiosity and Super-religiosity (I): Measures of Radical Religion." *NUMEN* 60(2/3): 165–194.

Aran, G. (2013b). "On Religiosity and Super-religiosity (II): The Case of Jewish Ultra-orthodoxy." *NUMEN* 60(4): 371–410.

Asad, T. (1988). "Towards a Genealogy of the Concept of Ritual." In *Vernacular Christianity: Essays in the Social Anthropology of Religion*, edited by Wendy James and Douglas H. Johnson, 73–87. Oxford Lilian Barber Press.

Asad, T. (1987). "On Ritual and Discipline in Medieval Christian Monasticism." *Economy and Society* 16(2): 159–203.

Augras, M. (2011). "Quizilas e preceitos—transgressão, reparação e organização dinâmica do mundo." In *Culto aos Orixás: Voduns e Ancestrais nas Religiões Afro-Brasileiras*, edited by Carlos Eugênio Marcondes de Moura, 159–196. São Paulo: Pallas Editora.

Barthes, R. (1975). "Towards a Psychosociology of Contemporary Food Consumption." In *European Diet, from Pre-industrial to Modern Times*, edited by E. Forster and F. Forster, 47–59. New York: Harper & Row.

Berger, P. (1985). *O Dossel Sagrado: elementos para uma teoria sociológica da religião.* São Paulo: Paulus.

Berkovitz, J.R. (2017). "Rabbinic Culture and the Historical Development of Halakhah." In *Cambridge History of Judaism*, vol. 7, edited by Jonathan Karp and Adam Sutcliffe, 349–377. New York: Cambridge University Press.

Berman, M.A. (1992). "Kosher Fraud Statutes and the Establishment Clause: Are They Kosher?" *Social Problems* 1: 71–73.

Besiroglu, L.; Karaca, S.; Keskin, I. (2014). "Scrupulosity and Obsessive-Compulsive Disorder: The Cognitive Perspective in Islamic Sources." *Journal of Religious Health* 53(1): 99–128.

Bildtgård, T. (2008). "Trust in Food in Modern and Late-Modern Societies." *Social Science Information* 47(1).

Birnbau, E.; Rosenberg, Sh. (2020). *O que é cashrut? Antologia do Pensamento Judaico sobre as Leis Dietéticas Judaicas.* São Paulo: Sêfer.

Bonchek, A. (2009). *Religious Compulsions and Fears: A Guide to Treatment.* Jerusalem: Feldheim Publishers.

Brown, B. (2014). "Jewish Political Theology: The Doctrine of Da'at Torah as a Case Study." *Harvard Theological Review* 107(3): 255–289.

Brown, B. (2011, Hebrew). *Rumo à democratização da liderança haredit? A doutrina do Daat Torá na virada dos séculos XX e XXI*. Jerusalem: Israeli Democracy Institute.

Burt, V.K.; Rudolph, M. (2000). "Treating an Orthodox Jewish Woman with Obsessive-Compulsive Disorder: Maintaining Reproductive and Psychologic Stability in the Context of Normative Religious Rituals." *American Journal of Psychiatry* 157(4).

Cardozo, Nathan. (2019). "Are You Really Eating Kosher? On Camouflage, Hypocrisy, and Hiding Behind the Kashrut Laws." In *Kashrut and Jewish Food Ethics*, edited by Shmuly Yanklowitz, 10–13. Boston: Academic Studies Press.

Caplan, L. (1987). "Introduction." In *Studies in Religious Fundamentalism*, edited by Lionel Caplan, 141–151. London: Palgrave Macmillan.

Chwarts, S. (2012). "A Eleição de Israel na Torá." Cadernos de Língua e Literatura Hebraica, n. 10: 141–151.

Cohen, A.K. (1968). *Transgressão e controle*. São Paulo: Livraria Pioneira Editora.

Cohen, A.; Susser, B. (2010). "The 'Sabbatical' Year in Israeli Politics: An Intra-religious and Religious-Secular Conflict from the Nineteenth through the Twenty-First Centuries." *Journal of Church and State* 52(3): 454–475.

Dan, J.O. (1997, Hebrew). "Haredismo triunfante." *Alpayim*, n. 15: 234–254.

Dein, S.; Loewenthal, K.M. (2013). "The Mental Health Benefits and Costs of Sabbath Observance among Orthodox Jews." *Journal of Religion Health* 52(1): 1382–1390.

Demirhan, Y.; Ulca, P.; Zenyuva, H. (2012). "Detection of Porcine DNA in Gelatine and Gelatine-Containing Processed Food Products—Halal/Kosher Authentication." *Meat Science* 90(3): 686–689.

Deutsch, N. (2009). "The Forbidden Fork, the Cell Phone Holocaust, and Other Haredi Encounters with Technology." *Contemporary Jewry* 29: 3–19.

Douglas, M. (1993/4). "Atonement in Leviticus." *Jewish Studies Quarterly* 1: 109–130.

Douglas, M. (1966). *Purity and Danger: An Analysis of Concepts of Pollution and Taboo*. London: Routledge & Kegan Paul.

Dundes, A. (2002). *The Shabbat Elevator and Other Sabbath Subterfuges*. Lanham, MD: Rowman and Littlefield.

Durkheim, E. (1996). *As formas elementares da vida religiosa*. São Paulo: Martins Fontes.

Eilberg-Schwartz, H. (1990). *The Savage in Judaism: An Anthropology of Israelite Religion and Ancient Judaism*. Bloomington: Indiana University Press.

Eisenstadt, S.N. (1997). "Sectarianism and Heterodoxy in Jewish History: Some Comparative Civilizational Notes." *Jewish Studies* 37: 7–59.

Eliade, M. (1999). *O sagrado e o profano*. São Paulo: Martin Fontes.

Ende, Sh. (2006). Cashrut e shabat na cozinha judaica: leis e costumes. São Paulo: Beit Chabad Central.

Even Shoshan. A. (2000). *Ha ′Milon Ha ′Chadash Be tesha prakim*. Jerusalem: Am Oved.

Ferziger, A.S. (2004). "Religious Zealotry and Religious Law: Rethinking Conflict and Coexistence." *Journal of Religion* 84(1): 48–77.

Fiddes, N. (1991). *Meat as a Natural Symbol*. New York: Routledge.

Fischer, J. (2015). "Keeping Enzymes Kosher: Sacred and Secular Biotech Production." *Science & Society*, May 4: 681–684.

Fishkoff, S. (2010). *Kosher Nation: Why More and More of America's Food Answers to a Higher Authority*. New York: Schocken.

Forst, B. (2013). *The Kosher Kitchen: A Practical Guide*. New York: Mesorah Publications.

Francione, G.L. (2013). *Introdução aos direitos dos animais*. Campinas: Editora da Unicamp.

Fletcher, M. (2013). *Do You Know Hilchos Shabbos? Practical Questions for the Whole Family*. New York: Menucha.

Freud, Z. (1959). *Obsessive Actions and Religious Practices*. The Standard Edition, vol. 9. Translated by James A. Strachey. London: Hogarth Press.

Friedman, J.L. (May 2009). "Walking with God: Realism, Fanaticism, and the Future of Jewish Law." *Marburg Journal of Religion* 14(1): 1–16.

Friedman, M. (1991). *The Haredi Society: Sources, Trends and Processes*. Jerusalem: Jerusalem Institute for Israeli Studies.

Friedman, M. (1990). "Jewish Zealots: Conservative versus Innovative." In *Religious Radicalism and Politics in the Middle East*, edited by Emanuel Sivan and Menachem Friedman, 127–142. Albany: State University of New York Press.

Fuks, Y.I. (2002, Hebrew). *Ha´kashrut, ha´mitbach ve ha´maachalim: halichot ve anhagot*. Jerusalem.

Garcia Parpet, Marie France. (2016). "Patrimonialização de produtos alimentícios na França: construções simbólicas e reinvenção do passado." In *Ensaios sobre a Antropologia da alimentação: saberes, dinâmicas e patrimônios*, edited by E. Woortmann and J. Cavignac, 57–90. Natal, EDUFRN. Brasília, ABA.

Geraldo, D.A. (2010). *O mercado kasher em São Paulo*. Master's dissertation, University of São Paulo.

Giddens, A. (1991). *As consequências da Modernidade*. São Paulo: UNESP.

Gluckman, M. (1954). *Rituals of Rebellion in South-East Africa*. Manchester: Manchester University Press.

Grandin, T. (1980). "Problems with Kosher Slaughter." *International Journal for the Study of Animal Problems* 1(6): 375–390.

Greenberg, D.; Huppert, J.D. (2010). "Scrupulosity: A Unique Subtype of Obsessive-Compulsive Disorder." In *David, in Current Psychiatry Reports*, 12: 282–289.

Greenberg, D.; Shefler, G. (2008). "Ultra-Orthodox Rabbinic Responses to Religious Obsessive-Compulsive Disorder." *Israel Psychiatry-Related Sciences* 45(3): 183–192.

Greenberg, D.; Witztum, E. (2001). *Sanity and Sanctity: Mental Health Work among the Ultra-Orthodox in Jerusalem*. New Haven, CT: Yale University Press.

Greenberg, M.B. (1984). "Are Religious Compulsions Religious or Compulsive: A Phenomenological Study." *American Journal of Psychotherapy* 38(4): 524–532.

Heilman, S. (2000). *Defenders of the Faith: Inside Ultra-Orthodox Jewry*. Berkeley: University of California Press.

Heilman, S. (1977). "Inner and Outer Identity: Sociological Ambivalence among Orthodox Jews." *Jewish Social Studies* 39(3) (Summer): 227–240.

Heilman, S.; Friedman, M. (1991). "Religious Fundamentalism and Religious Jews: The Case of the Haredim." In *Fundamentalisms Observed* edited by Martin Marty and R. Scott Appleby. Chicago: University of Chicago Press,.

Himle, J.A.; Chatters, L.M.; Taylor, R.J.; Nguyen, A. (2011). "The Relationship between Obsessive-Compulsive Disorder and Religious Faith: Clinical Characteristics and Implications for Treatment." *Psychology of Religion and Spirituality* 3(4): 241–258.

Hornstein, Rebecca Z. (2013). "When Kashrut Is Not 'Kosher': The Post Postville Struggle over Eating. Ethics and American Jewish Identity." *Religious Studies Honors Projects*. Paper 11.

Huppert, J.D.; Siev, J.; Kushner, E.S. (2007). "When Religion and Obsessive-Compulsive Disorder Collide: Treating Scrupulosity in Ultra-Orthodox Jews." *Journal of Clinical Psychology* 63(10): 925–941.

Joseph, N.B. (2002). "Feeding an Identity: Gender, Food, and Survival." *Nashim: A Journal of Jewish Women's Studies & Gender*, n. 5: 7–13.

Kapferer, B. (2004). "Ritual Dynamics and Virtual Practice: Beyond Representation and Meaning." *Source Social Analysis: The International Journal of Anthropology* 48(2): 35–54.

Karo, Josef. (1968). *Síntesis del Shuljan Aruj*. Buenos Aires: Editorial Sigal.

Katz, J. (1992). *The "Shabbes Goy": A Study in Halakhic Flexibility*. Philadelphia: Jewish Publication Society.

Keisar, A. (2017/8). *Thou Shalt Not Place Obstacles in Front of a Blind Man: What Is Written in the Torah, Prophets, Writings, Mishnah, Talmud, First and Last Sages about the Shedding of the Blood of Living Beings*. Jerusalem:

Kook, A.I. (1983). *The Vision of Vegetarianism and Peace from a Torah Perspective*. Collected and edited by David Hakohen. Jerusalem:

Kramer, D.C. (2009). *Jewish Eating and Identity through the Ages*. New York: Routledge.

Leroy, F.; Praet, I. (2017). "Animal Killing and Postdomestic Meat Production." *Journal of Agriculture and Environmental Ethics* 3: 67–86.

Liebman, Ch. (1987). "Orthodoxy Faces Modernity." *ORIM: A Jewish Journal at Yale* 2(2): 7–21.

Liebman, Ch. (1983). "Extremism as a Religious Norm." *Journal of the Scientific Study of Religion* 22(1): 75–86.

Lopes Cardozo, Nathan. (2012). "Halacha: The Microscopic Search for God." In Thoughts to Ponder, June 21. https://www.cardozoacademy.org/thoughtstoponder/halacha-the-microscopic-search-for-god-ttp-300/

Lytton, T.D. (2013a). "Chopped Herring and the Making of the American Kosher Certification System." *Jewish Review of Books* 44(1). https://jewishreviewofbooks.com/articles/91/chopped-herring-and-the-making-of-the-american-kosher-certification-system/#

Lytton, T.D. (2013b). *Kosher: Private Regulation in the Age of Industrial Food*. London: Harvard University Press.

Maccoby, H. (1999). *Ritual and Morality: The Ritual Purity System and Its Place in Judaism*. Cambridge: Cambridge University Press.

Melo Mendonça, P.S.; Oliveira Caetano, G.A. (2017). "Abate de bovinos: Considerações sobre o abate humanitário e jugulação cruenta." *PUBVET* 11(12): 1196–1209.

Milgrom, J. (1993). "The Rationale for Biblical Impurity." *JANES—Journal of the Ancient Near Eastern Society* 22(1) (January 1): 107–112.

Milgrom, J. (1991). *Leviticus*. The Anchor Bible, vol. 3. New York: Doubleday.

Mintz, S.W. (2001). Comida e antropologia: uma breve revisão. *Revista Brasileira de Ciências Sociais*, n. 16 (47): 31–41.

Nabil Md, Ahmad Roslia, Shalisah Sharipb, and Nur Sakinah Thomasc. (2019). "Scrupulosity and Islam: A Perspective." *Journal of Spirituality in Mental Health* (December): 1–25.

Pellarano, J. A. (2017). Industrialização e alimentação: Impactos da Revolução Industrial moderna em produção, distribuição, preparo e consumo de alimentos. *Anais da React—Reunião de Antropologia da Ciência e da Tecnologia*, n. 3(3): 111–123.

Pirutinksy, S.; Rosmarin, D.H.; Pargament, K.I. (2007). "Community Attitudes towards Culture-Influenced Mental Illness: Scrupulosity vs. Non-religious OCD among Orthodox Jews." *Journal of Community Psychology* 37(8): 949–958.

Regan, T. (2004). *The Case for Animal Rights* University of California Press.

Rifkin, J. (1992). *Beyond Beef: The Rise and Fall of the Cattle Culture*. New York: Plume.

Ruthven, M. (2007). *Fundamentalism: A Very Short Introduction*. New York: Oxford University Press.

Sacks, J. (1993). *One People? Tradition, Modernity, and Jewish Unity*. Washington, DC: Littman Library of Jewish Civilization.

Selby, J.J. (1997). *The Booming Kosher Food Market*. An Honors Thesis. Ball State University, Indiana.

Shemesh, Y. (2006). "Vegetarian Ideology in Talmudic Literature and Traditional Biblical Exegesis." *Review of Rabbinic Judaism* n. 9: 141–166.

Silber, M.K. (ed.). (1992). "The Emergence of Ultra-orthodoxy: The Invention of a Tradition." *Jewish Theologica Seminary of America*. Cambridge: Harvard University Press.

Singer, I.B. ([1963] 1978). *Breve sexta-feira*. São Paulo: Ed. Francisco Alves

Singer, P. (2010). *Libertação Animal*. São Paulo: Martin Fontes.

Soloveitchik, H. (1994). "Rupture and Reconstruction: The Transformation of Contemporary Orthodoxy." *Tradition* 28(4): 64–130.

Soloveitchik, J.B. (1983). *Halachic Man*. New York: Jewish Publication Society of America.

Spector, S.E. (2012). "Reexamining Kashrut: Taking into Consideration the Treatment of an Animal Prior to Slaughter." *Hebrew Union College—Jewish Institute of Religion*. Los Angeles Campus.

Sperber, Rabbi Daniel. (2019). "Eating as a Sacrament: The Eating Table and the Coffin." In *Kashrut and Jewish Ethics*, edited by Shmuli Yanklowitz. Brighton: Academic Studies Press.

Spero, M.H. (1977). "Anxiety and Religious Growth: A Talmudic Perspective." *Journal of Religion and Health* 16(1): 52–57.

Stolow, J. (2007). "Holy Pleather: Materializing Authority in Contemporary Orthodox Jewish Publishing." *Material Religion: The Journal of Objects, Art and Belief* 3 (November): 314–335.

Stolow, J. (2006). Aesthetics/Ascetics: Visual Piety and Pleasure in a Strictly Kosher Cookbook. *Postscripts* 2(1): 5–28.

Tek, C.; Ulog, B. (2001). "Religiosity and Religious Obsessions in Obsessive-Compulsive Disorder. *Psychiatry Research* 104(2): 99–108.

Tikochinsky, Sh. (2007, Hebrew). "Lekudim Be'Iun." *Eretz Acheret*, n. 41.

Topel, M. (2011). *Jewish Orthodoxy and its Discontents: Religious Dissidence in Contemporary Israel*. New York: University Press of America.

Topel, M. (2005). *Jerusalem and Sao Paulo: The New Jewish Orthodoxy in Focus*. New York: University Press of America, 2008.

Turner, Victor. (1974). *Dramas, Fields and Metaphors: Symbolic Action in Human Society*. Ithaca, NY: Cornell University Press.

Tzuberi, Ch. (2012). "'And the Woman Is a High-Priest': From the Temple to the Kitchen; From the Laws of Ritual Im/Purity to the Laws of Kashrut." In *Introduction to Seder Qodashim*, edited by Tal Ilan, Monica Brockhaus, and Tanja Hidde, 167–175. Tübingen: Mohr Siebeck.

Vaad Hakashrut. (2014/2015). *The Kashrut Commission, the Earth Sabbatical Year Commission: Verdicts and Guidance for Earth Sabbatical Halachot, Earth Sabbatical Year Laws, and List of Grocery Stores Respecting the Earth Sabbatical Year.* The Eda Charedit.

Vaya, M. (2011). *A verificação dos alimentos segundo a Torá.* Jerusalem: Machon Leanchalat Hahalachá.

Vaya, M. (2010). *Bedikas Hamazon—Laws and Practical Methods for Checking.* Jerusalem: Feldheim.

Waxman, Ch. I. (1991). "Toward a Sociology of Psak." *Tradition: A Journal of Orthodox Jewish Thought* 25(3) (Spring): 12–25.

Willard, B.E. (2003). "The American Story of Meat: Discursive Influences on Cultural Eating Practice." *Journal of Popular Culture* 36(1): 105–118.

Woortmann, E. (2016). "Memória alimentar: prescrições e proscrições." In *Ensaios sobre a antropologia da alimentação: saberes, dinâmicas e patrimônios*, edited by Ellen Woortman and Julie A, Cavignac, 57–90. Natal, EDUFRN.

Yerushalmi, H. (1992). *Zakhor: História Judaica e memória judaica.* Rio de Janeiro: Imago.

Zohar, A.H.; Goldman, E.; Calamary, R.; Mashiah, M. (2005). "Religiosity and Obsessive-Compulsive Behavior in Israeli Jews." *Behaviour Research and Therapy* 43(7): 857–868. DOI:10.1016/j.brat.2004.06.009.

Webpages Consulted

Aish. (n.d.). "Ask the Rabbi: Hunting." Accessed October 28, 2023. https://www.aish.com/atr/Hunting.html.

Beit Chabad Do Brasil. (n.d.). A "dieta" judaica na teoria e na prática—O que é cashrut? Beit Chabad. http://www.chabad.org.br/mitsvot/cashrut/principal_cashrut/in.dex1.html

Ben-Shachar. (2020). "Get Out of Our Uteruses!" *Haaretz.* January 2. https://www.haaretz.co.il/misc/article-print-page/.premium-1.8348981.

Cardozo, Nathan. "Halacha and 'Trivialities.'" David Cardozo Academy. August 20. https://www.cardozoacademy.org/thoughtstoponder/halacha-and-trivialities-ttp-140/.

Farm Forward. (2014). "Keeping Kosher Update." June 2.

Friedman, Yoel. "Waiter! There's a Bug in My Salad." Kosher Point. http://kosherpoint.passroads.com/waiter-theres-a-bug-in-my-salad.

Galahar, Ari. (2010). "Rabbi Yosef Comes Out against Wig-Wearing." Yediot Achronot, June 9. https://www.ynetnews.com/articles/0,7340,L-3949586,00.html.

Goldman, Moshe. (n.d.). "Do I Have to Eat Meat on Shabbat?" Chabad. https://www.chabad.org/library/article_cdo/aid/880198/jewish/Do-I-Have.

Lindell, Yosef. (2020). "Think Passover Guides Are Getting Stricter? Think Again." The Lehrhaus. April 2. https://thelehrhaus.com/timely-thoughts/think-passover-guides-are-getting-stricter-think-again/.

Lindell, Yosef. (2018). Editor's Introduction. The Lehrhaus. https://thelehrhaus.com/about-us/.

Melamed, Eliezer. (2014). "The Significance of Eating Meat." Israel National News. June 8. http://www.israelnationalnews.com/Articles/Article.aspx/15130.

Melamed, Zalman Baruch. (n.d.). The Torá world gateway. https://www.yeshiva.co/.

Maimônides, M.B. (n.d.). *The Guide for the Perplexed.* Accessed October 29, 2023. https://www.sefaria.org/Guide_for_the_Perplexed.

Nachmânides (Ramban). (n.d.). *Laws of Niddah* 9.25: www.sefaria.org.

Rotem, Tamar. (2012). "How Passover Rules Strike Fear in the Heart of the Hasidic Community." *Haaretz*. April 6. http://www.haaretz.com/israel-news/how-passover-rules-strike-fear-in-the-heart-of-the-hasidic-community-1.422990.

Scheinberg, Chaim Pinchas. ([5770]; 2009). "Clean for Pesach and Enjoy the Seder." https://www.yeshiva.co/midrash/13351.

Sefaria. (n.d.). Uma biblioteca viva de textos judaicos. www.sefaria.org .

Sharon, J. (2020). "Head of Chief Rabbinate Kashrut to Be Indicted for Bribery." Jerusalem Post. May 12. https://www.jpost.com/israel-news/head-of-chief-rabbinate-kashrut-to-be-indicted-for-bribery-627651.

Siegel-Itzkovich, Judy. (2009). "When Ritual Becomes Obsession." *Jerusalem Post*. August 9. https://www.jpost.com/health-and-sci-tech/health/when-ritual-becomes-obsession-150523.

Slifkin, N. (2012). "The Making of Haredim." *Rationalist Judaism*. January 26. http://www.rationalistjudaism.com/2012/01/making-of-haredim.html.

Slifkin, N. (2011). "The Novelty of Orthodoxy." *Rationalist Judaism*. October 30. http://www.rationalistjudaism.com/2011/10/novelty-of-orthodoxy.html.

Sorj, B. (2004). "Identidade e Identidade Judaica". Bernardo Sorj. Rio de Janeiro. May. https://bernardosorj.org/wp-content/uploads/2021/01/10identidadeeidentidadesjudaicas.pdf.

TOI Staff. (2019). "Senior Rabbinate Kashrut Official to Stand Trial for Bribery." *Times of Israel*. July 24. https://www.timesofisrael.com/senior-rabbinate-kashrut-official-to-stand-trial-for-bribery/.

Torczyner, Mordechai. (2014). "Judaism and Obsessive-Compulsive Disorder." YuTorah. March 24. https://www.yutorah.org/lectures/lecture.cfm/810961/rabbi-mordechai-torczyner/judaism-and-obsessive-compulsive-disorder/

Videos

Blue Apron. (2015). "How to Wash Lettuce." December 15. https://www.youtube.com/watch?v=JQBgOYg7VdI .

Enlace Judío. (2017). "¡Los insectos no son kosher!" Aprende cómo limpiar tus alimentos. November 8. https://www.facebook.com/watch/?v=1951829118179452.

OU Kosher. (n.d.). Insect-Free: A Guide to Home Vegetable Inspection—Leafy Vegetables (1 of 4). https://www.youtube.com/watch?v=IXvwxPjakwo.

STAR-K Kosher. (2014). "STAR-K Insect Checking Video." Introduction by Rabbi Boruch Beyer. https://www.youtube.com/watch?v=QI8rL9JQDjI.

World Gateway. https://www.yeshiva.co/.

Index